Feminism and Equality

Feminism and Equality

Edited by ANNE PHILLIPS

New York University Press
Washington Square, New York

Selection and editorial matter copyright © Anne Phillips 1987

First published in the USA in 1987 by
NEW YORK UNIVERSITY PRESS
Washington Square, New York, N.Y. 10003

Library of Congress Cataloging-in-Publication Data

Feminism and equality.
(Readings in social and political theory)
Bibliography: p.
Includes index.
1. Feminism. 2. Equality.   3. Sex differences (Psychology)
I. Phillips, Anne.   II. Series.
HQ1154.F4425 1987   305.4′2   87–11190

ISBN 0–8147–6604–8
ISBN 0–8147–6605–6 (pbk.)

Typeset in Sabon 10 on 11 pt
by Hope Services, Abingdon
Printed in Great Britain by
Billing & Sons Ltd, Worcester

Contents

Introduction

ANNE PHILLIPS

The words women have chosen to express their condition – inequality, oppression, subordination – all have their implications, for each carries its own version of the problem it describes. Inequality notes that women are denied what is granted to men. It focuses our attention on the injustices of letting men vote when women could not, of giving men access to higher-paid jobs while restricting women to low-status work, of encouraging boys to train as engineers while girls learn to type. Oppression, by contrast, carries with it a sense of the weight pressing down on women; alerting us not so much to the anomalies of female exclusion, as to a complex of ideological, political and economic forces that combine to keep women in their place. Subordination takes this one step further, identifying the agents in the process. Women don't just happen to have less than men; they are actively subordinated by the holders of power.

The terms are not mutually exclusive, but the particular weight attached to each in different periods is often a guide to the preoccupations of the moment. In the period defined as the contemporary women's movement (from the late 1960s to the present day) the concepts of oppression and subordination have been the more favoured – a shift reflected also in the language of 'liberation' rather than 'emancipation'. A hundred years ago one might have defined feminism as a movement towards the equality of the sexes; by now this is hardly apt. Equality remains of course central to feminist discussion, but its recurrence in the writing signals as much disagreement over its meaning as certainty over its goals.

A commitment to sexual equality does not of itself tell us what shape that equality should take. Equal pay for the jobs women do or equal shares in the jobs done by men? Equal opportunities to compete with men or numerical equality in each sphere of life? Equal responsibilities for housework and children or better conditions for women at home? Those who describe themselves as feminists have been almost as much at odds over such issues as their opponents; and the axes around which they have ranged themselves have been many and various. For the purposes of this collection I have concentrated on two broad sets of issues: a constellation of arguments around the notion of equal rights and equal opportunities, sometimes codified as the relationship between feminism and liberalism; and an ever-present tension in feminist thinking between what Sally Alexander has called 'the plea for equality and the assertion of sexual difference'.[1]

The first group of issues commands considerably more attention today than it did fifteen years ago, perhaps because of the very successes of the women's movement and the way these have enhanced equal opportunities and equal rights; perhaps conversely because of the failures. In the late 1960s and early 1970s, feminists on both sides of the Atlantic split between those who argued a relatively traditional equal rights case and those who anticipated a radical future; the proportions in which they divided varied enormously from country to country, with liberal or equal rights feminism much more prominent in America than Britain, but in both cases there was some kind of 'reform versus revolution' axis. The 'revolutionary' camp subdivided further into radical and socialist feminism – and it was between these two that arguments became most intense. This only confirms that the prior differentiation (between liberal feminists and others) was the more fundamental, for there was little discussion across that divide.

Subsequent gains and losses have altered the picture. In Britain – where liberal feminism was so weakly represented that one could hardly identify it as a force at all – the most lasting gains have been in areas that liberals might well claim as their own. This is most literally so with the legalization of abortion, where fifteen years of feminist campaigning did little more than hold onto an Act which had been introduced by a Liberal MP. But in the area of employment too, it was the rather conventional and unimaginative Equal Pay and Sex Discrimination Acts that edged the earnings of women at least marginally upwards. The more ambitiously transformative language (like building an alternative to the family, breaking the hold of patriarchal power) has tended to falter in a climate of economic and political retreat. And the most promising of recent developments fit quite easily with liberal ideals: local councils adopting equal opportunities policies for hiring and promotion; political parties bowing (at least a little!) to pressures for greater representation of women as councillors or MPs. In a final irony for those who once dismissed the inadequacies of liberal reform, a main lever of change in social policy in Britain has turned out to be the dauntingly respectable EEC.[2]

What British feminists saw across the Atlantic looked even odder. In the name of equal rights and equal opportunities, American women seemed to have scored extraordinary victories over at least some firms – and it is to the American experience of positive action that those involved in the fledgling equal opportunities industry in Britain have usually looked for their inspiration. At the same time America has been swept by a rising tide of New Right moralism, a politics that in its profoundly reactionary views on women and the family threatens to destroy the tentative gains around employment, abortion or nursery provision. In both Britain and America, feminists have had to ponder again the relationship with liberalism, not just as an academic interest in origins (what inspired Mary Wollstonecraft? was it liberalism that moved women to act?) but as a matter of urgent political concern. What exactly is the relationship between sexual equality and equal rights? Are equal rights and opportunities what in the end feminism is about? a step on the way? a travesty of the name? Is feminism essentially an extension of the liberal project? or something incomparably more?

The questions are further complicated by the second angle this collection pursues, that age-old dilemma of equality versus difference. When people first hear of feminism they often assume it denies sexual difference: 'anything he can do I can do too.' Yet as long as women bear children there is at least one inescapable difference between the sexes, and many recent writings have identified women's role in reproduction as the source and the mechanism of patriarchal power. What do such arguments imply? Do they mean we should aim to obliterate all difference, and if so, how far can we go? In 1970 Shulamith Firestone placed her hopes for the future in a 'cybernetic communism', where children would be born to technology, not mothers, cared for in 'households', not as a family affair.[3] More typically in the course of the seventies, it became commonplace to talk of the distinction between sex and gender: to use the former when referring to an inescapable biological difference, and the latter for the construction society puts upon it. That women bear children, for example, is a biological fact. That they then have exclusive responsibility for caring for those children reflects a particular and inegalitarian pattern of gender relations, and one that is open to change. In the eighties, this approach too has been seen as rather glib, with feminism moving much more thoroughly towards the assertion of sexual difference.

Androgyny is not fashionable in the women's movement today. Fifteen years ago the aspiration to equality might well have been expressed in the longing to be a 'person' instead of a 'woman', in a desire to escape the stereotypes and definitions of sex. Today the emphasis would be different, and partly, of course, because of the very existence of a movement that has helped women assert themselves with pride. Adrienne Rich, for example, gave theoretical expression to the politics of lesbian separatism when she argued that women have a fundamental attachment to one another, and that they are only wrenched into relationships with men through a complex of power relations that impose heterosexuality as the norm.[4] Mary Daly has portrayed men as parasites on women – or much more poignantly, as necrophiliacs draining off the energy from the women they have frozen into a living death. Only in throwing off this male power will women be able to develop their essential creativity, passion and powers of love.[5] Dale Spender has rewritten the feminist project as the assertion of women's experience and values over and against the different values of men.[6] These and other writings combine in a popular rendering that treats women as not only different from, but superior to, men, bearers of essentially 'female' qualities that sometimes replicate too closely for comfort the very stereotypes feminists once tried to avoid: emotional rather than rational; peace-loving rather than destructive; caring about people rather than things.[7] The kind of 'woman-centred culture' that is promised in such visions leaves little space for the petty politics of equal rights and opportunities. Any so-called feminism that tried to take the male world as it is and just get women into it would seem like pitiful stuff; in Mary Daly's eyes, for example, the token successes are 'double-crossing' the rest.

Parallel to this assertion of women's power and women's difference – if theoretically worlds apart – are the arguments of psychoanalytic theory, which have entered into American and British debate largely through translations of French feminist writing.[8] Here there is less obviously an essential woman and essential man: the emphasis (for example in the essay by Sally Alexander) is often on the very fragile and precarious nature of woman's sexual identity. But if sexual identity is precarious and shifting, it is still grounded in difference: to be a woman is not to be a man. We are brought back to the perennial and difficult question: if the sexes are different, in what sense and how can they be equal?

The meaning and implications of sexual equality are almost as much contested within feminism as they are by feminism's detractors, and indeed it is part of my project in putting together this collection to make this clear. On equality, as on many crucial issues, there is no single 'feminist' line, for feminism is a tradition rich in debate. My own comments are organized under three headings: first, I explore the scope and limitations of the concepts of equality and equal rights; second, I develop what has emerged as a specifically feminist critique of the liberal tradition, centring most commonly on the separation liberalism makes between the public and private; third, I examine the vexed area of equality versus difference. The readings are drawn from recent work by English-speaking feminists, the earliest dating from the mid-1970s. It is, I hope, one of the strengths of the collection that they stretch over Britain, North America and Australia, for even with the help of a common language, there has not always been as much communication as the broad similarities in the politics might lead one to expect.

EQUALITY AND EQUAL RIGHTS

Sexual oppression shares with racial oppression the tendency to operate on two different levels. In both cases there have been long periods of history when the oppressed were denied their very place in humanity; in both cases the successful negotiation of this major hurdle (as, for example, when women and black people are admitted to the category of those who can vote) seems to leave the structures of oppression intact. In the case of women's oppression it is the first aspect that has given liberal feminism its power and resonance, for the extraordinary denial of women as citizens is a gross expression of arbitrary power. The second aspect is what leads so many to view liberalism as inadequate, for while few societies today will dare to contest the legal equality of women with men, it still remains the case (in the snappy formulation of the United Nations) that 'women constitute one half of the world's population, perform nearly two-thirds of its work hours, receive one-tenth of the world's income, and own less than one-hundredth of the world's property.' Liberalism typically focuses its attention on formal equalities; what relevance can it have for women today?

The question-mark is not, as it happens, just a matter of past versus present. The equal rights project has shifted its focus with the victory of the suffrage campaigns, the removal (in most countries) of legal barriers to female participation in the labour force, the concession of women's right to hold property in their own name. But it would be too simple to say that nineteenth-

century feminists took the law as their target, while with hindsight
we transcend the naïveties of their view. As the so far unsuccessful
campaign for an Equal Rights Amendment in America warns us,
equal rights in a broader sense are still much contested. The
relationship between equal rights and women's liberation is an
issue that must concern us today.

That liberalism and feminism share some common history is
widely agreed in the literature, and the classic link between the two
is explored here in the essays by Juliet Mitchell, Zillah Eisenstein
and Carole Pateman. As liberalism developed through the seventeenth and eighteenth centuries in Europe and America, it rejected
the 'natural' order of things; it refused the divinely ordained right
of monarchs to govern; it challenged the patriarchal basis of
political power. Introducing a 'conception of individuals as free and
equal beings, emancipated from the ascribed, hierarchical bonds of
tradition', it seemed to cry out for application to women.[9] And
while early liberals hardly rushed to make this connection, their
principles seemed a basis for feminist ideals. If you believed, as John
Stuart Mill so cogently argued in 1869, that human beings should
be free to develop their faculties as they see fit, and not 'chained
down by an inexorable bond to the place they are born to', then
how with consistency could you deny this to women?[10] It may be
that men and women are different, that women cannot do all the
jobs done by men, that they find their greatest satisfaction inside the
home. But what tyranny to legislate them into this role!

Long before Mill spelt out these implications, women had seized
on the language of equality and made out a case of their own. The
notion that people had rights rather than just duties or responsibilities
was so apposite to women, while the attack on tyranny and
arbitrary power had an all too obvious bearing on the privileges of
men. And in the republican version that was to emerge in America
there was a further link, for republicanism emphasized the
responsibilities of citizenship, regarding virtue as participation in
public life. Here it clashed with what was to become the main
apologia for women's position: that doctrine of 'separate but equal'
which legitimated women's exclusion from politics in terms of their
supposedly superior qualities for domestic life (women were too
good to soil their hands on a vote). Attaching so much moral
weight to public activities, republicanism should not in principle
have followed this route, and as the extract from Zillah Eisenstein
shows, nineteenth-century feminists like Elizabeth Cady Stanton
were able to get considerable mileage out of this. Liberalism and
republicanism together offered a wealth of arguments against

sexual inequality, and if male practitioners were slow to follow through this point, feminists were rarely so tardy.

This said, there are limits to the liberal perspective, and a century and a half of debate with socialist critics have already alerted us to some of the problems. As Juliet Mitchell notes in 'Women and Equality', liberalism gave us a version of equality that was fundamentally bounded by the forms of the law. This, she argues, is the best that capitalism can offer: that whatever rights society enshrines within its laws, then these should apply equally to all. The fact that people occupy different positions in society is, and should be, irrelevant: indeed it is essential to the argument that 'there are differences, but these should not count.'[11] This is of course the strength of liberalism – that we are all of us citizens regardless of our status. But when the implication is that the differences no longer matter, then we have a concept of equality that abstracts from the sources and relations of power.

The tension between political equality on the one hand and social and economic equality on the other is, as I say, a familiar one, and it is part of what has been at stake in assessments of liberal feminism. Is it enough to talk of equal opportunities and rights, or does the obsession with formality obscure the realities of power?

The question would be relatively straightforward if it were a matter of liberalism being fine as far as it goes, but simply not going far enough. The case for giving at least partial support to liberal campaigns would then be psychologically compelling, for you have to be confident indeed in your longer-term projects to sniff at more limited gains. And to say that the struggle for equal rights is important, even if insufficient, is to voice an opinion on which many would agree: the equal right to a vote has not guaranteed women equal access to power, but this is not to say we'd be better off without it; the equal right to employment does not give women equal jobs or equal pay, but it was (and still is!) worth fighting against discriminatory laws. Can feminists not co-operate on the basics of equality, even if some pursue in addition their wider concerns?

The question is not that simple, for part of the accusation against liberalism is that it is counter-productive, that it mystifies and blocks any longer-term goals. Most closely associated with the Marxist tradition, this argument is developed in Michèle Barrett's exploration of 'Marxist-Feminism and the Work of Karl Marx'. Marx himself was no great advocate of equal rights, and indeed in his discussion of nineteenth-century demands for Jewish emancipation, he veered very close to total rejection. His general position, as Michèle Barrett notes, 'is to regard it as at best a limited project pending more fundamental human emancipation. At worst, he implies, such mere political emancipation distracts our attention from the degree to which we are all "imprisoned" together: emphasis on sectional political emancipation blinds us to more fundamental shared, *human*, emancipation.'[12] The implication for the women's movement is unclear, for in an omission that provided fertile ground for subsequent debate, Marx neither rebutted nor supported the arguments for women's rights. Had he turned his attention to the emergent women's movement, would that too have earnt disapproval, as a politics that was blind to the basis of power? Certainly many later socialists drew this conclusion, dismissing feminists as essentially 'bourgeois'.

The argument is not just about the limits of legal equality, for in an extension which has considerable bearing on today's discussions of equal rights, Marx also criticized the appeal to rights in the economic sphere. In a famous discussion of the Gotha Programme (drawn up by German socialists in 1875) he condemned as 'obsolete verbal rubbish' the demand that all members of society should have equal right to the proceeds of labour. Even this right – which far exceeded the usual liberal scope – was for Marx a 'right of inequality, in its content, like every other right'.[13] Right can only mean applying an equal standard to all – but what if we are different and unequal? What if I have a child to support and you have none? What if I am weak and you are strong? What if I need more than you?

The argument has particular pertinence to sexual equality, for the tension between calling for equal treatment or insisting on women's special needs is one that remains at the heart of feminist dilemmas. For women to have an 'equal right' to work, for example, they may actually need *more* than the men. They need maternity leave; they need workplace nurseries; they need extra safety conditions when pregnant; they may need time off for menstruation. Such arguments, of course, can be a hostage to fortune, for once you admit that women are different from men, you may diminish their chances at work. In the late nineteenth and early twentieth centuries the difficulty surfaced in the question of protective legislation: should women support the laws which 'protected' them from especially arduous labour (preventing them in Britain from working in the mines, and restricting their employment at night); or should they challenge women's exclusion from certain categories of often higher-paid work?[14] The dilemma proved an intractable one, with positions shifting over the years, and the general tension of equality versus difference is one to which I shall return. In this case as in many, principles alone did not settle the matter. As Marx, I think rightly, pointed out, if your treatment is equal in one respect, you will be unequally treated in another. There is a further dimension that is crucial here. When feminists talk of inequalities between women and men, they seem to imply that there is a unity of women: all women this, all men the other. This is most convincing when women are denied their rights under law: when, for example, they are deprived by virtue of their sex from the right to vote; when they are denied *as women* the right to certain kinds of employment; when regardless of their age, class, race, they are all in law subordinate to their husbands. Wherever the law employs sex to deny women rights, then all women are unequal to all men. What remains of this unity once women get their rights in law?

Again this is not a simple matter of past simplicities versus present sophistication, for even in the nineteenth century the unity of women was complex and troubled. While voting for men was on a ratepayers' basis, women's campaign for the vote seemed likely to enfranchise certain women before others; their campaign around the right of women to retain property on marriage had different consequences for those who owned capital and those who earnt a wage; their campaigns around the right of women to train as doctors or lawyers in practice only benefited middle-class women. All these gave cause for concern and the unity of women was not taken for granted.[15] But while the law could deny all women as women it gave a necessary cohesion to feminist demands.

The subsequent dismantling of overtly discriminatory laws did not destroy the only unity in women's condition, but it did shift the emphasis elsewhere. And while the first phase of the contemporary women's movement involved excited rediscovery of what women had in common, in recent years it is difference that has dominated debate. Contemporary statistics on the distribution of income reveal gross inequality between the sexes, but still women themselves vary in their incomes and power. And while as mothers, wives and daughters women may face similar patterns of oppression, it would be naive to pretend that all the problems are the same. A feminism that focuses too exclusively on what seem to be similarities between women can pass over in silence the divisions by race and by class; its preoccupations may then express only minority concerns.

Black women and working-class women have long argued that under cover of a unitary female experience, the women's movement has spoken for the white middle class, in a politics that reflects this constituency alone. In this collection, Bell Hooks draws on such arguments to suggest that the language of equality is simplistic and glib. 'Since men are not equals in white supremacist, capitalist, patriarchal class structure which men do women want to be equal to?'[16] When feminism defines itself as a movement to gain social equality with men, it fudges the crucial questions: relying on the abstractions of equal opportunities, it obscures the real problems that beset women's lives.

Bell Hooks proposes an alternative definition: feminism as a struggle to end sexist oppression. Such a formulation, she argues, will focus attention more directly on the other forms of oppression, and thus link up the politics around sex, class and race. A partial feminism, she is suggesting, simply will not do. The ways in which women are discriminated against, exploited and oppressed, rest on combinations of all three of these factors, so unless the politics of socialism and anti-racism can be integrated into women's struggle, the movement will still speak to the middle class alone. You cannot say that feminism is about women and then just leave it at that, as if class or race are problems for others to take up. If you do, you end up with the kind of liberal or 'bourgeois' feminism that dominates the American movement – and for Bell Hooks this is not really feminism at all.

In thinking through some of these problems we can see that they share common ground with the socialist critique of liberalism: the notion that equality is only equality under the law; the idea that formal equality legitimizes real inequalities; the idea that it abstracts from differences of race and of class. But the feminist debate on liberalism has not just divided into socialist and liberal camps. Partly of course because radical feminism (which is not represented in this volume) stands outside either tradition. But also because the different contexts in which arguments have developed have shaped the political concerns. As already noted, equal rights/liberal feminism had few adherents in the emergence of the Women's Liberation Movement in Britain, which had little time for what it saw as a 'women into boardrooms' approach, and placed itself more definitively within a radical or socialist tradition. At the risk of gross oversimplification I would say that because British feminism was so much engaged in debate with the socialist tradition, it had to challenge the tendency to regard *any* feminism as 'bourgeois'. Operating in a field where equality was too often prefaced by the denigratory 'mere', it moved towards a greater accommodation with the basic ideas of equality or equal rights.

Thus when Juliet Mitchell wrote her essay on 'Women and

Equality' in 1976, she was simultaneously criticizing equality and defending its relevance for today. She made no bones about the link between feminism and 'bourgeois' thought, and while she explored the limits, she saw equality as fundamental to feminist thought. Part of her project was to rescue equal rights as worthy and far from complete: if equal rights could never be more than rights before the law, still they 'have by no means been won yet nor their possible extent envisaged.'[17] Her final plea is definite, if carefully circumscribed. 'A new society that is built on an old society that, within its limits, has reached a certain level of equality clearly is a better starting point than one that must build on a society predicated on privilege and unchallenged oppression.'[18]

In similar vein, Michèle Barrett explores with sympathy Marx's critique of liberalism, yet refuses to dismiss the equal rights approach. With all the criticisms that can be levelled at 'mere' political emancipation, who, she asks, 'would care to argue against a systematic political project of eliminating racism and sexism from the working class on the grounds that such inequalities were not of prime significance?'[19] The point is as much to query Marx in the light of feminism as it is to query feminism in the light of Marx. And to this extent it reflects what became an important characteristic of feminist thinking in Britain: a more sceptical questioning of socialism's claims.

The idea that capitalism is totally, or even primarily, responsible for women's condition has taken a battering in recent debates; the associated idea that feminism finds its natural home inside the socialist camp has likewise been held up to question. Socialist, and more specifically Marxist, theory has been criticized for the way it can subsume all forms of oppression under a more 'primary' class exploitation, leaving issues of either sexual or racial equality as subsidiary concerns. Equal rights or liberal feminism may smooth over and deny class differences between women, but socialism smooths over conflicts between women and men. In noting and criticizing this, British feminists became more resistant to the complaint that the women's movement was 'bourgeois', more reluctant to condemn an equal rights line.

Juliet Mitchell and Michèle Barrett write as women who are both feminists and at the same time socialists, who, whatever their position on women's oppression, would see political emancipation as a limited goal. Neither, however, wants to claim feminism as necessarily socialist, and indeed Barrett notes her reservations over any 'easy alliance' of the two. It is implicit in both arguments that there are different feminisms – this is more explicitly developed in the 1986 collection edited by Juliet Mitchell and Ann Oakley on *What Is Feminism?* [20] – and that each has a legitimate claim to the name. Thus while Bell Hooks regards liberal feminism as a 'contradiction that must be resolved',[21] Mitchell and Barrett see it as a feminism that is different from theirs.

It is, as I say, important to bear in mind the political contexts. If liberal feminism was a bystander in Britain, in America it often dominated the stage. There was, and is, a powerful and active liberal-feminist lobby, organized largely under the umbrella of the National Organization for Women (NOW) which was launched in 1966, and focusing recently upon the campaign for the ERA. It is harder to tolerate what is a dominant position, and for those American feminists outside this mainstream the impulse has been much more to explode the tradition – either from without or else from within. One consequence of this is that where liberalism has been more politically important, the engagement has provoked a fuller feminist response. Juliet Mitchell and Michèle Barrett explore what is in a sense a universal critique of liberalism: arguments that could apply equally whether we were looking at the relationship between rich and poor, white and black, male and female, Christian and Jew. In the writings of Carole Pateman or Zillah Eisenstein what emerges is a more specifically feminist critique.

FEMINIST CRITIQUES OF LIBERALISM

With all the uncertainties as to what the terms mean, it is when feminists talk of equality and equal rights that they most closely approximate the liberal tradition. When they talk instead of the personal as political, they are profoundly at odds with liberal ideas. The relationship between public and private has become the real bone of contention between liberal and feminist thinking, and it is the focus of most feminist critiques.

Like all abbreviated statements, 'the personal is political' has had to carry a wide range of meanings. Partly a rebuttal of those who dismissed as trivial questions like who does the housework or who sleeps with whom; partly a reminder that in the most private corners of our existence the state and economy still hold sway. Partly saying that the kind of 'consciousness-raising' activities that became associated with recent feminism were as politically crucial as anything else; partly saying that change does not come from personal lives alone. The basic point is clear. If all aspects of our lives are up for question, then nothing is outside the political sphere.

For liberals this is anathema, for to make no distinction between private life and public affairs is the very antithesis of their thinking. Liberalism is that doctrine *par excellence* that tries to keep things separate, to demarcate the personal from the political sphere. For most liberals, the state is a necessary evil. Individuals cannot be trusted to regulate themselves, and the state must therefore play a referee role. But since governments and laws are by their very nature a restraint on our freedom, the question is when they can justly intervene. When is it legitimate, asked John Stuart Mill, to subject 'individual autonomy to external control'?[22] And what is irreducibly a private affair? Liberalism is not anarchism; it does not aspire to eliminate the state. But it guards jealously the autonomy of the individual, watching out for encroachments on the private sphere.

When this translates into police officers refusing to protect a woman beaten by her husband on the grounds that domestic quarrels are a private affair – or indeed into employers refusing a woman time off work to look after her sick child on the grounds that personal problems should not intrude on her work – we can see why feminists get worried. The private is very often taken to mean the family, and in the family men and women are unequal. In the name of freedom, liberalism can exempt from political interference the arena in which women are most subordinate and controlled. In its desire to keep separate the worlds of public and private, it offers us 'equality' in the former while hypocritically ignoring our real difference in the latter. The split between public and private may present itself as a neutral, 'sex-free' distinction, but its effects are unequal between women and men.

Feminists have not argued that liberalism alone makes this distinction. In her book *Public Man, Private Woman* Jean Bethke Elshtain traces the split from Plato to the present day, and argues that the distinctions between public and private are 'fundamental . . . ordering principles of all known societies, save, perhaps, the most simple'.[23] In the *Radical Future of Liberal Feminism* Zillah Eisenstein also sees the split between public and private as going far beyond the liberal tradition, though in her case this is because it is a defining feature of the patriarchal order, whose universality has been expressed 'in the sexual assignment of private and public life, to woman and man, respectively'.[24] The notion that there are separate spheres of public and private existence – and the sleight of hand through which one becomes male and the other female – has a much longer history than the 300 odd years through which liberalism has been with us. What is disturbing about liberalism is that on the face of it, it should have been so different. Liberalism, as Carole Pateman notes, 'is an individualist, egalitarian, conventionalist doctrine; patriarchalism claims that hierarchical relations of subordination necessarily follow from the natural characteristics of women and men.'[25] How did liberalism then end up so badly? Denied entry by the front door, patriarchy crept in at the back. Instead of rejecting all forms of natural authority, early liberals restricted themselves to saying that government and the family were separate realms. John Locke, for example, fully accepted that fathers had a natural authority over their children, and indeed that husbands had a natural authority over wives. Where he broke with more obviously patriarchal theorists was in refusing the relevance of this to the state. Political authority, he argued, was conventional: free and equal beings had created a ruler to regulate their lives, and what they had created they had some right to control. But in a malignant failure of imagination, he then drew on this contrast to exclude women from any role in the state. If they were 'naturally' subordinate in the family, they could not be included among consenting adults: it was men who had created, and should monitor, their government, men who were the citizens of John Locke's state.

Locke here was perhaps breaking his own rules, for having suggested that the principles of the family should not be extended to the state, he then excluded women from the latter precisely because of their role in the former. Later liberals (and to the shame of the tradition this was very much later) queried this anomaly, arguing that women too should share in political life. But as a number of feminists have argued – including in this collection Zillah Eisenstein and Carole Pateman – liberalism then got caught in another dilemma. John Stuart Mill, for example, rejected the idea that women's position as wives and mothers should exclude them from participation in public affairs, but he hoped and expected that women would still stay in their sphere. Arguing that legal equality need not prevent women from 'choosing' to be wives and mothers, and conversely that their continuing as wives and mothers need not unfit them for public concerns, nineteenth-century liberals turned a blind eye to the fact that women and men occupied separate spheres. Yet as Carole Pateman notes, 'Mill's acceptance of a sexually ascribed division of labour, or the separation of domestic from public life, cuts the ground from under his argument for enfranchisement . . . How can wives who have "chosen" private life develop a public spirit?'[26] Locke, after all, had a point.

The issue connects with socialist complaints against the liberal tradition. How can we be politically equal despite all our difference, when the differences undermine the formality and make it pretence? Feminist writers, however, have picked up on another dimension, and in a particularly enlightening essay, Carole Pateman shows why this is so. Liberals make not one, but two, distinctions between the private and public: the prior distinction between family and the public, and then a subsequent one within the public itself. Much of the discussion (either among liberals or between liberals and socialists) has focused on the latter, the connection between what Marx called civil society and the state. What is the appropriate relationship between private enterprise and public regulation? Do inequalities in the private sphere (between, say, landlord and tenant, employer and employee) matter as long as we are equal in political rights? 'Private' in this sense is not about the family; abstracting entirely from the domestic sphere, it refers to the market, to the economy, to our 'social' as opposed to our 'political' life. And because the family is now completely out of the picture, liberalism can more plausibly pretend that we are indeed the private and isolated individuals on which its theories rest. In seemingly universal concern over the limits of the state and the freedoms of the individual, liberalism talks in effect of a world occupied by men.

There are two kinds of point here. Liberalism pretends we can be equal in the public sphere when our differences are overwhelming in the private: it exhorts women to apply for good jobs while treating the babies as their private affair; it offers them equality with one hand and takes it away with the other. This is damning enough, but feminists have more up their sleeves. Having pushed the familial into the background, liberalism creates a fictional world of autonomous atoms, each propelled by his (*sic*) own interests and desires, each potentially threatened by the others.

This kind of radical individualism is not of course without its attractions to feminists. Zillah Eisenstein argues that 'all feminism is liberal at its root in that the universal feminist claim that woman is an independent being (from man) is premised on the eighteenth-century liberal conception of the independent and autonomous self.'[27] When nineteenth-century feminists insisted that women had rights of their own, they were refusing to be subsumed under fathers or husbands. When twentieth-century feminists said that women had needs and desires of their own, they were refusing to be sacrificed to children or lovers. Asserting the self is part of the politics, and it is this – as much as the common language of equal rights – that provides the link between liberal and feminist traditions. The question Zillah Eisenstein poses is, how far can this go? Women straddle public and private worlds in different ways from men, and they cannot so readily conceive of themselves in public terms alone. Could feminism really throw in its lot with the market mentality of the liberal tradition? Can it consistently adhere to the individualist view?

The way Eisenstein herself puts this is somewhat formalistic: that because feminism is about women as a 'sex-class', it cannot express its politics in terms of individuals alone. When it tries none the less to keep within the contours of the liberal tradition it keeps posing questions it cannot resolve. Elizabeth Cady Stanton, for example, thought of individuals as islands alone, and much of her argument for women's right to education and the vote was based on her perception that women do in the end have to rely on themselves. But she also knew that the problem for women was not an individual condition, that women were constrained and defined by being mothers and wives. Eisenstein argues that the adherence to liberalism prevented her from pursuing this further, so that despite knowing comments on marriage and motherhood Stanton kept coming back to the liberal solutions, as if equality can be achieved in the public sphere alone. But even if she never acknowledged it herself, her ideas transcended the liberal tradition.

'Liberal feminism, by dint of speaking of women as a group, is in contradiction with "the principles of liberalism," which do not see people as groups, only individuals.'[28] Put like this, the argument is over-strained, for not all liberals are as radically individualist as this comment suggests, nor is it so obviously contradictory to say that women are oppressed as a group, but should be freed in the future to compete as individuals with men. The real power of the argument lies behind the formal contrast between liberal individualism and feminist groupiness, and rests on the idea that feminism has its own and different conception of individuality. 'Connection and related-ness,' Zillah Eisenstein suggests, are what characterize feminism, 'between people, between politics and economics, between ideology and actual social conditions.'[29] A politics based upon female experience must surely eschew the extremer versions of atomistic individualism, pointing instead towards a new relationship of public to private, and recognizing collectivity even as it claims independence.

The argument is plausible, but it leads us back to the question 'which feminism?'. Does the nature of women's politics point in a specific direction, or are there many feminisms, of which some at least may remain resolutely allied to their liberal friends? In *Public Man, Private Woman* Jean Bethke Elshtain criticizes liberal feminists for doing just what Eisenstein suggests they could not, for swallowing the 'market' perspective on life. And while she too notes the contradictory elements in their thinking, she criticizes them for trying to have it both ways: trying

> to condemn woman's second-class status and the damaging effects of her privatization and, simultaneously, to extol or celebrate the qualities that have emerged within the sphere women are to be 'freed' from. The result of all this is a confused admixture: a tough-minded market language of self-interest coupled with evocations to softer virtues, precisely the combination which plagued the Suffragists. Because the only politics liberal feminists know is the rather crass utilitarianism they implicitly or explicitly adopt, they have thus far failed to articulate a transformative feminist vision of public and private.[30]

The argument here is that many feminists are indeed appallingly, crassly, individualist – and that they do not escape this by trying to cover their tracks.

Elshtain's account of liberal feminism is much less sympathetic than that of Eisenstein – if we were to try to fit them into pre-feminist categories, then the former is arguing from a conservative perspective, the latter from a socialist one. Their differences in respect to liberalism hinge on contrasting approaches to the public/private split, for as already noted, Zillah Eisenstein sees this as a function of patriarchal rule, while Jean Bethke Elshtain regards it as necessary to life. The private for her is the site of caring and concern; the pity is that the public has not reflected these values. The kind of reconstruction she proposes is one that would create an 'ethical polity': public life informed by social and moral responsibilities; private life lending of its values, but still keeping its autonomy clear.

There is a major dispute here, and it is one that leads on to the question of equality and difference. What Elshtain most objects to in the present version of the public/private split is not so much that it keeps women out of public affairs, as that it keeps out the values that women express. Largely because of their role as mothers, women have become the guarantors of a deeper humanity, carrying a sense of community, of belonging, of selflessness and care. Feminism should be building on this, not capitulating to a narrower self-interest. Yet as Elshtain sees it – and here she echoes what many *anti*-feminists would also say – the contemporary women's movement often took the second, more damaging road. Stridently asserting their own individual needs, women sacrificed the most helpless among them. They brought up their children outside the family, condemning them to the insecurities of a casual collectivity; pushed them prematurely into nurseries in order to further the mothers' careers. 'The feminist political thinker must . . . ask at what price she would gain the world for herself or other women', and she must utterly reject 'those victories that come at the cost of the bodies and spirits of human infants'.[31] 'The reflective feminist must be as concerned with the concrete existences and self-understandings of children as she is with female subjects.'[32] '*As* concerned' is an interesting emphasis: why is this particularly the challenge to feminists, as opposed to socialists or liberals or anyone else?

I cannot enter here into the rewriting of women's movement history, and shall merely second a comment from Denise Riley's essay on 'The Serious Burdens Of Love'. 'We have always been told that feminism is indifferent to the problems of mothers and children; and that charge has not ever been true.'[33] In a thoughtful review of the kinds of question feminists have raised over the decades, Riley argues that the needs of women and children can neither be treated as one, nor assumed to be essentially opposed. But if we give up on the case for improved social provision for children, if we end up just glorying in our creativity as mothers, we retreat from the challenge feminism sets. The new celebration of motherhood that is becoming commonplace among feminists 'tells us what we already know: that there are passions and surprises bound up with child-care as well as the exhaustion and isolation dwelt on by women's liberation. But it tells us in a debased language which produces a flat sociology of the emotions, and does so at the expense of thought about practical needs.'[34] Elshtain's emphasis on children leads her towards the status quo: children need the family, and while she sometimes seems to go along with current ideas of shared parenting, she does not clarify the mechanisms that would bring this about. Riley's emphasis on children confirms rather the importance of social provision, for even shared parenting is not a solution when the sharing couple so often comes to grief. Neither writer could be accused of ignoring mothers and children, but still the conclusions they reach are poles apart. The contrast cannot be reduced to one of equality versus difference, but it takes us directly into this debate.

EQUALITY AND DIFFERENCE

It is one of the oddities in the tension between equality and difference that representatives from each end of the spectrum can make their case for being the more radical. Advocates of stricter equality have argued – with considerable force – that once feminists admit the mildest degree of sexual difference, they open up a gap through which the currents of reaction will flow. Once let slip that pre-menstrual tension interferes with concentration, that pregnancy can be exhausting, that motherhood is absorbing, and you are off down the slope to separate spheres. It was with good reason that prominent suffragists (like Millicent Garrett Fawcett) argued against emphasizing women's maternal role: the whole point of the movement was to get women out of their stereotyped domesticity, to assert their claims in the public sphere.

But those who have argued for a feminism grounded in sexual difference have their own very plausible case. The politics of equality directs energies to the spheres that are occupied by men, while the predominantly female activities around housework or child-care remain obscured as always from view. Women are called on to fit themselves into slots devised for the men, and their own needs are in the process ignored. Why should equality mean women shaping themselves to a world made for men? Why shouldn't the world be made to change its tune?

The confusion around which is more progressive is well exemplified in Ellen DuBois's discussion of the American suffrage movement. From the standpoint of today, it seems extraordinary that nineteenth-century feminists had no strategy for the family: that they uncritically accepted women's role as mothers and wives and concentrated on getting the vote. How could they not see that women's oppression was based in the family? How could they accept their domestic role? 'No suffragist of whom I am aware', writes Ellen DuBois, 'including the otherwise iconoclastic Elizabeth Cady Stanton, seriously suggested that men take equal responsibilities with women for domestic activities. "Sharing housework" may be a more uniquely twentieth-century feminist demand than "smashing monogamy".'[35] But at the time, she argues, this might have been the more radical stance. Instead of saying that women earned their equality as citizens by working as equals outside the home, the suffragists confronted and discredited the notion that being a mother and wife disqualified you from having a vote. 'Leave the family out of it', they said; 'accept us as individuals in our own right.' Arguing for full citizenship regardless of their familial status ('there are differences but these should not count!'), they refused to be defined in the traditional way. And if to twentieth-century ears this can sound like capitulation to domestic drudgery, it was dramatically contested at the time.

In the history of the women's movement there has usually been a class dimension to equality versus difference. In the nineteenth century, for example, it was middle-class women who felt themselves most acutely victimized by the doctrine of separate spheres, for they were the ones whose femininity was most explicitly defined through denying them useful work. The feminism this generated was primarily about challenging exclusion, claiming access to public life, the right to vote and to study and to work. And in Britain at least, it was left to the organizations of working-class women (like the Women's Co-operative Guild) to take up more domestic concerns: issues like contraception, divorce, provision for mothers and children. When in the 1920s British feminists were asked to choose between the older tradition of 'equal rights' and a 'new feminism' centred on motherhood, the case for the latter was very often put in terms of class. 'What rights had the working-class mother?' asked Dora Russell.[36] Those feminists who previously refused to engage with issues of maternity on the grounds that this would help push women back into the home were now identified as the voice of middle-class women. In the name of the working-class mother the emphasis was then reversed.

The example typifies the problems, for in effect neither position was satisfactory. The equality end of the feminist spectrum had tended to highlight women as workers, while the difference end has highlighted women as mothers. Since most women in practice are both, stressing either aspect to the exclusion of the other is usually a dangerous choice. Thus if the call for better contraceptive advice, more midwives, improved ante-natal care, 'family endowment' and so on, marked an important and welcome emphasis on the problems women faced as mothers, it also ran the risk of denying women's need for paid work. When the working mother came under threat in the 1940s and 1950s – with wartime nurseries shut down and women encouraged to see their place in the home – feminists by and large were ill prepared in her defence. Campaigns for paid employment had become too closely identified with the limited needs of better-off women, and feminism had temporarily lost the language in which to assert women's equal right to work.[37] Equality and difference had become too counter-posed in the politics, with, in this instance, unfortunate results.

The main thrust of the debate in contemporary feminism has come from the influence of psycho-analytic theory on the one hand and the celebration of a woman-identified woman on the other. Here the discussion moves on to a new level. The earlier arguments were usually put in terms of which aspects of women's lives feminists should concentrate their activities upon: those where women were claiming an equality with men? or those that were traditionally the woman's concern? The argument was not so much about whether men and women were in principle different, for while this was continually discussed, it was not really the issue at stake. Today's arguments, by contrast, do imply a more essentialist line on sexual difference.

Anything stronger than 'imply' would expose me too roughly to critical complaint. Most exponents of a woman-identified politics remain officially agnostic over the extent to which women are essentially and ineradicably different from men, though in practice the differences are treated as enduring facts of life. Those influenced by psycho-analysis are much more likely to come clean about sexual difference being inevitable, but the content of this difference is shifting and obscure. In this collection, for example, Jean Bethke Elshtain argues that the 'sex distinction is ineliminable and important',[38] but her analysis of this only tells us that boys and girls learn who they are by noting that they have different bodies. A '*sexual difference*', she suggests, 'is neither an affront, nor an outrage, not a narcissistic injury. A *sexual division*, on the other hand, one that separates the sexes and locks each into a vector of isolated, alienated activity *is* both a deep wound to the psycho-sexual identity of the human subject as well as a specific damage of an overly rigidified system of stratification and specialization.'[39] I am inclined to agree, but until we see more clearly what is entailed by this sexual difference it is hard to decide whether it matters.

Sally Alexander sees subjectivity and sexual identity as 'constructed through a process of differentiation, division and splitting, and best understood as a process which is always in the making, is never finished or complete.'[40] The process is none the less fundamentally different for the little girl/woman and the little boy/man. Her main concern in the essay is with how the unconscious enters politics, and in particular with the way our understanding of self and sexual identity changes our understanding of class. Thought-provoking as this is, its implications for feminism still need to be spelt out: what – other than *a* difference – does this sexual difference imply? The more content that feminist writers put into the notion of difference, the more worried I become; but the less content, the more confused!

In its various forms (and in this collection it is only the influence
of psycho-analysis that is even partially represented) the renewed
interest in difference has become one of the central preoccupations
of contemporary thought. Of the issues covered in this collection, it
seems most likely to set the terms of future debate, for it is a tension
built into the feminist project. Men and women are different; they
are also unequal; feminists will continue to debate and disagree
over how far the inequality stems from the difference, and how far
the difference can or should be eliminated.

My object in writing this introduction has been to open out,
rather than wrap up, debate, and I make no apologies if my
comments pursue no very definite line. The caution is deliberate, for
feminism is a tradition with many variations, with the opaqueness
of equality partly the cause. It should I trust be clear that I align
myself with those who consider equal rights as only part of the
picture, but to say this is not to give much away. The whole
relationship between public and private is a crucial area for feminist
action, but extreme alternatives (simply obliterating the distinction
as in 'the personal is political' or celebrating the private as the
feminine sphere) can too easily lead us off route. There is, to
borrow a phrase from Denise Riley's essay, a 'necessary stitched-
togetherness' in feminist thinking, because the goals are complex
and diffuse.

NOTES

1 See below, ch. 8, p. 162.
2 See Catherine Hoskins, 'Women, European Law and Transnational
  Politics', *International Journal of the Sociology of Law*, vol. 14, nos. 3–
  4 (1986), pp. 299–315.
3 Shulamith Firestone, *The Dialectic of Sex* (Jonathan Cape, London,
  1971).
4 Adrienne Rich, 'Compulsory Heterosexuality and the Lesbian Existence',
  Signs 5, no. 4 (Summer 1980), pp. 631–60.
5 Mary Daly, *Gyn/Ecology: The Metaethics of Radical Feminism* (Beacon
  Press, Boston, 1973).
6 Dale Spender, *Women of Ideas (And What Men Have Done To Them)*
  (Routledge and Kegan Paul, London, 1982).
7 For a critical discussion of this school of thought see Hester Eisenstein,
  Contemporary Feminist Thought (Unwin, London and Sydney, 1984);
  and Lynne Segal, *Is The Future Female? Troubled Thoughts on
  Contemporary Feminism* (Virago, London, 1987).

8 E.g. Elaine Marks and Isabelle de Courtivron (eds), *New French Feminisms: an Anthology* (University of Massachusetts Press, Amherst, 1980).
9 See below, ch. 5, p. 103.
10 John Stuart Mill, 'The Subjection of Women' (1869), reprinted in *Three Essays* (Oxford University Press, London, 1975), p. 445.
11 See below, ch. 1, p. 42.
12 See below, ch. 2, p. 50.
13 Karl Marx, 'Critique of the Gotha Programme' (1875), reprinted in *Marx and Engels: Selected Works in One Volume* (Lawrence and Wishart, London, 1968), p. 320.
14 See Anne Phillips, *Divided Loyalties: Dilemmas of Sex and Class* (Virago, London, 1987), for a fuller discussion.
15 Ibid.
16 See below, ch. 3, p. 62.
17 Below, ch. 1, p. 42.
18 Ibid.
19 Below, ch. 2, p. 50.
20 Juliet Mitchell and Ann Oakley (eds), *What Is Feminism?* (Basil Blackwell, Oxford, 1986).
21 Below, ch. 3, p. 75.
22 John Stuart Mill, 'On Liberty' (1859), reprinted in *Three Essays* (Oxford University Press, London, 1975), p. 16.
23 Jean Bethke Elshtain, *Public Man, Private Woman: Women in Social and Political Thought* (Princeton University Press, New Jersey, 1981), p. 6.
24 Zillah Eisenstein, *The Radical Future of Liberal Feminism* (Longman, New York, 1981), p. 22.
25 Below, ch. 5, p. 105.
26 Ibid., p. 116.
27 Eisenstein, *The Radical Future of Liberal Feminism*, p. 4.
28 Ibid., p. 191.
29 Ibid.
30 Elshtain, *Public Man, Private Woman*, pp. 248–9.
31 Ibid., p. 331.
32 Ibid., p. 333.
33 See below, ch. 9, p. 179.
34 Ibid., pp. 180–1.
35 See below, ch. 6, p. 130.
36 For a fuller discussion see Anne Phillips, *Divided Loyalties*, pp. 98–106. Olive Banks covers similar ground in relation to both American and British movements in *Faces of Feminism* (Martin Robertson, Oxford, 1981), ch. 9.
37 See Denise Riley, *War In The Nursery* (Virago, London, 1983).
38 See below, ch. 7, p. 148.
39 Ibid., p. 155.
40 See below, ch. 8, p. 171.

1

Women and Equality

JULIET MITCHELL

As a number of people, such as Charles Fourier and Karl Marx, have commented, the position of women in any given society can be taken as a mark of the progress of civilization or *humanization* within that society. There may be slave societies, like that of the Ptolemies, in which there is an elite of privileged women, but it is not such an elite that we are talking about when we consider the position of women in general as the index of human advance: men and women actually become human in relation to each other and if one sex is denigrated as a sex then humanity itself is the loser. I do not mean this in the simple sense that any exploitation or oppression diminishes the dignity of the whole society – though that is, of course, the case – but in the rather special sense that it is precisely in his transformation of the functions of sexuality and reproduction and communication into emotional relationship and language that at a basic level man as an animal becomes man as a human being. If we consider that within this process women as a social group have been oppressed, then we can see the depth of the problem. However, rather than hesitating at the edge because the question is too large for contemplation, it is obviously worth considering smaller, specific aspects. In this essay I shall present a selective history of the conscious protest that women have made against their position.

Biological differences between men and women obviously exist, but it is not these that are the concern of feminism. Society in its preliminary organization distinguishes the sexes as social groups in many different ways. But, so far as it is known, whatever the way, women are always disadvantaged in this distinction. Opposition to this situation is always a possibility, but I think that it is important to separate conscious from unconscious opposition. Modern

Reprinted with permission from *The Rights and Wrongs of Women*, edited with an introduction by Juliet Mitchell and Ann Oakley (Penguin, London, 1976), pp. 379–99.

feminism, particularly in America, is anxious to trace its own history and in doing so has identified medieval witches, among others, as its ancestors. Witches defended female crafts and medical skills against encroaching male professionalism and a violently patriarchal church. Witchcraft is one cultural form of female protest and a history of this and other forms would be very interesting. But my argument is that feminism as a conscious political ideology is not trans-historical. It cannot be generalized as just any form of female protest. That is to say that it is not produced by the general conditions of all societies which for their functioning (indeed for their existence) divide men and women as social groups. Instead feminism arises only in very particular historical circumstances. An exemplary instance of these circumstances would seem to be found in England in the seventeenth century.

There are several implications to the thesis that feminism arises in the type of historical conditions found in England in the seventeenth century. I think that not the least of these is the suspicion that I am discussing what is known in the women's movement as 'bourgeois feminism'. Not only am I ignoring, for the reasons just stated, the heroic struggles of women in other social contexts, but in claiming that feminism, if it is to be given any precise meaning, starts as an awareness by middle-class women I am ignoring the massive contribution of working-class women to its formation. I seem to be confirming the current media myths that it is only privileged women who protest. But some distinctions here are mandatory.

'Bourgeois feminism' in the mid-twentieth century must indicate a tendency within the women's movement that believes that its demands can be met within the context of the present capitalist society. It is not that the feminists in the seventeenth century were not largely from the bourgeois class – they were – but that such a perspective had a very different meaning in that period. Of course working-class women, ex-slave women, women from the *lumpen*-proletariat and so on contributed to, reshaped and developed feminism, but in its essential meaning it seems to me to have been the conception of middle-class women or, at least, a conception that initially spoke to and for them. If we look at the moment in which they first formulate it I suggest that even the most ardent socialist feminist will have nothing to be ashamed of in her origins. However, such a demonstration does involve a very selective history. In trying to pinpoint this bourgeois tradition I shall select those to demonstrate it best. Furthermore I have elicited one aspect of bourgeois thought that seems to me to make the connection between the rise of feminism and the ideology of capitalism most clearly – this aspect is the concept of equality.

All democratic countries have as one of their highest aspirations the attaining of equality among their citizens, but in no democratic country in the world do women have equal rights with men. England has been a democratic country for over 300 years, equality has been a guiding principle; yet this is how the authors of a recent survey of women's rights in Britain introduce their researches:

> At no level of society do [women] have equal rights with men. At the beginning of the nineteenth century, women had virtually no rights at all. They were the chattels of their fathers and husbands. They were bought and sold in marriage. They could not vote. They could not sign contracts. When married, they could not own property. They had no rights over their children and no control over their own bodies. Their husbands could rape and beat them without fear of legal reprisals. When they were not confined to the home, they were forced by growing industrialization to join the lowest levels of the labour force. *Since then, progress towards equal rights for women has been very slow indeed.* (My italics)[1]

The authors go on to document how in work, education, social facilities and under law women are treated as men's inferiors and, despite such appearances as equal pay acts, equality is never attained.

Equal rights are an important tip of an iceberg that goes far deeper. That they are only the tip is both a reflection of the limitation of the concept of equality and an indication of how profound and fundamental is the problem of the oppression of women. The position of women as a social group in relation to men as another social group goes far deeper, then, than the question of equal rights, but not only are equal rights an important part of it but they have the most intimate connection with the whole history of feminism as a conscious social and political movement.

What then could be seen to be the strengths and limitations of the concept of equality? I plan to give a parallel account: first, the meaning of the concept of equality followed by an attempt to relate it to the history of feminism and then some suggestions on how we must, while never undervaluing it, go beyond equality. In using England one is fortunate in that England does present something of a model – an exemplary case – of the historical connections I want to make. But, with obviously important variations, all capitalist and later industrial capitalist countries have crucial similarities and it should be possible to slot another particular example into the general framework provided by English history.

The economic development of capitalism is always uneven and the ideological world view that goes with economic development will likewise be uneven and not necessarily develop in a parallel manner. I do not intend to consider, except cursorily, the material economic and social base either of the development of capitalism or of the position of women, but only some particular ideologies and politics that go with it. One consequence of the uneven development of any ideological world view has an effect intrinsic to the presentation of this argument here: as I am tracing a continuity in ideas, the discontinuities will get short shrift. The material position of women and the attitudes towards them have zigzagged like a cake-walk or the proverbial snail up the side of a well – two slithers up and one slither down, sometimes one up and two down, as the authors quoted earlier record:

> . . . progress towards equal rights for women has been very slow indeed. There have even been times when the tide seemed to turn against them. The first law against abortion was passed in 1803. It imposed a sentence of life imprisonment for termination within the first fourteen weeks of pregnancy. In 1832 the first law was passed which forbade women to vote in elections. In 1877 the first Trades Union Congress upheld the tradition that women's place was in the home whilst man's duty was to protect and provide for her.[2]

Certainly both the history of feminism and the ideology of equality in general and for women in particular offer a monument to the law of uneven development. It is a monument I shall largely pass by in selecting the continuous track.

Equality as a principle – never as a practice – has been an essential part of the political ideology of all democratic capitalist societies since their inception. In being this it has expressed both the highest aspiration and the grossest limitation of that type of society. The mind of liberal and social-democratic man soars into the skies with his belief in equality only to find that it must return chained, like the falcon, to the wrist whence it came. For it is not only that capitalist society (which produces its own version of both liberal and social democratic thought) cannot produce the goods or practise what it preaches but that the premise on which it bases its faith in equality is a very specific and a very narrow one. The capitalist system establishes as the premise of its ideological concept of equality the economic fact of an exchange of commodities: a commodity exchanged for another of roughly equal value. In overthrowing the noble landlords of a preceding period the newly arising and revolutionary bourgeoisie made free and equal access to the production and exchange of commodities the basis of man's estate: individual achievement replaced aristocratic birth.

In England in the late fifteenth century, the absolutist monarchy first overcame the multiplicity of feudal lords and the multifariousness of competing jurisdictions of secular and temporal powers. As happened later in France, for example, the central power of the still largely feudal monarch created and integrated large economic areas and established an equality of duties. The notion of equality of duties stands midway between a system of privilege asserted by feudal landlords and the concept of equality of rights propounded by the capitalist middle classes in the seventeenth century in England and the late eighteenth century in France. The legal edifice which enshrined the new equality of rights replaced the harmony between a law of privilege and economic privilege with a complete disjuncture between legal equality and economic disparity – if disparity is not too mild a word to fit the bill.

In bourgeois ideology everyone has access to the dominant entrepreneurial class; in the capitalist economy that it expresses, of course, the majority of the people do not. For the accumulation of capital – which is the rationale of capitalism – profits must be made; for profits to be made there is one particular commodity that cannot be equally exchanged and it is the only commodity that the majority of the population possess – the commodity of labour power. In a capitalist system the person who has only one commodity to sell (his labour power) is thought to be doing this in a free and equal way – no one enforces his labour and he is paid a 'fair' wage for the job. But in fact, if profits are to be made and capital to accumulate, there is no way in which a wage could be *equal* to the preferred labour power – the labour power must produce *more* than the wage answers for, else where is the profit to come from? (The worker's labour power, which is in a sense himself, produces a surplus.) The freedom to work is little more than the freedom not to go hungry: the equal bargaining power of employer and employee is the right of the employer to hire or dismiss the employee and the right of the employee to be dismissed or go on strike – without a wage.

Under capitalism 'equality' can only refer to equality under the law. Because it cannot take into account the fundamental inequities of the class society on which it is based, the law itself must treat men as a generalizable and abstract category, it must ignore not only their individual differences, their different needs and abilities, but the absolute differences in their social and economic positions. Since the seventeenth century the law has expressed this, its precondition.

Bourgeois, capitalist law is a general law that ensures that everybody is equal before it: it is abstract and applies to all cases and all persons. As the political theorist Franz Neumann writes: 'A minimum of equality is guaranteed, for if the law-maker must deal with persons and situations in the abstract he thereby treats persons and situations as equals and is precluded from discriminating against any specific person.'[3] In writing further of the concept of political freedom with which the bourgeois concept of equality is very closely linked, Neumann continues to analyse this particular capitalist notion of law in these terms:

> The generality of the law is thus the precondition of judicial independence, which, in turn, makes possible the realization of the minimum liberty and equality that inheres in the formal structure of the law.
>
> The formal structure of the law is, moreover, equally decisive in the operation of the social system of a competitive-contractual society. The need for calculability and reliability of the legal and administrative system was one of the reasons for the limitation of the power of the patrimonial monarchy and of feudalism. The limitation culminated in the establishment of the legislative power of parliaments by means of which the middle classes controlled the administrative and fiscal apparatus and exercised a condominium with the crown in changes of the legal system. A competitive society requires general laws as the highest form of purposive rationality, for such a society is composed of a large number of entrepreneurs of about equal power. Freedom of the commodity market, freedom of the labour market, free entrance into the entrepreneurial class, freedom of contract, and rationality of the judicial responses in disputed issues – these are the essential characteristics of an economic system which requires and desires the production for profit, and ever renewed profit in a continuous, rational capitalistic enterprise.[4]

The law, then, enshrines the principles of freedom and equality – so long as you do not look at the particular unequal conditions of the people who are subjected to it. The concept 'equal under the law' does not apply to the economic inequities it is there to mask. The law is general. Therefore, as *men* – employer and employee – are equal, the law does not consider the inequality of their position. Equality always denies the inequality inherent in its own birth as a concept. The notions of equality, freedom or liberty do not drop from the skies; their meaning will be defined by the particular historical circumstances that give rise to them in any given epoch. Rising as the slogan of a bourgeois revolution, equality most emphatically denies the new class inequalities that such a revolution sets up – the equality exists only as an abstract standard of measurement between people reduced to their abstract humanity under the law.

Those seem to me to be some of the limitations of the concept of equality – what of its strengths? When a rising bourgeoisie is struggling against an old feudal order, that is, before it has firmly constituted itself as the dominant class, in its aspirations it does in some sense represent all the social classes that were subordinate previously: its revolution initially is a revolution on behalf of all the oppressed against the then dominant class – the nobility. The ideological concepts that the bourgeoisie will forge in this struggle are universalistic ones – they are about *most* people and the society most people want. New formulations about 'human nature' will jostle with old ones and eventually set themselves as permanent truths. New values, such as a belief in the supremacy of reason, will be treated as though they have always been the pinnacle to which men try to ascend. These ideas will seem to be not only timeless, but classless. Equality is one of them. Equality is the aspiration of the bourgeoisie at the moment when as the revolutionary class it momentarily represents all classes.

The liberal universalistic concept of equality, encapsulating the highest and best aspirations of the society, is represented by these words of Jeremy Taylor's:

> If a man be exalted by reason of any excellence in his soul, he may please to remember that all souls are equal, and their differing operations are because their instrument is in better tune, their body is more healthful or better-tempered; which is no more praise to him than it is that he were born in Italy.[5]

Taylor recognizes that there are differences but these should not count. It is this universalistic aspect of the concept that has continued in the most ennobled liberal and social-democratic thought within capitalism; because it is instituted as a demand of the revolutionary moment it soars above the conditions that create it, but because this revolution is based on these conditions – the conditions of creating two new antagonistic 'unequal' classes – to these conditions it must eventually return trapped by the hand that controls even its flight.

A history of the concept of equality would run in tracks very similar to a history of feminism. First introduced as one of the pinnacles of the new society's ideology in revolutionary England of the seventeenth century, the notion of equality next reached a further high in the era of enlightenment in the eighteenth century and then with the French Revolution. Feminism likewise has both the continuity and the fits and starts of this trajectory. Feminism as a conscious, that is self-conscious, protest movement, arose as part of a revolutionary bourgeois tradition that had equality of mankind as its highest goal. The first expressions of feminism were endowed with the strengths of the concept of equality and circumscribed by its limitations. Feminism arose in England in the seventeenth century as a conglomeration of precepts and a series of demands by women who saw themselves as a distinct sociological group and one that was completely excluded from the tenets and principles of the new society. The seventeenth-century feminists were mainly middle-class women who argued their case in explicit relation to the massive change in society that came about with the end of feudalism and the beginning of capitalism. As the new bourgeois man held the torch up against absolutist tyranny and argued for freedom and equality, the new bourgeois woman wondered why she was being left out.

Writing on marriage in the year 1700, Mary Astell asked:

> If Absolute Sovereignty be not necessary in a State how comes it to be so in a Family? or if in a Family why not in a State; since no reason can be alleg'd for the one that will not hold more strongly for the other,

> If *all Men are born free*, how is it that all Women are born slaves? As they must be if the being subjected to the *inconstant, uncertain, unknown, arbitrary Will* of Men, be the perfect Condition of Slavery?[6]

How could men proclaim social change and a new equality in the eyes of the Lord and consistently ignore one half of the population? It is to the values of the revolutionary society and against those of the old that the feminists appealed. The old society was represented by arbitrary rule, superstition, irrational custom and pointless pedantry of argument – more problematic was the continued use of two otherwise respected sources – Aristotle and the Bible.

Aristotle's contribution to the debate on the status of women can be summarized by his comment: '. . . and woman is, as it were, an impotent male, for it is through a certain incapacity that the female is female' and the arguments the women made against this were organized around a thorough refutation of any *natural* inferiority: there was no physical, 'bodily' difference in men and women's minds (it was left to the nineteenth century to try to prove by measurement that there was a physiological sexual defect here). The power of reason was the mark of mankind's superiority over the beasts, if women were deficient in this it could only be as a result of their lack of educational and social opportunities for improving their minds.

Considerable ingenuity was spent reinterpreting the assumed mysogyny of the Bible. Mary Astell demonstrated that St Paul in crucial passages was arguing not literally, but allegorically, yet beneath the sophistication of her own argument there is a simple appeal to the new common-sensical aspect of reason: 'For the Earthly *Adam's* being *Form'd* before *Eve*, seems as little to prove her Natural Subjection to him, as the Living Creatures, Fishes, Birds and Beasts being Form'd before them both, proves that Mankind must be subject to these Animals.'[7]

The feminists ask for the equal status that they insist any reasonable person must grant they should have by right of all the professed values of the society. As the anonymous author of 'An Essay in Defence of the Female Sex' writes in her dedication to Princess Ann of Denmark: 'I have only endeavour'd to reduce the Sexes to a Level, and by Arguments to raise Ours to an Equality at the most with Men.'[8] The arguments for equality are still valid in all democratic societies and few of these feminist demands for equal rights (mainly to education and professional employment) have been adequately met. But the demands for equality are permeated with something more radical still.

I want to select three aspects of the seventeenth-century feminists' arguments that make it clear this was the beginning of political feminism. First, in rejecting women as naturally different from men they are forced to define women as a distinct *social* group with its own socially defined characteristics. Second, as a result of this they see that men *as a social group* oppress women as a social group — they are not against men as such, but against the social power of men; women's oppression as they put it is due to 'the Usurpation of Men, and the Tyranny of Custom'. Finally while they want to be let into men's privileged sphere they also want men to learn something from women; though they wouldn't have used exactly these terms the feminization of men is as important as the masculinization of women – they do not undervalue female powers only their abuse. In the quotation from the anonymous author that I have just cited we should note that there are two clauses: she wants to be equal to men *and* her arguments have endeavoured 'to reduce the Sexes to a Level'. There is a current Chinese slogan that says 'anything a man can do a woman can do too'; feminism in the seventeenth century, as today, would add: 'anything a woman can do a man can do too' – though the seventeenth-century terms for this sexual 'levelling' are slightly different.

The mental agility of women is valuable. 'I know' (writes our anonymous author) 'our Opposers usually mis-call our Quickness of Thought, Fancy and Flash, and christen their own Heaviness by the specious Names of Judgement and Solidity: but it is easy to retort upon 'em the reproachful ones of Dulness and Stupidity with more Justice',[9] and she goes on to claim that potentially the women's world of care-for-others could be as much a repository of the highest values of civilization as the men's world of pursuing material gain – there is nothing in itself wrong with domesticity; it is only women's enforced exclusive confinement thereto and men's self-imposed exclusion therefrom that creates the evil; but given this exclusiveness then indeed it is evil. As the Duchess of Newcastle somewhat fancifully wrote in 1662:

> . . . men are so unconscionable and cruel against us, as they endeavour to Barr us all Sorts or kinds of Liberty, as not to suffer us Freely to associate amongst our own sex, but, would fain Bury us in their houses or Beds, as in a Grave; the truth is, we live like Bats or owls, Labour like Beasts, and Dye like worms.[10]

The early feminists do not consciously congregate as a political movement but they do propose to establish female groups usually for educational and self-educational purposes – they want to develop 'friendship' among women. (The urge for female friendship bears a resemblance to the desire for sisterhood as it is advocated in the Women's Movement today.) Clearly a larger rebellion crossed their minds:

> . . . women are not so well united [writes Mary Astell] as to form an Insurrection. They are for the most part Wise enough to Love their Chains, and to discern how very becomingly they sit. They think as humbly of themselves as their Masters can wish, with respect to the other Sex, but in regard to their

own, they have a Spice of Masculine Ambition, every one would Lead, and none will Follow . . . therefore as to those Women who find themselves born for Slavery, and are so sensible of their own Meanness to conclude it impossible to attain to anything excellent, since they are, or ought to be, the best acquainted with their own Strength and Genius, She's a Fool who would attempt their Deliverance and Improvement. No, let them enjoy the great Honor and Felicity of their Tame, Submissive and Depending Temper! Let the Men applaud, and let them glory in, this wonderful Humility![11]

It was left to later generations of women to try to devise a way of solving the problem of the masculine ambition to lead and of overcoming the apathy of feminine contentment – both are struggles that still continue. But less ironic and more strident than Mary Astell, the Duchess of Newcastle could wish she 'were so fortunate, as to persuade you to make a frequentation, association, and combination amongst our sex, that we may unite in Prudent consuls, to make ourselves as Free, Happy and famous as Men . . .'[12] In fact a number of groups were formed and though they lacked the larger political unity and range of reference, such 'frequentations' do bear some resemblance to the small groups which are the distinctive unit of organization within feminism today.

The seventeenth-century feminists are today frequently criticized for only wanting the liberation of the women of their own social class. Certainly whenever they explicitly thought of the labouring classes, it did not occur to them to consider that their own demands for access to education, the world of business and the professions were strikingly inappropriate for women (or men) of a lower class. When they talked of freeing 'half the world' they were oblivious of class differences. Yet I think to criticize them for being blinkered by their bourgeois vision is ahistorical and inaccurate. In so far as they came from the revolutionary class of that epoch and that they pointed out the oppressions that still existed, they did speak for all women. I said earlier that at the point where it is challenging an old order a revolutionary class speaks a universalistic language initially on behalf of all oppressed groups. If this is true in general it must be true for women – the seventeenth-century feminists appealed in a universalistic language on behalf of women to the highest concepts of freedom and humanity of which their society was capable. Even the very precepts of a revolutionary change, in any era, cannot transcend the social conditions that give rise to them. In demanding entry into a male world, the end of men's social oppression of women and equality between the sexes, the women were truly revolutionary. They had explanations, but they did not have a theory of how women came to be an oppressed social group, but still today we lack any such full theoretical analysis. They understood clearly enough that in their own time they were being made to live like bats and they saw the contradictions between this oppression and the ideology of liberty and equality; at that historical point to go beyond such insight and such forceful protest could only be millenarianism – as they well knew. In a final dedication to Queen Anne of her book on marriage, Mary Astell addresses the future: 'In a word, to those Halcyon, or if you will *Millennium* Days, in which the Wolf and the Lamb shall feed together, and a Tyrannous Domination which Nature never meant, shall no longer render useless if not hurtful, the Industry and Understanding of half Mankind!'[13]

When feminism next really reached a new crescendo, with Condorcet and Mary Wollstonecraft and the French Revolution, it was the hurtfulness, not the uselessness, of the oppression of women that was uppermost in the writers' minds. The principles were clear; Condorcet was emphatic in stating them. 'Either no member of the human race has real rights, or else all have the same; he who votes against the rights of another, whatever his religion, colour or sex, thereby adjures his own.'[14] It is as bad to be tyrants as to be slaves; men and women are degraded by the oppression of women. But what is new to the argument, and best expressed in Mary Wollstonecraft's *A Vindication of the Rights of Women* (1792) is the constant analysis of the damage done to women and therefore to society by conditioning them into inferior social beings. The theme is present in the seventeenth century, but a hundred years of confirmation has made its mark: 'femininity' has been more clearly defined as fragility, passivity and dependence – economic and emotional. Wollstonecraft inveighs against such false refinement:

> In short, women, in general . . . have acquired all the follies and vices of civilization, and missed the useful fruit . . . Their senses are inflamed, and their understandings neglected, consequently they become the prey of their senses, delicately termed sensibility, and are blown about by every momentary gust of feeling. Civilized women are therefore so weakened by false refinement, that, respecting morals, their condition is much below what it would be were they left in a state near to nature.[15]

Between the end of the seventeenth and the end of the eighteenth centuries it would seem that among the middle classes the social definition of sexual differences had been more forcefully asserted; the behavioural characteristics of 'masculinity' and 'femininity' had drawn further apart. Behind Wollstonecraft's energetic analysis is a dilemma with which we are still familiar: if a woman strives not to fall for the lure of feminine subservience she is labelled 'masculine', in which case what happens to her legitimate femininity or 'femaleness'? How can one be a woman, indeed womanly, and avoid the social stereotypes? The answer is a concept of humanity which more urgently unifies the social characteristics of men and women: 'A wild wish has just flown from my heart to my head, and I will not stifle it, though it may excite a horse-laugh. I do earnestly wish to see the distinction of sex confounded in society, unless where love animates the behaviour.'[16]

In fact Wollstonecraft, while asserting equality as a human right, has to some degree moved away from what I have characterized as an essentially liberal position into one that we might desribe as radical humanism. Though, like the seventeenth-century writers, her highest good is reason and she demonstrates that women are inferior because they have been subjugated – not, as is usually argued, that they are subjugated because they are inferior – yet there is a new political dimension to her feminism. Where her English predecessors were demanding the practice consistent with the revolutionary values of their society, Wollstonecraft, living in the double context of by then reactionary Britain yet having the inspiration of the French Revolution, wanted not a change *within* society, but a change *of* society:

> I do not believe that a private education can work the wonders which some sanguine writers have attributed to it. Men and women must be educated, in a great degree, by the opinions and manners of the society they live in . . . It may . . . fairly be inferred, that, till society be differently constituted, much cannot be expected from education.[17]

> Rousseau exerts himself to prove that all *was* right originally: a crowd of authors that all *is* now right: and I, that all *will be* right.[18]

In Wollstonecraft the millennium has come down firmly from heaven to earth.

The writer to whom I wish to refer finally in this sketch of the relationship between feminism and the concept of equality is John

Stuart Mill. To offer a somewhat sweeping generalization, after Mill, in England the feminist struggle moves from being predominantly the utterances of individuals about a philosophical notion of equality to being an organized political movement for the attainment, among other things, of equal rights. Of course, the one does not exclude the other, it is a question of emphasis.

In a lucid and powerful manner, Mill's essay, 'The Subjection of Women' (1869), written at the height of the Victorian repression of women, resumes with a new coherence the arguments with which we have become familiar. Thus he has a clear perspective on the argument that maddened the earlier writers, that women's characteristics and social status were 'natural':

> What is now called the nature of women is an eminently artificial thing – the result of forced repression in some directions, unnatural stimulation in others.[19]

> So true is it that unnatural generally means only uncustomary, and that everything which is usual appears natural. The subjection of women to men being a universal custom, any departure from it quite naturally appears unnatural.[20]

Mill also looks back with clarity on the history of democracy and of women's rights – or rather lack of them.

Where the seventeenth-century women looked to their own new society for change and Wollstonecraft, with the example of the first radical years of the French Revolution at hand, looked to change her society, Mill, writing from within an industrial capitalism that had hardened into fairly extreme conservatism had to stand aside and argue from the best of the past and the hope of the future. Most importantly, the justice and morality he wants have not yet been found in the world:

> Though the truth may not yet be felt or generally acknowledged for generations to come, the only school of genuine moral sentiment is society between equals.[21]

> We have had the morality of submission, and the morality of chivalry and generosity; the time is now come for the morality of justice.[22]

But Mill's lucidity, unlike Wollstonecraft's exuberance, forces him to constrict his own vision. Although at one moment he speculates that the reason why women are denied equal rights in society at large is because men must confine them to the home and the family, he does not pursue the implications of this insight and instead programmatically demands these rights. When it comes down to it, his equality is, quite realistically, equality under the law:

> . . . on women this sentence is imposed by actual law, and by customs equivalent to law. What, in unenlightened societies, colour, race, religion or, in the case of a conquered country, nationality, are to some men, sex is to all women; a peremptory exclusion from almost all honourable occupations, but either such as cannot be fulfilled by others, or such as those others do not think worthy of their acceptance.[23]

> . . . the principle which regulates the existing social relations between the two sexes – the legal subordination of one sex to the other – is wrong in itself, and now one of the chief hindrances to human improvement.[24]

I am not arguing against Mill's position, but trying to indicate a lack that is implicit in this perspective. Mill's concept of human beings that are freed from the artificial constraints of a false masculinity or femininity is somehow more abstract than that of the earlier feminists. The seventeenth-century women thought if men and women were equal they could gain some quality from each other. Mary Wollstonecraft's vision combined in one being the best of a female world with the best of a male world. Mill correctly argues that we cannot know what men and women will be like when released from present stereotypes but out of this correctness comes an elusive feeling that Mill, seeing so accurately women's miserable subordination, failed to see their contribution. This turns on the question of the importance of the reproduction and care of human life – Mill does not see, as Wollstonecraft does, that there might be a gain in men really becoming fathers (instead of remote, authoritarian figureheads) as well as in women being freed to pursue the so-called 'masculine' virtues. That Mill's concept of humanity is abstract, that he did not seem to consider the contribution of 'femaleness' once freed of its crippling exclusiveness to oppressed women, may have been because he was a man; it may just as easily have been because of the different social circumstances from which he wrote. Because he was not living at the moment when the bourgeoisie was the revolutionary class, the universalistic aspect of such thought of which I spoke earlier must turn to abstraction, there is no other way in which it can refer to all people.

John Stuart Mill in a sense expresses the best and the last in the high liberal tradition. His ideals represent the best his society is capable of but they can no longer be felt to represent that society –

as a consequence there is a sort of heroic isolation to his philosophy. Because of his isolation, because of his abstraction, in this field Mill's thought pinpoints and 'fixes' the essence of liberalism:

> The old theory was, that the least possible should be left to the individual agent; that all he had to do should, as far as practicable, be laid down for him by superior powers. Left to himself he was sure to go wrong. The modern conviction, the fruit of a thousand years of experience, is that things in which the individual is the person directly interested, never go right but as they are left to his own discretion; and that any regulation of them by authority except to protect the rights of others, is sure to be mischievous. This conclusion, slowly arrived at, and not adopted until almost every possible application of the contrary theory has been made with disastrous result, now (in the industrial department) prevails universally in the most advanced countries, almost universally in all that have pretensions to any sort of advancement. It is not that all processes are supposed to be equally good, or all persons to be equally qualified for everything; but that freedom of individual choice is now known to be the only thing which procures the adoption of the best processes, and throws each operation into the hands of those who are best qualified for it.[25]

Mill's philosophy is an overriding belief in the individual and in the right of the individual to fulfil his or her maximum potential, Mill's concept of equality is therefore an equality of opportunity. As a politician he fought for equal rights for women under the law.

Since Mill wrote there has, I think, been, in an uneven way, a decline in the tradition of liberal thought. Today, exactly three-quarters of the way through the twentieth century, 'equality' would seem to have become a somewhat unfashionable concept. Equal rights are still strenuously fought for but equality as a principle of a just and free society rarely elicits the eloquent support it once received. I am neither a philosopher nor a political scientist and I am ill equipped to analyse why this should be the case. I can, however, point to some observations we all might make.

The concept of equality as a high ideal flourishes as a revolutionary aspiration when it is confronted with two types of conservatism – as Mill's was in Victorian England. One type of conservatism is a direct reflection of the economic conditions of a society once the society had settled down after its revolutionary open-endedness. When class distinctions have rigidified, then the conservative ideology of capitalism can bear a striking resemblance to the old order the revolutionary bourgeoisie once overthrew. In its naked crudity this conservatism is found in Arthur Young's statement: '. . . everyone but an idiot knows that the lower classes must be kept poor, or they will never be industrious'[26] or in a verse of a hymn popular in England in the years before the First World War:

> The rich man in his castle,
> The poor man at his gate,
> God made them high or lowly
> And ordered their estate.[27]

The best liberal traditions of liberty, equality and individualism such as those represented by Mill rarely engaged directly with conservatism of this sort, but their presence as an alternative *within* the same society hopefully acts to circumscribe the possible power of such reactionary stances.

There is another conservative tradition that is more testing for the liberal conception of individualism and equality and that is Tory radicalism. Where conservative conservatism argues that there are generic differences which must be the basis of inequalities between groups of people, Tory radicalism, like liberalism and, for that matter socialism and communism, argues that there are differences between individuals. The litmus test here for establishing a distinction between the political philosophies is to see what happens to these individual differences. Tory radicalism always offers a place in the past, a romantic golden age when society was small enough for all these differences to flourish – merely as differences, be they handicaps or advantages. The liberal concept that I have presented here, argues that we are all different but these differences can only be realized in their infinite variety if we are given equal opportunities to make what we individually and differently can of them – they cannot be the basis of different treatment. The socialist, and communist, perspectives suggest that 'equality' in capitalist society is based on class inequality; in a classless society there will still be differences or inequalities, inequalities between individuals, strengths or handicaps of various kinds. There will be differences between men and women, differences among women and among men; a truly just society based on collective ownership and equal distribution would take these inequalities into account and give more to he who needed more and ask for more from he who could give more. This would be a true recognition of the individual in the qualities that are essential to his humanity.

When the liberal concept of equality – the ideal of a revolutionary bourgeoisie – has to oppose not conservatism, as it did in Mill's case, but a system of thinking such as that of socialism which looks to a new future, then its own radicalism is weakened and that is what has been happening in a somewhat sporadic fashion since the last part of the last century.

A crisis in the history of the concept of equality can, I think, be marked by one book that epitomizes the problem: the publication of the Halley Stewart lectures that the socialist historian, R. H. Tawney gave in 1929. The book, entitled *Equality*, is a most moving document – a humanitarian plea for equality as, quite simply, a correct, indeed *the* correct principle of civilization. The framework within which Tawney argues for equality is that of moral and ethical philosophy, the terms in which he assesses the progress of equality are those of poverty and disparity of opportunity particularly in education. There is no underlying analysis of a class-antagonistic society and even in the lengthy epilogue written in 1950 the racial minorities in Britain are not mentioned, the position of women is not hinted at. Yet Tawney's own recommendations transcend the limitations of his belief in equality: he must argue for redistribution of wealth and for more collective provision of social services. His argument follows the liberal tradition but starts to look beyond it and sees that the freedom of privilege must be controlled; that freedom in a class society is ultimately freedom for one class to exploit another.

It was not malicious oversight that made Tawney fail to see women as a deprived group – when he was writing women were simply not seen as a group at all. Ten years before he wrote and roughly fifteen years after his epilogue they were seen as a group once more. Feminism had in both cases pointed to the fact. In 1974, using the very criteria by which Tawney estimated the march of equality – poverty – a survey carried out in Britain found that women were the single most impoverished social group. The survey was not carried out by feminists, but feminism had made the investigators conscious of this category: women were found both to be a distinct social group and an under-privileged one.

The fight for equal rights for women today takes place against this weakening of the liberal conception of equality. It is important both to remember that ideal and to realize its limitations. Too many revolutionary groups would skip the present and think that given both a falseness in the conception and its ultimate unrealizability, 'equality' is not something to be fought for: too many not-so-revolutionary groups think that equal rights are attainable under class-antagonistic systems and are adequate. Equal rights will always only be rights before the law but these have by no means been won yet nor their possible extent envisaged. A new society that is built on an old society that, within its limits, has reached a certain level of equality clearly is a better starting point than one that must build on a society predicated on privilege and unchallenged oppression.

ACKNOWLEDGEMENT

I am greatly indebted to Hilda Smith of the University of Maryland, Washington, DC, for introducing me to the seventeenth-century feminists, and for letting me read her excellent work on the subject prior to its publication.

NOTES

 1 Anna Coote and Tess Gill, *Women's Rights: A Practical Guide* (Penguin, 1974), pp. 15–16.
 2 Ibid., p. 16.
 3 Franz Neumann, 'The Concept of Political Freedom', in *The Democratic and the Authoritarian State* (The Free Press of Glencoe, New York, 1964), p. 167.
 4 Ibid., pp. 167–8.
 5 Quoted in R. H. Tawney, *Equality* (Allen and Unwin, 1964), p. 48.
 6 Mary Astell, *Reflections Upon Marriage* (1700), no pagination.
 7 Ibid.
 8 Anon., *An Essay in the Defence of the Female Sex* (1696).
 9 Ibid., p. 17.
10 Margaret Lucas, Duchess of Newcastle, 'Female Orations', in *Orations of Divers Sorts* (1662), pp. 225–6.
11 Astell, *Reflections Upon Marriage*.
12 Lucas, 'Female Orations'.
13 Astell, *Reflections Upon Marriage*.
14 Caritat, Marquis de Condorcet, 'Sur l'admission des femmes au droit de cite' (1790), quoted in Tomalin, *The Life and Death of Mary Wollstonecraft* (Weidenfeld and Nicolson, 1974), p. 104.
15 Mary Wollstonecraft, *A Vindication of the Rights of Women* (1792), (Everyman Library, 1970), p. 67. (Penguin edn 1975.)
16 Ibid., p. 63.
17 Ibid., p. 25.

18 Ibid., p. 18.
19 John Stuart Mill, *The Subjection of Women* (1869) (Everyman Library, 1970), p. 238.
20 Ibid., p. 230.
21 Ibid., p. 259.
22 Ibid., p. 259.
23 Ibid., p. 316.
24 Ibid., p. 219.
25 Ibid., pp. 234–5.
26 Arthur Young, quoted in Tawney, *Equality*, p. 94.
27 From the hymn 'All Things Bright and Beautiful'.

2

Marxist-Feminism and the Work of Karl Marx

MICHÈLE BARRETT

Any commemorative essay, let alone one whose subject is the greatest revolutionary thinker of modern history, tends to court the danger of hagiography. On the question of feminism, however, even the most committed Marxists now suspect that our idol has feet of clay. Many feminists, indeed, see this weakness as one which vitiates the whole of Marx's work. Gone are the days when 'the woman question' could be answered from the writings of Marx; his treatment of the issue is now widely regarded as scattered, scanty and unsatisfactory. The situation is scarcely improved by the fact that much of what is attributed to Marx, particularly in relation to a programme for the emancipation of women, was in fact the work of Engels. It is not entirely clear how far Marx himself accepted arguments such as those eventually set out in Engels's *The Origin of the Family, Private Property and the State* (1884).

The fact that Engels took such an interest in questions about the family and the oppression of women makes it difficult to take a charitable view of Marx's own failings in this area. He cannot be 'let off the hook' by saying that gender inequality had yet to be discovered at the time he lived and wrote. In any case such an argument does Marx a disservice that borders on insult. Marx's ability to penetrate the appearance of social relations and expose their underlying exploitative character is the basis of the explanatory value of Marxism. We can see this ability applied to a broad enough range of phenomena to be conscious of its *not* being applied to questions of gender. To exonerate Marx by an appeal to a supposedly 'pre-feminist' culture is both to underestimate the currency of feminist ideas in the nineteenth century and to underestimate the usual level of perception of Marx.

In order to consider the place of Marx's thought in the tradition

Reprinted with permission from *Marx: One Hundred Years On*, edited by Betty Matthews (Lawerence and Wishart, London, 1983), pp. 199–219.

of socialist feminism we shall need to look at several different types of question, ranging from general philosophical orientation to specific formulations and analyses.

I EGALITARIANISM AND HUMANISM

Many people see a 'natural' sympathy between all struggles against oppression. Class struggle, anti-racist struggle, feminist struggle are all self-evidently directed against inequality and towards human liberation and hence may be expected to enjoy relationships of mutual support. The history of these struggles is less the history of easy alliances, however, than it is a history of distance and division. Alliances have to be built in a mood of conscious solidarity and are not naturally given by the simple fact of oppression.

The vocabulary of 'inequality' comes from liberalism rather than Marxism and there is considerable evidence that Marx is misrepresented when he is portrayed as a gladiator of egalitarianism. In fact, Marx regarded the notion of 'equality' as not merely an idea that historically coincided with bourgeois rule but as a *bourgeois idea*. This is the point he makes in the well-known discussion of 'ruling class and ruling ideas':

> If now in considering the course of history we detach the ideas of the ruling class from the ruling class itself and attribute to them an independent existence, if we confine ourselves to saying that these or those ideas were dominant at a given time, without bothering ourselves about the conditions of production and the producers of these ideas, if we thus ignore the individuals and world conditions which are the source of the ideas, we can say, for instance, that during the time that the aristocracy was dominant, the concepts honour, loyalty, etc. were dominant, during the dominance of the bourgeoisie the concepts freedom, equality, etc. The ruling class itself on the whole imagines this to be so.[1]

Equality, justice and rights are not embraced in the abstract by Marxism. Engels's lengthy polemic against Dühring makes it very clear that what might be called 'ethical socialism' – socialism based upon truth and justice as goals – differs sharply from the Marxist view of socialism as the historically given mission of the proletariat.[2] Marx and Engels both display an antipathy to the doctrine of egalitarianism which they identify as part of the political arsenal of the ascendent bourgeoisie. As Allen Wood puts it: 'On the basis of the texts, I think we must regard Marx as an opponent of the ideal of equality, despite the fact that he is also and not any the less an opponent of all forms of social privilege and oppression.'[3] Wood inclines to the view that it would be in keeping with 'the spirit of Marxism' to regard movements based on the concept of equality – such as feminism or anti-racism – as progressive. This, in a sense, is the view generally held on the left today. We cannot be too confident, though, that Marx would have agreed with it. The nineteenth century saw several manifestations of the call for women's suffrage. Marx, however, having plenty of opportunities to identify himself with this movement, failed to do so. Just as he was happy to leave the theorization of 'the woman question' to Engels, so he left its political profile to others such as his daughter Eleanor. The implication must obviously be that, to say the least, he regarded such issues as marginal.

Neither Marx nor Engels saw fit to attempt to rebut the classic statements in favour of women's rights. Wollstonecraft and Mill remain unanswered where similarly egalitarian and liberal arguments on other topics are despatched with vigour. It is not perhaps surprising that, although Marx and Engels might be ready enough to approve the organization of *women workers*, they did not see that the cause of socialism had much in common with that of women's rights. Engels noted in the early 1890s that 'The foremost English champions of the formal rights of women . . . are in a large measure directly or indirectly interested in the capitalist exploitation of both sexes.'[4] It is no coincidence that this last reference is from Yvonne Kapp's biography of Eleanor Marx, for – such is the paucity of research on the attitudes of Marx and Engels to feminist issues – it is an invaluable source of information on Marx and Engels too.

It can be argued that feminism as a modern political doctrine is based principally on a philosophy of egalitarianism.[5] Underlying many feminist political positions is the variant of humanism that demands equal rights for all individuals. Historically, feminism has arisen as part of bourgeois liberal ideology, though undoubtedly most feminists today would resist Marx's implication that this renders feminism a bourgeois notion *tout court*. One way of posing a philosophical distance between feminist thought and that of Marx, is in terms of egalitarianism. The dominant traditions of feminism are couched in terms of morality, justice or equal rights, and attempts to draw up a model of male dominance with an explanatory value to match that of Marxism's historical materialism have been, so far, problematic. The claim of Marxism, of course, is to provide a scientific account of the exploitation we experience, with a view to overthrowing it; it is precisely this claim to a scientific status that differentiates Marxism from 'ethical' or egalitarian political doctrines.

In so far as egalitarianism is a source of conflict and disagreement betwen feminism and Marx, it might be thought that humanism would be a point of philosophical agreement. Attempts to develop rigorously non-humanist versions of feminism and Marxism have proved extremely difficult. On the Marxist side there is considerable scope for movement since the later Marx is patently more amenable to an anti-humanist reading than the early Marx. My own view would be that both feminism and the approach of Marx himself are essentially humanist in orientation. This would not necessarily make them compatible, however, since there could be substantial differences of emphasis. Feminism could be said to rest, ultimately, on an appeal to justice within the category of humanity. It relies on a notion of the self-evident fairness of distributing rights and opportunities equally among humans. The case is the same for anti-racist philosophy. The humanism in Marx's thought, notwithstanding the disavowals of egalitarianism, is in some respects similar. The theory of alienation (to be discussed in more detail later) is the obvious example to take. It argues that certain categories of people (labourers under a capitalist labour process for instance) are deprived of what belongs to them by virtue of their humanity.

Marx's writings are shot through with various aspects of humanist philosophy. One elementary example is the sharp distinction Marx draws between humanity on the one hand and the animal kingdom on the other. Humans have the ability to transform nature through labour, they can plan and execute their projects and are not limited by patterns of instinctual behaviour. This insistence on the distinctive abilities of humans gives rise, as Timpanaro's work suggests, to a certain 'triumphalism' in Marxism.[6] There are difficulties with this variant of humanism in that it partakes of a typically bourgeois complacency and conceit over the superiority of humanity. Raymond Williams is critical of Marx's use of 'man's conquest of nature':

. . . in both its moderate and its extreme forms, the notion of the 'conquest of nature' belongs not simply to Marxism but to a whole period of bourgeois thought. Indeed it became an almost inevitable generalization from the extraordinary achievements in material transformation of the industrial revolution and of advances in the physical sciences . . . But it

can now be clearly seen that this triumphalist version is, in an
exceptionally close correspondence, the specific ideology of
imperialism and capitalism, whose basic concepts – limitless
and conquering expansion; reduction of the labour process to
the appropriation and transformation of raw materials – it
exactly repeats.[7]

It is significant that this version of humanism is predicated upon
the centrality of *labour*. Although in principle human labour is
exactly that – neither male nor female – there is a tendency in
Marx's more specific analyses to imply that labour power is
generally male. Many anthropologists would now insist, as indeed
Engels did, that women played a dominant part in the transformation
of nature in societies where survival depended less on the construction of iron bridges and more on maintaining adequate food
supplies. In the analysis of capitalism, however, we tend to find (a
point to be dealt with in more detail later) an assumption that the
wage labourer is a man. The 'triumphalist' element of Marx's
humanism is one that has lent itself, in its application to specific
societies, to a marked gender imbalance.

A rather more complex issue arises if we consider another aspect
of Marx's humanism – the one classically thought of when
humanism is identified with atheism or secularism. Marx was
implacably opposed to religion in any version. Those who speak of
'Christian Marxism', for instance, are invoking a Marxism that
Marx himself would not recognize. So central to his philosophy
was Marx's demystification of religion that he claimed that '. . . the
criticism of religion is the presupposition of all criticism.'[8] Marx
saw religion as necessarily involving the impoverishment of
humanity, as necessarily alienating. Although it could be argued
that philosophical anti-Christianity is not historically a feature of
feminism – indeed the reverse would be true if we look to the
nineteenth-century development of evangelical influences on feminism[9] – certain problems do arise in the relationship between Marx's
anti-religious humanism and the equal-rights humanism more
characteristic of feminism.

Feminist humanism tends to be based on notions of justice and
equality within the human species. Marx's humanism is in the main
directed towards a future human liberation or emancipation. Marx
argues that this is why the proletariat has the transcending purpose
that he ascribes to it. The proletariat, as the utterly exploited class
has literally nothing to lose – it is the *universal* class and is hence
capable of bringing about a revolution that, in liberating itself,

must liberate everyone.[10] Only then is it possible to speak of *human* emancipation. Marx's critique of religion is an important prerequisite of his theory of human emancipation, since religion (here Marx follows Feuerbach) provides a prime case of the alienation from humanity of all that is conceived of as good. The creation of Gods must be at the expense of humanity.

The relationship between religion, alienation and emancipation is explored in Marx's analysis of 'the Jewish question' and his discussion there is of particular relevance to feminism. Essentially Marx argues that the call for emancipation of the Jews is a call for merely 'political' emancipation: it would not amount to human emancipation. He writes:

> So we do not say to the Jews, as Bauer does: you cannot be emancipated politically without emancipating yourselves radically from Judaism. Rather we say to them: because you can be politically emancipated without completely and consistently abandoning Judaism, this means that political emancipation itself is not human emancipation. If you Jews wish to achieve political emancipation without achieving human emancipation, then the incompleteness and contradiction does not only lie in you, it lies in the nature and category of political emancipation. If you are imprisoned within this category, then you are sharing in something common to everyone.[11]

The underlying problem is − to put it another way − human alienation: if all religion is dehumanizing then Judaism is no different from Christianity. As Karl Löwith puts it: 'What is needed for a genuine emancipation of the Jews, as of the Christians, is not freedom of religion decreed by the state, but human freedom from religion as such.'[12]

The key point in all this for a consideration of feminism is Marx's distinction between *political emancipation* and human emancipation. The goal of 'equality' is directed towards political emancipation and, as we have seen, Marx considered this not merely a limited category but a mystificatory one. He analyses the bourgeois liberal state as resting on the very inequalities − he cites 'birth, class, education and profession'[13] as examples − that it denies to be salient political differences. There can be little doubt that the categories of race and gender would − had Marx considered them in this context − form two further distinctions of civil society and its systems of rank. Marx's general position on the political emancipation of the Jews is to regard it as at best a limited project pending more fundamental human emancipation. At worst, he implies, such mere political emancipation distracts our attention from the degree to which we are all 'imprisoned' together: emphasis on sectional political emancipation blinds us to more fundamental shared, *human*, emancipation.

It must be noted that Marx's position on the Jewish question would be regarded as somewhat reductionist today. He would have had little sympathy for our efforts to engage with anti-semitism as an autonomous political ideology. On the basis of his own arguments it would be difficult to see – *pace* the spirit of human emancipation – how he would have supported a political movement aimed solely at abolishing the particular and specific oppressions of gender. My reading of Marx suggests that the feminist movement would undoubtedly fall within the circumscribed, if not illusory, gains to be obtained from 'mere' political emancipation.

Unless, of course, we adopt an extremely devout adherence to Marx's texts, this does not necessarily resolve our difficulties. We need to consider further whether Marx was right to be so critical of political emancipation or whether we might wish to conceive it as more progressive than he did. Secondly we might want to question the exclusively class-based orientation he has towards human liberation.

On the merits of egalitarian political emancipation versus the revolutionary potential of immiseration, readers no doubt have their own views. Decades of labourism and welfarism and feeble attempts to provide 'equality of opportunity' have tended to bear out Marx's gloomy predictions on the value of abolishing inequalities of earning, occupation, political rights and so on. Who, however, would care to argue against a systematic political project of eliminating racism and sexism from the working class on the grounds that such inequalities were not of prime significance? Marx's arguments on the place of 'political emancipation' need to be considered over his whole lifetime and changing views, and in the light of political developments over the last century. Let us leave in suspension, then, for the moment, whether Marx's critical conception of political emancipation is adequate to its task.

The second question I raised concerned Marx's account of human liberation or emancipation. This is based directly, in this early work, on the theory of alienation and this must now be considered. For although Marx casts this theory in terms that only engage directly with the labour process and the wage relation, it is widely interpreted, and has become popularized, as a far more general theory. In particular, it is often argued that Marx's writings on alienation, and indeed the philosophical humanism and ethical emphasis in his early writings, constitute his major influence on feminism and other liberation movements.

II OPPRESSION AND LIBERATION

Marx's theory of alienation has proved one of the most popularly resonant of his works. Although there is a considerable gulf between the various colloquial uses of the word 'alienation' and the complex theory of self-objectification Marx himself elaborated under this heading, it remains the case that Marx here propounded a doctrine that goes straight to the heart of much radicalism. What finer and more elegant expression of injustice could take the place of Marx's words:

> Labour produces works of wonder for the rich, but nakedness for the worker. It produces palaces, but only hovels for the worker; it produces beauty, but cripples the worker; it replaces labour by machines but throws a part of the workers back to a barbaric labour and turns the other part into machines. It produces culture, but also imbecility, and cretinism for the worker.[14]

We can observe these processes today as Marx saw them in 1844. The significance of Marx's approach is that he identified the causal relationship between the enrichment of the product and the impoverishment of labour: he explained what might otherwise appear as coincidence, irony, tragedy. Marx's explanation is as simple as the basis of his hostility to religion: 'The more man puts into God, the less he retains in himself'. As he puts it: '. . . the more the worker externalizes himself in his work, the more powerful becomes the alien, objective world that he creates opposite himself, the poorer he becomes himself in his inner life and the less he can call his own.'[15]

Marx's theory of alienation is effective as a general theory of oppression and liberation for the reason that it has a strong *relational* character. It enables us to understand oppression not as an arbitrary imposition but as a process involving the oppressed. C. J. Arthur rightly notes that what distinguishes an alienating situation from one based on robbery and brute force is that '. . . the workers, in effect, continually *reproduce the conditions of their subservience.*'[16] It is this dimension of alienation theory that has made it so relevant to feminism, as indeed it has had its influence on work such as Fanon's on interior colonization. Feminist theory and practice has tended to emphasize the necessity of engaging with subjectivity and consciousness as well as with external structures and it has attempted analyses of how an oppressed group comes to live out the dynamics of oppression in forms of collusion. It is to these concerns that Marx's account of alienation speaks so eloquently. The engagement of feminism with psycho-analysis, even – through Simone de Beauvoir – with existentialist concerns of authenticity and good faith is widely recognized. But Marx's explorations of alienation, and his deployment of even such relatively crude concepts as 'false consciousness' have made an indispensable early contribution to twentieth-century feminist thought.

It must be said, however, that this contribution has been extracted from the most general bearings of Marx's theory rather than from any explicit and detailed argument. Marx himself, unfortunately, poses the issue in such a way that a number of difficulties arise in *applying* the theory of alienation to the specific oppression of women. Consider the following passage:

> The alienation of man and in general of every relationship in which man stands to himself is first realized and expressed in the relationship with which man stands to other men. Thus in the situation of alienated labour each man measures his relationship to other men by the relationship in which he finds himself placed as a worker.[17]

To ask whether Marx intends 'man' to mean humanity or men is of more consequence than some 'tedious feminist pedantry'. If the generic meaning is intended Marx forgets that *precisely* the relationship in which a woman is placed *as a worker* differs from that in which a man is placed. (To what extent does the theory of alienation apply to a full-time housewife? How do we analyse the dual role of many women, as wage-labourers but also as creators of use values in the home?) Later Marx writes that 'The infinite degradation in which man exists for himself is expressed in his relationship to woman as prey and servant of communal lust . . .',[18] recognizing that his use of 'man' is not the generic one. The more salient point, however, is the general significance of labour to Marx's definition of what it is to be human rather than animal. If, as we shall see later, Marx tends to construe the labourer as male, this will raise problems at some level in the applicability of the theory of alienation to questions of gender.

Ideology

A parallel example can be seen, although I wish to mention it only briefly here, in Marx's account of ideology. Nothing could be more apposite to the present hegemonic dominance of men in the media and in ideological and cultural processes than Marx's well-known remarks on 'ruling ideas':

> The ideas of the ruling class are in every epoch the ruling ideas, i.e. the class which is the ruling *material* force of society, is at the same time its ruling *intellectual* force. The class which has the means of material production at its disposal, has control at the same time over the means of mental production, so that thereby, generally speaking, the ideas of those who lack the means of mental production are subject to it.[19]

Certainly it is suggestive to consider the extent to which men could be said to control 'the means of mental production'. Virginia Woolf, for example, has constructed an argument along these lines in her well-known *A Room of One's Own*.[20] It would be another matter, however, to elaborate in respect of gender the arguments that Marx's outlines in theorizing the relationship of ideology to the mode of production. So we are left with an insight, a suggestive or illuminating metaphor, but scarcely a body of concepts or a theoretical account of gender ideology.

The theory of alienation, and Marx's early writings in general, have had a tremendous impact on political liberation movements outside the class struggle. These early works are held by many to represent the true revolutionary spirit of Marxism. It is easy to see how theories of 'human liberation' can be identified with a political stance such as feminism, and equally easy to see how the early Marx is read as just such a theory. Whether or not one subscribes to the view that Marx's mature works, including the detailed analysis of capitalism, constitutes a rejection of this youthful and idealistic humanism, it is necessary to consider the implication of Marx's later work for feminism. If, as I have suggested, the early work is difficult to apply to the question of gender, then we may be even less confident about the later works. In particular, I want to discuss the conception of the family employed by Marx in his analysis of wage labour under capitalism.

III THE FAMILY AND WAGE-LABOUR

In theory, for Marx, both capital and labour are abstract categories and must be assumed to be sexless. In practice, however, although capital retains this conceptual purity, labour is historically constituted as the labour of concrete men and women. There can be little doubt that Marx tended to assume a 'typical' wage-labourer who was male. This is because he tended to assume a rather naturalistic approach to the family without giving adequate consideration to this. It is perhaps not surprising that in Marx's early works, including those written with Engels, we find a naturalistic conception of sexual relations and the family. The *Economic and Philosophical Manuscripts* and *The German Ideology* tend to discuss phenomena such as 'the communal possession of women' exclusively from the point of view of the possessing men. Marx sees 'man's relationship to woman' as an index of the general level of culture – but the entire discussion is couched rather as if women were a barometer of the state of male civilization.[21] Certainly there are flashes of perceptiveness in these early works, just as there are in the iconoclastic discussion of the family in *The Communist Manifesto*, but it may reasonably be suspected that the best of these are indebted to the contribution of Engels.

Marx himself, in his later work, continues to use an analysis which casts female wage-labour as intrinsically problematic. In *Capital*, for instance, he refers frequently to the labour of women and children as little other than a threat to the male worker. They are always invoked in terms of the moral degradation of women workers or in terms of the negative impact they have on male resistance. In a typical passage Marx writes, 'By the excessive addition of women and children to the ranks of the workers, machinery at last breaks down the resistance which the male operatives in the manufacturing period continued to oppose to the despotism of capital.'[22]

Marx's persistent assumption that the balance of forces in the labour–capital struggle was upset by women glutting the labour market was maintained over a curiously long period of time. *Capital* (volume 1) was published in 1867 and yet seems surprisingly unaffected by some key passages in Engels's much earlier work *The Condition of the Working Class in England* (1844). The employment of women in large numbers was scarcely a new phenomenon, yet Marx describes it with an air of shock and surprise that is not strictly appropriate to the situation he is discussing. The tone of

Marx's account suggests that the mass employment of women was an innovative strategy of capitalists in the mid-nineteenth century. Yet the data existed for Marx to see clearly that women had been wage-labourers from the earliest moments of wage-labour. For one thing, it was known that they tended to earn less, so it must have been known that they earned something.[23]

Underlying Marx's 'common-sense' misapprehensions about female wage-labour is his assumption that the norm from which to begin was the situation where a male worker's wage covered the reproduction of his family. Marx, as we see in the crucial passage where he puts forward the nub of his argument on the family and wage-labour, assumes as a baseline that there is a (pre-given) housewife engaged in domestic labour in the home.

> In so far as machinery dispenses with muscular power, it becomes a means of employing labourers of slight muscular strength, and those whose bodily development is incomplete, but whose limbs are all the more subtle. The labour of women and children was, therefore, the first thing sought for by capitalists who used machinery. That mighty substitute for labour and labourers was forthwith changed into a means for increasing the number of wage-labourers by enrolling, under the direct sway of capital, every member of the workman's family, without distinction of age or sex. Compulsory work for the capitalist usurped the place, not only of the children's play, but also of free labour at home within moderate limits for the support of the family.[24]

At this point Marx explains in a footnote how, since women's domestic work has to be replaced by buying ready-made things, this situation raises the overall cost of keeping the family. The simple implication of this leads to difficulties, however, since domestic labour is not entirely replaceable with bought goods. As is now abundantly clear to most women who work for wages and work in the home, houswork does not disappear as soon as wage-labour begins. This point is glossed over by Marx (as indeed it was by Engels) who goes on to make a more substantial argument using this supposedly typical situation – before the 'fall' of women into wage-labour – of a male breadwinner supporting his family on a single wage. A male breadwinner *must* be assumed for Marx's argument to hold:

> The value of labour-power was determined, not only by the labour-time necessary to maintain the individual adult labourer,

but also by that necessary to maintain his family. Machinery, by throwing every member of that family on to the labour-market, spreads the value of the man's labour-power over his whole family. It thus depreciates his labour-power. To purchase the labour-power of a family of four workers may, perhaps, cost more than it formerly did to purchase the labour-power of the head of the family, but, in return, four days' labour takes the place of one, and their price falls in proportion to the excess of the surplus-labour of four over the surplus-labour of one. In order that the family may live, four people must now, not only labour, but expend surplus-labour for the capitalist. Thus we see, that machinery, while augmenting the human material that forms the principal object of capital's exploiting power, at the same time raises the degree of exploitation.[25]

What is not clear here is the implication of Marx having bound together his assumptions on women's domestic contribution to these broad generalizations on the value of labour power. Eldred and Roth suggest, from an inspection of this and similar passages from *Capital*, that Marx by implication vitiates the category 'value of labour power' in assuming that the women and children's labour power 'have no value in themselves.'[26] Few Marxists would accept this suggestion, though it does indicate that disputes over the value of labour power, the analysis of domestic labour and determination of female wages are of more than incidental significance. The 'domestic labour debate', however ensnared it may have become in irresolvable technicalities, was important for these reasons.[27]

The political implications of these debates are clearly of the utmost importance. Marx's view has naturally supported the argument that the standard of living of the working class is raised by a so-called 'family wage' system in which a male wage-labourer earns sufficient to reproduce his family without women or children being obliged to seek wage work. Critics of such a system − if 'system' it can be said to be when the history of wage-labour in Britain shows such a situation to be a rarity enjoyed only by a 'labour aristocracy' − can marshall various rather different arguments. In the first place Marx was in error in his assumption that women's employment 'cheapened' the value of labour power since his comparison was with the fictitious situation of the woman as exclusively a housewife; in the second place he failed to see that the contribution made by domestic labour cannot be traded off against wage-labour but exists where the housewife is also a wage-labourer; in the third place, such a strategy has tended merely to exacerbate the badly paid and marginal position of women workers thereby worsening rather than ameliorating the threat they objectively pose to male workers.[28] This last argument amounts to nothing less than the claim that Marx's unreflectively sexist presuppositions in regard to women, work and the family have contributed to one of the major divisions within the working class and the organized labour movement.

The difficulty in assessing these problems is that so much hangs on errors of omission. Marx persists, to the end of his life and in his posthumous writings,[29] in the assumption that the individual of whom he speaks is male and that occasionally cognizance will need to be taken of his wife and family. This is scarcely an unspeakable crime; on the other hand it is not what we might expect from a mind that did not rest at appearances, commonsense and an unreflective absorption of personal experience on any other matter. The problem has some light thrown on it by considering – some might think rather belatedly – the question of the relationship between Marx's work and that of Engels and the attitudes they both held on this issue.

IV MARX AND ENGELS

Charles Wolfson has commented on a tendency for the 'errors' of Marxism to be laid at the door of Engels rather than at that of the 'great man' himself.[30] On the question of women, however, there is little danger of this occurring and indeed many feminists find the work of Engels by far the most useful of the texts of the Marx–Engels canon.

It is not necessary here to review the contribution made by Engels's much-debated account of *The Origin of the Family, Private Property and the State*. There exist several excellent discussions of this work from a contemporary feminist point of view[31] and perhaps the most striking aspect of the text is the purchase it still has on debate in this field. Scarcely a Marxist-feminist text is produced that does not refer somewhere to Engels's argument, and if one had to identify one major contribution to feminism from Marxism it would have to be this text, flawed and disputed as it is.

In general the writing of Engels often reads as more sympathetic to what we now identify as feminism than does the writing of Marx. Engels appears to be more modern in his touch on these questions and one has less sense of a Victorian patriarch worthily espousing doctrines that he believes correct rather than believes in. Random examples are somewhat unfair, and can be misleading, but they illustrate the point. Engels can deride Dühring's solemn comment on the demand for prostitution: '. . . *nothing of the kind is possible for the women*'. He simply remarks that 'I would not care, for anything in the world, to have the thanks which might accrue to Herr Dühring from the women for this compliment' and wonders how Dühring has managed to get by for so long without having heard of men living on the 'petticoat-pension'.[32] These sentiments would not disgrace a 'male Marxist' in 1983, let alone in 1878, and they are characteristic of Engels's empathy with women. Although no doubt a thorough search would reveal many sexist remarks in Engels's correspondence and private papers, one suspects that there would be little to match those 'howlers' that can be found in Marx.[33]

Nor is it irrelevant that it is Engels rather than Marx who has done most to settle fairly the question of the relationship between Marxist and utopian socialism. On the whole Marx sought to clarify the differences but Engels, although arguing that utopian socialism arose too early to rest on a proper analysis of industrial capitalism, is unstinting in his efforts to express solidarity with the earlier utopians against their critics. Owenite socialism, as Barbara Taylor has argued,[34] was in many ways more concerned with themes taken up in twentieth-century feminism than was Marxism, especially in its insistence on integrity and non-exploitativeness in personal relationships. Whatever differences arise between Owenism and Marxism, Engels was at least utterly open in his admiration, going so far as to say that 'Every social movement, every real advance in England on behalf of the workers links itself to the name of Robert Owen.'[35]

A comparison between Marx and Engels on 'the woman question' tends to favour the latter both in terms of personal and political attitudes and because of Engels's willingness to problematize the familial and sexual arrangements that Marx tended to take for granted. There is, of course, much controversy on whether the personal and family lives of Marx and Engels are relevant to an assessment of the value of their work for feminism. This is an issue on which, by and large, feminism's insistence that 'the personal is political' leads to different conclusions from those normally found among commentators. An acute instance arises over the paternity of Frederick Demuth – Engels on his death-bed having been reported as saying that Demuth was Marx's son rather than, as had been assumed privately, Engels's. A typical response to this is given by Terrell Carver who simply denies that the evidence exists to substantiate the claim. Carver's reference to the 'story' is prefaced by the following:

> Had Engels and Marx lived impeccably proletarian lives they would probably have had no time for their intellectual labours, and in any case subsequent critics might have attacked them for belieing their own middle-class origins and becoming phonies. The life-style of any radical critic of contemporary social arrangements is bound to look incongruous.[36]

In other words, personal conduct is completely irrelevant. Yvonne Kapp, in her discussion of the issue, maintains that Demuth *was* Marx's son, but insists that ' . . . Marx's importance to the history of mankind is not lessened by one jot because he fathered Frederick Demuth.'[37] In this Yvonne Kapp is right and Carver surely wrong – the issue is *relevant* although the outcome does not diminish Marx's *importance*. It does throw light, however, on Marx's unwillingness to challenge adequately the 'natural' family unit. Supposing that Kapp is right, the Demuth issue does identify the secrecy and hypocrisy that formed part of Marx family life.

The feminist critique of such hypocrisy is not the normal moralistic one: it simply demands that revolutionaries practise what they preach. These questions are relevant to an understanding of Marx because they help us to identify how and why his critique of the family is so flawed and contradictory. It could not be proved that his practice in this was the result of his theory, or vice versa, but the relationship between them is worthy of note.

.I say this not to score a point or to reiterate the painful fact that, as far as feminism is concerned, Marx's feet really are made of clay. To speak of 'Marxist-feminism' is not to invoke a systematic and integrated approach to the oppression of women in capitalism or in any other mode of production. The meaning that I would attach to it is that one's feminism exists alongside the recognition that Marxism provides an unrivalled explanation and analysis of the capitalist society in which we live. The task, if it be possible, of synthesizing Marxism and feminism was not attempted by Marx and to suggest that it was is to belittle feminism. We would do well, however, to heed Marx's views on comparable questions and refrain from taking too sanguine a view of this integrative project. Marx's discussion of the limitations of 'political emancipation' should alert us to the fundamental issue of what *kind* of feminism we are struggling for and in what context. Marx himself, as I argued earlier, poses this question in a way that is distinctly awkward for feminism in that it forces us to decide whether we seek a set of egalitarian demands or whether we can rise to the challenge of conceptualizing a truly revolutionary politics of gender. It is, of course, an ironic tribute to Marx's stature that his work raises the central feminist question – political emancipation or revolutionary liberation – in the course of discussing *not* the family or the position of women, but in polemicizing on the Jewish question.

ACKNOWLEDGEMENTS

My thanks to Mary McIntosh and William Outhwaite for their helpful comments on this essay.

NOTES

1 Marx and Engels, *The German Ideology* (Lawrence and Wishart, London, 1974), p. 65.
2 Engels, *Anti-Dühring* (Progress, Moscow, 1977), p. 347.
3 'Marx and Equality', in *Issues in Marxist Philosophy*, vol. 4 (Social and Political Philosophy), John Mepham and David-Hillel Ruben (eds) (Harvester, Brighton, 1981), p. 196.
4 Yvonne Kapp, *Eleanor Marx*, vol. 2 (*The Crowded Years*) (Lawrence and Wishart, London, 1976; Virago, London, 1979), p. 85.
5 See the discussion of 'Women and Equality' by Juliet Mitchell in *The Rights and Wrongs of Women*, Juliet Mitchell and Ann Oakley (eds) (Penguin, Harmondsworth, 1976), pp. 379–99.
6 Sebastiano Timpanaro, *On Materialism* (NLB, London, 1975).
7 Raymond Williams, 'Problems of Materialism', *New Left Review*, 109 (1978), pp. 8–9.
8 Karl Marx, 'Toward the Critique of Hegel's Philosophy of Right', in *Karl Marx and Frederick Engels: Basic Writings*, ed. L. S. Feuer (Fontana, London, 1969), p. 303.
9 See Olive Banks, *Faces of Feminism* (Martin Robertson, Oxford, 1981).
10 Marx and Engels, *The German Ideology* (Lawrence and Wishart, London, 1974).
11 Marx, 'On the Jewish Question', in *Karl Marx: Early Texts*, ed. David McLellan (Blackwell, Oxford, 1979), p. 100.
12 *Max Weber and Karl Marx*, Tom Bottomore and William Outhwaite (eds) (Allen and Unwin, London, 1982), p. 78.
13 'On the Jewish Question', p. 93.
14 Marx, 'Economic and Philosophical Manuscripts', in *Karl Marx: Early Texts*, ed. McLellan, p. 136.

15 'Economic and Philosophical Manuscripts', p. 135.
16 *The German Ideology* (editor's introduction), p. 16.
17 'Economic and Philosophical Manuscripts', p. 141.
18 Ibid., p. 147. In the German Marx tends to use *Mensch* as the generic term and where, as here, a distinction between women and men is made or their relation noted he uses the specific, *Mann*.
19 *The German Ideology*, p. 64.
20 Penguin, Harmondsworth, 1972.
21 'Economic and Philosophical Manuscripts', p. 147.
22 *Capital*, vol. 1 (Lawrence and Wishart, London, 1970), p. 402.
23 The kind of data I have in mind is that collected in, for example, Alice Clark, *The Working Life of Women in the Seventeenth Century* (Cass, London, 1977) and Ivy Pinchbeck, *Women Workers and the Industrial Revolution 1750–1850* (Cass, London, 1930).
24 *Capital*, vol. 1, pp. 394–5.
25 Ibid., p. 395.
26 Michael Eldred and Mike Roth, *Guide to Marx's Capital* (CSE, London, 1978), p. 70.
27 The following articles contain summaries as well as discussion of this debate: Sue Himmelweit and Simon Mohun, 'Domestic Labour and Capital', *Cambridge Journal of Economics*, 1 (1977), Maxine Molyneux, 'Beyond the Domestic Labour Debate', *New Left Review* 116 (1979), Eva Kaluzynska, 'Wiping the Floor with Theory', *Feminist Review*, 6 (1980). On the question of the value of labour power and female wages the most salient text is Veronica Beechey's 'Some Notes on Female Wage Labour in the Capitalist Mode of Production', *Capital and Class*, 3 (1977).
28 These arguments are elaborated in more detail in 'The "Family Wage": Some Problems for Socialists and Feminists' by myself and Mary McIntosh, *Capital and Class*, 11 (1981).
29 See, e.g., his discussion of private proprietors in *Grundrisse* (Penguin, Harmondsworth, 1973), pp. 474–6.
30 *The Labour Theory of Culture* (Routledge, London, 1982), p. 1.
31 For a general consideration see Rosalind Delmar, 'Looking Again at Engels' *Origin of the Family, Private Property and the State*', in *The Rights and Wrongs of Women*, J. Mitchell and A. Oakley (eds) (Penguin, Harmondsworth, 1976).
32 Engels, *Anti-Dühring*, p. 393.
33 Some examples may be found in a collection that contains some items for good reason rarely anthologized, *The Essential Marx: The Non-Economic Writings*, ed. Saul Padover (Mentor, New York, 1978).
34 *Eve and the New Jerusalem* (Virago, London, 1982).
35 *Anti-Dühring*, p. 319 (part of the extracts from *Anti-Dühring* reprinted as Engels's pamphlet, *Socialism: Utopian and Scientific*).
36 *Engels* (Oxford UP, Oxford, 1981), p. 72.
37 *Eleanor Marx*, Vol. 1 (*Family Life*) (Lawrence and Wishart, London, 1972); Virago, London, 1979, pp. 289–97.

3
Feminism: A Movement to End Sexist Oppression

BELL HOOKS

A central problem within feminist discourse has been our inability to either arrive at a consensus of opinion about what feminism is or accept definition(s) that could serve as points of unification. Without agreed-upon definition(s), we lack a sound foundation on which to construct theory or engage in overall meaningful praxis. Expressing her frustrations with the absence of clear definitions in a recent essay, 'Towards A Revolutionary Ethics', Carmen Vasquez comments:

> We can't even agree on what a 'Feminist' is, never mind what she would believe in and how she defines the principles that constitute honor among us. In key with the American capitalist obsession for individualism and anything goes so long as it gets you what you want, Feminism in American has come to mean anything you like, honey. There are as many definitions of Feminism as there are feminists, some of my sisters say, with a chuckle. I don't think it's funny.[1]

It is not funny. It indicates a growing lack of interest in feminism as a radical political movement. It is a despairing gesture expressive of the belief that solidarity between women is not possible. It is a sign that the political naïvety which has traditionally characterized woman's lot in male-dominated culture abounds.

Most people in the United States think of feminism or the more commonly used term 'women's lib' as a movement that aims to make women the social equals of men. This broad definition, popularized by the media and mainstream segments of the movement, raises problematic questions. Since men are not equals in white supremacist, capitalist, patriarchal class structure, which men do women want to be equal to? Do women share a common

Reprinted with permission from Bell Hooks, *Feminist Theory: From Margin to Center*, copyright © 1984 by Bell Hooks (South End Press, Boston), pp. 17–31.

vision of what equality means? Implicit in this simplistic definition of women's liberation is a dismissal of race and class as factors that, in conjunction with sexism, determine the extent to which an individual will be discriminated against, exploited, or oppressed. Bourgeois white women interested in women's rights issues have been satisfied with simple definitions for obvious reasons. Rhetorically placing themselves in the same social category as oppressed women, they were not anxious to call attention to race and class privilege.

Women in lower-class and poor groups, particularly those who are non-white, would not have defined women's liberation as women gaining social equality with men since they are continually reminded in their everyday lives that all women do not share a common social status. Concurrently, they know that many males in their social groups are exploited and oppressed. Knowing that men in their groups do not have social, political, and economic power, they would not deem it liberatory to share their social status. While they are aware that sexism enables men in their respective groups to have privileges denied them, they are more likely to see exaggerated expressions of male chauvinism among their peers as stemming from the male's sense of himself as powerless and ineffectual in relation to ruling male groups, rather than an expression of an overall privileged social status. From the very onset of the women's liberation movement, these women were suspicious of feminism precisely because they recognized the limitations inherent in its definition. They recognized the possibility that feminism defined as social equality with men might easily become a movement that would primarily affect the social standing of white women in middle- and upper-class groups while affecting only in a very marginal way the social status of working-class and poor women.

Not all the women who were at the forefront of organized women's movement shaping definitions were content with making women's liberation synonymous with women gaining social equality with men. On the opening pages of *Woman Power: The Movement for Women's Liberation*, Cellestine Ware, a black woman active in the movement, wrote under the heading 'Goals': 'Radical feminism is working for the eradication of domination and elitism in all human relationships. This would make self-determination the ultimate good and require the downfall of society as we know it today.'[2]

Individual radical feminists like Charlotte Bunch based their analyses on an informed understanding of the politics of domination and a recognition of the interconnections between various systems

of domination even as they focused primarily on sexism. Their
perspectives were not valued by those organizers and participants
in women's movement who were more interested in social reforms.
The anonymous authors of a pamphlet on feminist issues published
in 1976, *Women and the New World*, make the point that many
women active in women's liberation movement were far more
comfortable with the notion of feminism as a reform that would
help women attain social equality with men of their class than
feminism defined as a radical movement that would eradicate
domination and transform society:

> Whatever the organization, the location or the ethnic com-
> position of the group, all the women's liberation organizations
> had one thing in common: they all came together based on a
> biological and sociological fact rather than on a body of ideas.
> Women came together in the women's liberation movement
> on the basis that we were women and all women are subject
> to male domination. We saw all women as being our allies
> and all men as being the oppressor. We never questioned the
> extent to which American women accept the same materialistic
> and individualistic values as American men. We did not stop
> to think that American women are just as reluctant as
> American men to struggle for a new society based on new
> values of mutual respect, cooperation and social responsibility.[3]

It is now evident that many women active in the feminist movement were interested in reform as an end in itself, not as a stage in
the progression towards revolutionary transformation. Even though
Zillah Eisenstein can optimistically point to the potential radicalism
of liberal women who work for social reform in *The Radical Future
of Liberal Feminism*, the process by which this radicalism will
surface is unclear. Eisenstein offers as an example of the radical
implications of liberal feminist programs the demands made at the
government-sponsored Houston conference on women's rights
issues which took place in 1978:

> The Houston report demands as a human right a full voice
> and role for women in determining the destiny of our world,
> our nation, our families, and our individual lives. It specifically
> calls for (1) the elimination of violence in the home and the
> development of shelters for battered women, (2) support for
> women's business, (3) a solution to child abuse, (4) federally
> funded nonsexist child care, (5) a policy of full employment
> so that all women who wish and are able to work may do so,

(6) the protection of homemakers so that marriage is a partnership, (7) an end to the sexist portrayal of women in the media, (8) establishment of reproductive freedom and the end to involuntary sterilization, (9) a remedy to the double discrimination against minority women, (10) a revision of criminal codes dealing with rape, (11) elimination of discrimination on the basis of sexual preference, (12) the establishment of nonsexist education, and (13) an examination of all welfare reform proposals for their specific impact on women.[4]

The positive impact of liberal reforms on women's lives should not lead to the assumption that they eradicate systems of domination. Nowhere in these demands is there an emphasis on eradicating the politic of domination, yet it would need to be abolished if any of these demands were to be met. The lack of any emphasis on domination is consistent with the liberal feminist belief that women can achieve equality with men of their class without challenging and changing the cultural basis of group oppression. It is this belief that negates the likelihood that the potential radicalism of liberal feminism will ever be realized. Writing as early as 1967, Brazilian scholar Heleith Saffioti emphasized that bourgeois feminism has always been 'fundamentally and unconsciously a feminism of the ruling class', that:

> Whatever revolutionary content there is in petty-bourgeois feminist praxis, it has been put there by the efforts of the middle strata, especially the less well off, to move up socially. To do this, however, they sought merely to expand the existing social structures, and never went so far as to challenge the status quo. Thus, while petty-bourgeois feminism may always have aimed at establishing social equality between the sexes, the consciousness it represented has remained utopian in its desire for and struggle to bring about a partial transformation of society; this it believed could be done without disturbing the foundations on which it rested . . . In this sense, petty-bourgeois feminism is not feminism at all; indeed it has helped to consolidate class society by giving camouflage to its internal contradictions . . .[5]

Radical dimensions of liberal women's social protest will continue to serve as an ideological support system providing the necessary critical and analytical impetus for the maintenance of a liberalism that aims to grant women greater equality of opportunity within the present white supremacist capitalist, patriarchal state. Such liberal women's rights activism in its essence diminishes feminist struggle. Philosopher Mihailo Markovic discusses the limitations of liberalism in his essay, 'Women's Liberation and Human Emancipation':

> Another basic characteristic of liberalism which constitutes a formidable obstacle to an oppressed social group's emancipation is its conception of human nature. If selfishness, aggressiveness, the drive to conquer and dominate, really are among defining human traits, as every liberal philosopher since Locke tries to convince us, the oppression in civil society – i.e. in the social sphere not regulated by the state – is a fact of life and the basic civil relationship between a man and a woman will always remain a battlefield. Woman, being less aggressive, is then either the less human of the two and doomed to subjugation, or else she must get more power-hungry herself and try to dominate man. Liberation for both is not feasible.[6]

Although liberal perspectives on feminism include reforms that would have radical implications for society, these are the reforms which will be resisted precisely because they would set the stage for revolutionary transformation were they implemented. It is evident that society is more responsive to those 'feminist' demands that are not threatening, that may even help maintain the status quo. Jeanne Gross gives an example of this co-optation of feminist strategy in her essay 'Feminist Ethics from a Marxist Perspective,' published in 1977:

> If we as women want change in all aspects of our lives, we must recognize that capitalism is uniquely capable of co-opting piecemeal change . . . Capitalism is capable of taking our visionary changes and using them against us. For example, many married women, recognizing their oppression in the family, have divorced. They are thrown, with no preparation or protection, into the labor market. For many women this has meant taking their places at the row of typewriters. Corporations are now recognizing the capacity for exploitation in divorced women. The turnover in such jobs is incredibly high. 'If she complains, she can be replaced.'[7]

Particularly as regards work, many liberal feminist reforms simply reinforced capitalist, materialist values (illustrating the flexibility of capitalism) without truly liberating women economically. Liberal women have not been alone in drawing upon the dynamism of feminism to further their interests. The great majority of women who have benefited in any way from feminist-generated social reforms do not want to be seen as advocates of feminism. Conferences on issues of relevance to women, that would never have been organized or funded had there not been a feminist movement, take place all over the United States and the participants do not want to be seen as advocates of feminism. They are either reluctant to make a public commitment to feminist movement or sneer at the term. Individual African-American, Native American Indian, Asian-American, and Hispanic American women find themselves isolated if they support feminist movement. Even women who may achieve fame and notoriety (as well as increased economic income) in response to attention given their work by large numbers of women who support feminism may deflect attention away from their engagement with feminist movement. They may even go so far as to create other terms that express their concern with women's issues so as to avoid using the term feminist. The creation of new terms that have no relationship to organized political activity tend to provide women who may already be reluctant to explore feminism with ready excuses to explain their reluctance to participate. This illustrates an uncritical acceptance of distorted definitions of feminism rather than a demand for redefinition. They may support specific issues while divorcing themselves from what they assume is feminist movement.

In a recent article in a San Francisco newspaper, 'Sisters – Under the Skin,' columnist Bob Greene commented on the aversion many women apparently have to the term 'feminism.' Greene finds it curious that many women 'who obviously believe in everything that proud feminists believe in dismiss the term "feminist" as something unpleasant; something with which they do not wish to be associated.' Even though such women often acknowledge that they have benefited from feminist-generated reform measures which have improved the social status of specific groups of women, they do not wish to be seen as participants in feminist movement:

> There is no getting around it. After all this time, the term 'feminist' makes many bright, ambitious, intelligent women embarrassed and uncomfortable. They simply don't want to be associated with it.
>
> It's as if it has an unpleasant connotation that they want no connection with. Chances are if you were to present them

with every mainstream feminist belief, they would go along
with the beliefs to the letter – and even if they consider
themselves feminists, they hasten to say no.[8]

Many women are reluctant to advocate feminism because they are
uncertain about the meaning of the term. Other women from
exploited and oppressed ethnic groups dismiss the term because
they do not wish to be perceived as supporting a racist movement;
feminism is often equated with white women's rights effort. Large
numbers of women see feminism as synonymous with lesbianism;
their homophobia leads them to reject association with any group
identified as pro-lesbian. Some women fear the word 'feminism'
because they shun identification with any political movement,
especially one perceived as radical. Of course there are women who
do not wish to be associated with women's rights movement in any
form so they reject and oppose feminist movement. Most women
are more familiar with negative perspectives on 'women's lib' than
the positive significations of feminism. It is this term's positive
political significance and power that we must now struggle to
recover and maintain.

Currently feminism seems to be a term without any clear
significance. The 'anything goes' approach to the definition of the
word has rendered it practically meaningless. What is meant by
'anything goes' is usually that any woman who wants social
equality with men regardless of her political perspective (she can be
a conservative right-winger or a nationalist communist) can label
herself feminist. Most attempts at defining feminism reflect the class
nature of the movement. Definitions are usually liberal in origin
and focus on the individual woman's right to freedom and self-
determination. In Barbara Berg's *The Remembered Gate: Origins
of American Feminism*, she defines feminism as a 'broad movement
embracing numerous phases of woman's emancipation.' However,
her emphasis is on women gaining greater individual freedom.
Expanding on the above definition, Berg adds:

> It is the freedom to decide her own destiny; freedom from sex-
> determined role; freedom from society's oppressive restrictions;
> freedom to express her thoughts fully and to convert them
> freely into action. Feminism demands the acceptance of
> woman's right to individual conscience and judgment. It
> postulates that woman's essential worth stems from her
> common humanity and does not depend on the other
> relationships of her life.[9]

This definition of feminism is almost apolitical in tone; yet it is the type of definition many liberal women find appealing. It evokes a very romantic notion of personal freedom which is more acceptable than a definition that emphasizes radical political action. Many feminist radicals now know that neither a feminism that focuses on woman as an autonomous human being worthy of personal freedom nor one that focuses on the attainment of equality of opportunity with men can rid society of sexism and male domination. Feminism is a struggle to end sexist oppression. Therefore, it is necessarily a struggle to eradicate the ideology of domination that permeates Western culture on various levels as well as a commitment to reorganizing society so that the self-development of people can take precedence over imperialism, economic expansion, and material desires. Defined in this way, it is unlikely that women would join feminist movement simply because we are biologically the same. A commitment to feminism so defined would demand that each individual participant acquire a critical political consciousness based on ideas and beliefs.

All too often the slogan 'the personal is political' (which was first used to stress that woman's everyday reality is informed and shaped by politics and is necessarily political) became a means of encouraging women to think that the experience of discrimination, exploitation, or oppression automatically corresponded with an understanding of the ideological and institutional apparatus shaping one's social status. As a consequence, many women who had not fully examined their situation never developed a sophisticated understanding of their political reality and its relationship to that of women as a collective group. They were encouraged to focus on giving voice to personal experience. Like revolutionaries working to change the lot of colonized people globally, it is necessary for feminist activists to stress that the ability to see and describe one's own reality is a significant step in the long process of self-recovery; but it is only a beginning. When women internalized the idea that describing their own woe was synonymous with developing a critical political consciousness, the progress of feminist movement was stalled. Starting from such incomplete perspectives, it is not surprising that theories and strategies were developed that were collectively inadequate and misguided. To correct this inadequacy in past analysis, we must now encourage women to develop a keen, comprehensive understanding of women's political reality. Broader perspectives can only emerge as we examine both the personal that is political, the politics of society as a whole, and global revolutionary politics.

Feminism defined in political terms that stress collective as well as individual experience challenges women to enter a new domain – to leave behind the apolitical stance sexism decrees is our lot and develop political consciousness. Women know from our everyday lives that many of us rarely discuss politics. Even when women talked about sexist politics in the heyday of contemporary feminism, rather than allow this engagement with serious political matters to lead to complex, in-depth analysis of women's social status, we insisted that men were 'the enemy,' the cause of all our problems. As a consequence, we examined almost exclusively women's relationship to male supremacy and the ideology of sexism. The focus on 'man as enemy' created, as Marlene Dixon emphasizes in her essay, 'The Rise and Demise of Women's Liberation: A Class Analysis,' a 'politics of psychological oppression' which evoked world views which 'pit individual against individual and mystify the social basis of exploitation.'[10] By repudiating the popular notion that the focus of feminist movement should be social equality of the sexes and emphasizing eradicating the cultural basis of group oppression, our own analysis would require an exploration of all aspects of women's political reality. This would mean that race and class oppression would be recognized as feminist issues with as much relevance as sexism.

When feminism is defined in such a way that it calls attention to the diversity of women's social and political reality, it centralizes the experiences of all women, especially the women whose social conditions have been least written about, studied, or changed by political movements. When we cease to focus on the simplistic stance 'men are the enemy,' we are compelled to examine systems of domination and our role in their maintenance and perpetuation. Lack of adequate definition made it easy for bourgeois women, whether liberal or radical in perspective, to maintain their dominance over the leadership of the movement and its direction. This hegemony continues to exist in most feminist organizations. Exploited and oppressed groups of women are usually encouraged by those in power to feel that their situation is hopeless, that they can do nothing to break the pattern of domination. Given such socialization, these women have often felt that our only response to white, bourgeois, hegemonic dominance of feminist movement is to trash, reject, or dismiss feminism. This reaction is in no way threatening to the women who wish to maintain control over the direction of feminist theory and praxis. They prefer us to be silent, passively accepting their ideas. They prefer us speaking against 'them' rather than developing our own ideas about feminist movement.

Feminism is the struggle to end sexist oppression. Its aim is not to benefit solely any specific group of women, any particular race or class of women. It does not privilege women over men. It has the power to transform in a meaningful way all our lives. Most importantly, feminism is neither a lifestyle nor a ready-made identity or role one can step into. Diverting energy from feminist movement that aims to change society, many women concentrate on the development of a counter-culture, a woman-centred world wherein participants have little contact with men. Such attempts do not indicate a respect or concern for the vast majority of women who are unable to integrate their cultural expressions with the visions offered by alternative woman-centred communities. In *Beyond God the Father*, Mary Daly urged women to give up 'the securities offered by the patriarchal system' and create new space that would be woman-centred. Responding to Daly, Jeanne Gross pointed to the contradictions that arise when the focus of feminist movement is on the construction of new space:

> Creating a 'counterworld' places an incredible amount of pressure on the women who attempt to embark on such a project. The pressure comes from the belief that the only true resources for such an endeavor are ourselves. The past which is totally patriarchal is viewed as irredeemable . . .
>
> If we go about creating an alternative culture without remaining in dialogue with others (and the historical circumstances that give rise to their identify) we have no reality check for our goals. We run the very real risk that the dominant ideology of the culture is re-duplicated in the feminist movement through cultural imperialism.[11]

Equating feminist struggle with living in a counter-cultural, woman-centred world erected barriers that closed the movement off from most women. Despite sexist discrimination, exploitation, or oppression, many women feel their lives as they live them are important and valuable. Naturally the suggestion that these lives could be simply left or abandoned for an alternative 'feminist' lifestyle met with resistance. Feeling their life experiences devalued, deemed solely negative and worthless, many women responded by vehemently attacking feminism. By rejecting the notion of an alternative feminist 'lifestyle' that can emerge only when women create a subculture (whether it is living space or even space like women's studies that at many campuses has become exclusive) and insisting that feminist struggle can begin wherever an individual woman is, we create a movement that focuses on our collective experience, a movement that is continually mass-based. Over the past six years, many separatist-oriented communities have been formed by women so that the focus has shifted from the development of woman-centred space towards an emphasis on identity. Once woman-centered space exists, it can be maintained only if women remain convinced that it is the only place where they can be self-realized and free. After assuming a 'feminist' identity, women often seek to live the 'feminist' lifestyle. These women do not see that it undermines feminist movement to project the assumption that 'feminist' is but another pre-packaged role women can now select as they search for identity. The willingness to see feminism as a lifestyle choice rather than a political commitment reflects the class nature of the movement. It is not surprising that the vast majority of women who equate feminism with alternative lifestyle are from middle-class backgrounds, unmarried, college-educated, often students who are without many of the social and economic responsibilities that working-class and poor women who are laborers, parents, homemakers, and wives confront daily. Sometimes lesbians have sought to equate feminism with lifestyle but for significantly different reasons. Given the prejudice and discrimination against lesbian women in our society, alternative communities that are woman-centered are one means of creating positive, affirming environments. Despite positive reasons for developing woman-centered space (which does not need to be equated with a 'feminist' lifestyle) like pleasure, support, and resource-sharing, emphasis on creating a counter-culture has alienated women from feminist movement, for such space can be in churches, kitchens, etc.

Longing for community, connection, a sense of shared purpose, many women found support networks in feminist organizations. Satisfied in a personal way by new relationships generated in what was called a 'safe', 'supportive' context wherein discussion focused on feminist ideology, they did not question whether masses of women shared the same need for community. Certainly many black women as well as women from other ethnic groups do not feel an absence of community among women in their lives despite exploitation and oppression. The focus on feminism as a way to develop shared identity and community has little appeal to women who experience community, who seek ways to end exploitation and oppression in the context of their lives. While they may develop an interest in a feminist politic that works to eradicate sexist oppression, they will probably never feel as intense a need for a 'feminist' identity and lifestyle.

Often emphasis on identity and lifestyle is appealing because it creates a false sense that one is engaged in praxis. However, praxis within any political movement that aims to have a radical transformative impact on society cannot be solely focused on creating spaces wherein would-be-radicals experience safety and support. Feminist movement to end sexist oppression actively engages participants in revolutionary struggle. Struggle is rarely safe or pleasurable.

Focusing on feminism as political commitment, we resist the emphasis on individual identity and lifestyle. (This should not be confused with the very real need to unite theory and practice.) Such resistance engages us in revolutionary praxis. The ethics of Western society informed by imperialism and capitalism are personal rather than social. They teach us that the individual good is more important than the collective good and consequently that individual change is of greater significance than collective change. This particular form of cultural imperialism has been reproduced in feminist movement in the form of individual women equating the fact that their lives have been changed in a meaningful way by feminism 'as is' with a policy of no change need occur in the theory and praxis even if it has little or no impact on society as a whole, or on masses of women.

To emphasize that engagement with feminist struggle as political commitment we could avoid using the phrase 'I am a feminist' (a linguistic structure designed to refer to some personal aspect of identity and self-definition) and could state 'I advocate feminism.' Because there has been undue emphasis placed on feminism as an identity or lifestyle, people usually resort to stereotyped perspectives on feminism. Deflecting attention away from stereotypes is necessary if we are to revise our strategy and direction. I have found that saying 'I am a feminist' usually means I am plugged into preconceived notions of identity, role, or behavior. When I say 'I advocate feminism' the response is usually 'what is feminism?' A phrase like 'I advocate' does not imply the kind of absolutism that is suggested by 'I am.' It does not engage us in the either/or dualistic thinking that is the central ideological component of all systems of domination in Western society. It implies that a choice has been made, that commitment to feminism is an act of will. It does not suggest that by committing oneself to feminism, the possibility of supporting other political movements is negated.

As a black woman interested in feminist movement, I am often asked whether being black is more important than being a woman; whether feminist struggle to end sexist oppression is more important than the struggle to end racism and vice versa. All such questions are rooted in competitive either/or thinking, the belief that the self is formed in opposition to an other. Therefore one is a feminist because you are not something else. Most people are socialized to think in terms of opposition rather than compatibility. Rather than see anti-racist work as totally compatible with working to end sexist oppression, they are often seen as two movements competing for first place. When asked 'Are you a feminist?' it appears that an affirmative answer is translated to mean that one is concerned with no political issues other than feminism. When one is black, an affirmative response is likely to be heard as a devaluation of struggle to end racism. Given the fear of being misunderstood, it has been difficult for black women and women in exploited and oppressed ethnic groups to give expression to their interest in feminist concerns. They have been wary of saying 'I am a feminist.' The shift in expression from 'I am a feminist' to 'I advocate feminism' could serve as a useful strategy for eliminating the focus on identity and lifestyle. It could serve as a way women who are concerned about feminism as well as other political movements could express their support while avoiding linguistic structures that give primacy to one particular group. It would also encourage greater exploration in feminist theory.

The shift in definition away from notions of social equality towards an emphasis on ending sexist oppression leads to a shift in attitudes in regard to the development of theory. Given the class nature of feminist movement so far, as well as racial hierarchies, developing theory (the guiding set of beliefs and principles that become the basis for action) has been a task particularly subject to the hegemonic dominance of white academic women. This has led many women outside the privileged race/class group to see the focus on developing theory, even the very use of the term, as a concern that functions only to reinforce the power of the elite group. Such reactions reinforce the sexist/racist/classist notion that developing theory is the domain of the white intellectual. Privileged white women active in feminist movement, whether liberal or radical in perspective, encourage black women to contribute 'experiential' work, personal life stories. Personal experiences are important to feminist movement but they cannot take the place of theory. Charlotte Bunch explains the special significance of theory in her essay, 'Feminism and Education: Not by Degrees':

> Theory enables us to see immediate needs in terms of long-range goals and an overall perspective on the world. It thus

gives us a framework for evaluating various strategies in both the long and the short run and for seeing the types of changes that they are likely to produce. Theory is not just a body of facts or a set of personal opinions. It involves explanations and hypotheses that are based on available knowledge and experience. It is also dependent on conjecture and insight about how to interpret those facts and experiences and their significance.[12]

Since bourgeois white women had defined feminism in such a way as to make it appear that it had no real significance for black women, they could then conclude that black women need not contribute to developing theory. We were to provide the colorful life stories to document and validate the prevailing set of theoretical assumptions.[13] Focus on social equality with men as a definition of feminism led to an emphasis on discrimination, male attitudes, and legalistic reforms. Feminism as a movement to end sexist oppression directs our attention to systems of domination and the inter-relatedness of sex, race, and class oppression. Therefore, it compels us to centralize the experiences and the social predicaments of women who bear the brunt of sexist oppression as a way to understand the collective social status of women in the United States. Defining feminism as a movement to end sexist oppression is crucial for the development of theory because it is a starting point indicating the direction of exploration and analysis.

The foundation of future feminist struggle must be solidly based on a recognition of the need to eradicate the underlying cultural basis and causes of sexism and other forms of group oppression. Without challenging and changing these philosophical structures, no feminist reforms will have a long-range impact. Consequently, it is now necessary for advocates of feminism to collectively acknowledge that our struggle cannot be defined as a movement to gain social equality with men; that terms like 'liberal feminist' and 'bourgeois feminist' represent contradictions that must be resolved so that feminism will not be continually co-opted to serve the opportunistic ends of special interest groups.

NOTES

1 Carmen Vasquez, 'Towards a Revolutionary Ethics', in *Coming Up* (January 1983), p. 11.
2 Cellestine Ware, *Woman Power: The Movement for Women's Liberation* (Tower Publications, New York, 1970), p. 3.

3 *Women and the New World* (Advocators, Detroit, 1976), p. 33.
4 Zillah Eisenstein, *The Radical Future of Liberal Feminism* (Longman, New York and London, 1981), p. 232.
5 Helieth Saffioti, *Women In Class Society* (Monthly Review Press, New York, 1978), p. 223.
6 Mihailo Markovic, 'Women's Liberation and Human Emancipation', in Carold Gould and Mary Wartofsky (eds), *Women and Philosophy* (G. P. Putnam, New York, 1976), pp. 145–67.
7 Jeanne Gross, 'Feminist Ethics from a Marxist Perspective', in *Radical Religion*, III. 2 (1977), pp. 52–6.
8 Bob Greene, 'Sisters Under the Skin', in *San Francisco Examiner*, 15 May 1983, p. 3.
9 Barbara Berg, *The Remembered Gate: Origins of American Feminism* (OUP, New York, 1979).
10 Marlene Dixon, 'The Rise and Demise of Woman's Liberation: A Class Analysis', in *Women in Class Struggle* (Synthesis Publications, San Francisco, 1980), p. 61.
11 Gross, 'Feminist Ethics from a Marxist Perspective', p. 54.
12 Charlotte Bunch, 'Feminism and Education: Not By Degrees', *Quest*, V. 1 (1979), pp. 7–18.
13 An interesting discussion of black women's responses to feminist movement may be found in the essay 'Challenging Imperial Feminism', by Valerie Amos and Pratibha Parmar, *Feminist Review*, 17 (1984).

4

Elizabeth Cady Stanton: Radical-Feminist Analysis and Liberal-Feminist Strategy

ZILLAH EISENSTEIN

Elizabeth Cady Stanton (1815–1902)[1] has often been called the philosopher of nineteenth-century feminism, but there has been little examination of the theory she expounded.[2] It is my purpose here to define the radical feminist as well as the liberal influences that construct her theory. Her radical-feminist understanding of woman's oppression, the recognition of women as part of a sexual class, is found in her discussions of marriage, motherhood, and divorce. In these writings, she begins to question the division of public and private life as male and female spheres. However, the liberal and republican influences in Stanton's thought cannot help her in this feminist endeavor because they seek to protect the relationship between the state and the family as a sexual division. Liberalism and republicanism reproduce the patriarchal division between public and private life as male and female, respectively, by emphasizing the important role of the (male) citizen in public life. Stanton's analysis of the family and marriage allows her to recognize a relationship between these sexual spheres, but their separation in liberal and republican thought[3] causes confusion in her presentation.

I argue that the demand for the vote for women reflects Stanton's liberal, republican, and radical-feminist commitments. However, it was her understanding of woman as an oppressed sexual class that underlay the demand for the vote *for women*. I also argue that Stanton's theory of liberal individualism underpins her feminist

Reprinted with permission from Zillah R. Eisenstein, *The Radical Future of Liberal Feminism*, copyright © 1981 by Zillah Eisenstein (Northeastern University Press), ch. 7, pp. 145–73. This version has been edited with Zillah Eisenstein's permission.

analysis. I specifically want to draw attention to the possibility of distinguishing, in Stanton's thought, between the idea of the independent individual, which is so crucial to feminist theory, and the liberal ideology of emancipation, meaning the formal rights given the individual within the state. Stanton's feminism owes its origins to her view of liberal individualism, although this theory instigates, rather than completes, her radical-feminist analysis of women's oppression within the system of patriarchy. A study of Stanton's theoretical work allows us to understand the contribution of liberalism to the development of the radical-feminist position and its limitations.

One cannot write of Stanton's sexual politics without addressing her position on the enfranchisement of blacks because the two issues were entwined for her. She believed that the exclusion of women and blacks from citizenship, on the basis of their ascribed status by race and/or sex, was a violation of the liberal promise of equality of opportunity as a universal goal. The exclusion of blacks and women from citizen rights involved the same question for her: the right of an individual to an independent and self-fulfilling life. Stanton as well as Susan B. Anthony and Sarah Grimke were sensitized to their own sexual oppression through their earlier anti-slavery involvement. Most active feminists of their period had been abolitionists first.

Only when Stanton felt that the abolitionist struggle did not recognize the question of women's rights as of equal import with their own struggle did she disassociate herself from it. When the world Anti-Slavery Convention of 1840 in London refused to seat the women in the American delegation,[4] Lucretia Mott and Elizabeth Cady Stanton, the decision was made to begin a women's rights movement. The feminist movement began to build its autonomous base in reaction to the sexism of the abolitionist movement, although the actual split between abolitionists and feminists did not come until 1866–7.[5] The critical issue that brought the split centered upon the vote for the black *man*. Stanton wrote to Susan B. Anthony in 1865 that she feared that black men would be enfranchised without women: '. . . but I fear one and all will favor enfranchising the negro without us. Woman's cause is in deep water. With the league disbanded, there is pressing need of our Woman's Rights Convention. Come back and help. There will be a room for you. I seem to stand alone.'[6] Stanton also wrote to Martha Wright in 1865 arguing that, as feminists, they must insist on women's right to the vote along with the right of black men. They should not defer to the 'negro's hour'.

We have fairly boosted the negro, over our own heads, and now we had better begin to remember that self-preservation is the first law of nature. Some say, 'Be still, wait, this is the negro's hour.' But I believe this is the hour for everybody to do the best thing for reconstruction. A vote based on intelligence and education for black and white, man and woman – that is what we need.[7]

Stanton saw no sense in distinguishing among the various categories of disenfranchised citizens. All the disenfranchised suffered alike. She therefore questioned enfranchisement for the black man that excluded the black woman. In a letter to Wendell Phillipps in 1865, she wrote:

You say, 'this is the negro's hour.' I will not insist that there are women of that race, but ask, Is there not a danger that he, once entrenched in all his inalienable rights, may be an added power to hold us at bay? Why should the African prove more just and generous than his Saxon compeers? Again, if the two millions of Southern black women are not to be secured in their rights of person, property, wages, and children, then their emancipation is but another form of slavery.[8]

She could not defer to 'the negro's hour' because she believed black men would rule black women if women were not enfranchised at the same time. This formulation reveals her early understanding of patriarchy: that white and black men share a sexual partnership as males, which on the basis of the historical record, Stanton did not trust.

It is her espousal of the notions of self-sovereignty and independence that makes Stanton both an abolitionist and a feminist. It is a commitment to the liberal conception of the independent and autonomous self that connects the political struggles for racial and sexual emancipation. For Stanton, the logic of liberal theory demands equality of opportunity for black and white, man and woman. Liberalism as an ideology recognizes individuals and their particular rights. Stanton wished to force the liberal-democratic state to make good on its individualist promise.

Her radical-feminist position, however, would not allow her to defer the question of women's rights to abolitionist demands. Her liberal-political strategy of enfranchisement could not help her overcome the state's pitting of sex interests against race interests. Nor could it address how the state *used* the patriarchal stance of many abolitionists to fight women's enfranchisement. Neither analysis, radical-feminist or liberal-individualist, could fully help Stanton develop a strategy that could aid her in achieving political victory.

WOMEN'S 'RIGHTS' AGAINST 'THE ARISTOCRACY OF SEX'

Stanton wanted to give women the possibility of achieving something for themselves. Individual freedom, personal independence, and the equality of opportunity, which were in practice privileges only open to men, would have to be opened to women if they were to remain valid as political ideals for her. She pointed out that in the Preamble to the Constitution these rights were extended to people in general, not merely to men.

> This is declared to be a government 'of the people.' All power it is said, centers in the people. Our state constitutions also open with the words, 'We the People.' Does any one pretend to say that men alone constitute races and peoples? When we say parents, do we not mean mothers as well as fathers? When we say children, do we not mean girls as well as boys? When we say people, do we not mean women as well as men?[9]

The ideology of liberal democracy requires that freedom and equality apply to 'all' persons equally. The very basis of individual rights is that everyone supposedly shares them alike. Stanton takes the language of the Constitution seriously and demands that women be able to enjoy personal independence. Her demand, however, requires freeing women from their present subservient, dependent status by destroying the arbitrary rule by men. 'When we place in the hands of one class of citizens the right to make, interpret and execute the law for another class wholly unrepresented in the government, we have made an order of nobility.'[10] White males are the nobility in America, according to Stanton: '. . . they are the privileged order, who have legislated as unjustly for women and negroes as have the nobles of England for their disfranchised classes.'[11] As long as women are denied representation in government, government will remain an oligarchy of males rather than a republic of the people.[12] 'I detest the words royalty and nobility and all the ideas and institutions based on them.'[13] The 'rule of men' resonates with the outworn dogma of divine-right rule. 'Hence, he takes upon himself the responsibility of directing and controlling the powers of woman, under that all-sufficient excuse of tyranny, "divine right".'[14] Just as men used the liberal idea of individual sovereignty to dislodge the power of the king, Stanton now extends this notion along with natural-rights doctrine to dislodge the power of men.

According to natural-rights doctrine, women should have the individual right to self-determination. Natural rights are a component part of individuals and cannot be taken from them. Stanton therefore argues that women bring their rights into the world with them: '. . . every individual comes into this world with rights that are not transferable. He does not bring them like a pack on his back, that may be stolen from him, but they are a component part of himself, the laws which insure his growth and development.'[15] Because Stanton believes 'her rights were born with her' and apply universally,[16] she cannot accept 'the man-made constitution, the man-interpretation thereof, the man-amendment submitted by a convention of aristocrats'[17] that denies her these rights. The right to govern one's own destiny is woman's at birth and cannot rightfully be denied her. In a phrase reminiscent of Mary Wollstonecraft, Stanton describes the rule of men as the 'aristocracy of sex.'[18] In her eyes it is the most harmful form of rule, for it is based on force rather than reason. 'Of all kinds of aristocracy, that of sex is the most odious and unnatural; invading, as it does, our homes, desecrating our family altars, dividing those whom God has joined together, exalting the son above the mother who bore him, and subjugating, everywhere moral power to brute force.'[19]

Stanton takes the liberal ideas of nineteenth-century America in much the same way Wollstonecraft took eighteenth-century English liberalism and applies them to women because she believes that women should share in the newborn liberties of their time.

> In gathering up the threads of history in the last century, and weaving its facts and philosophy together, one can trace the *liberal social ideas*, growing out of the political and religious revolutions in France, Germany, Italy and America; and their tendency *to substitute for the divine right of kings, priests, and orders of nobility, the higher and broader one of individual conscience and judgment,* in all matters pertaining to this life and that which is to come. It is not surprising that in so marked a transition period from the old to the new, as seen in the eighteenth century, *that women, trained to think and write and speak, should have discovered that they, too, had some share in the new-born liberties suddenly announced to the world.*[20]

This position against the anachronistic rule of men led Stanton to fight against the Fifteenth Amendment to the Constitution, which would enfranchise black men, but not women. As such, the Fifteenth Amendment, in Stanton's view, would establish the aristocracy of sex, once again.

A government, based on the principle of caste and class, cannot stand. The aristocratic idea, in any form, is opposed to the genius of our free institutions, to our own declaration of rights, and to the civilization of the age. All artificial distinctions, whether of family, blood, wealth, color, or sex, are equally oppressive to the subject classes and equally destructive to national life and prosperity.[21]

Women's exclusion from citizenship contradicts the universal promise of equality of opportunity. Stanton asks, 'While all men, everywhere, are rejoicing in new-found liberties, shall women alone be denied the rights, privileges, and immunities of citizenship?'[22]

This concern with citizenship inspired the 'Declaration of Sentiments and Resolutions,' drawn up at Seneca Falls in 1848. The feminists present at this first meeting wrote: 'We hold these truths to be self-evident: that all men and women are created equal. . . .'[23] Women citizens of the United States were therefore entitled to all the rights of citizenship. As late as 1902, Stanton was still fighting this battle. She writes of this in her letter to Theodore Roosevelt in which she complains of the tyranny of 'taxation without representation.' 'In the beginning of our nation, the fathers declared that no just government can be founded without the consent of the governed, and that "taxation without representation is tyranny." Both of these grand declarations are denied in the present position of woman, who constitutes one half of the people.'[24] Stanton wanted women to have an equal chance with men in the 'race of life.' To create equality of opportunity with men, women had to be recognized as citizens.

LIBERAL INDIVIDUALISM AND FEMINISM

Stanton believed that personal merit and not artificial inheritance or family position should decide one's place in life. An individual should work hard to make his or her mark on the world. One's particular individuality will be expressed by one's performance. 'Nothing adds such divinity to character as the recognition of one's self-sovereignty; the right to an equal place, everywhere conceded – a place earned by personal merit, not an artificial attainment by inheritance, wealth, family and position.'[25] To attain such results, one needs certain personal qualities. Speaking of her father in an entry in her diary in 1898, she writes of the importance of a person's self-assertion and drive: 'It is those with push who have the rougher time, and it is generally these last that get the so-called honors of life. . . . When such men or women attain success, it is *due to pure personal merit*. But he would have attained still higher honors if he had been more self-asserting.'[26]

Woman is instead reared for obedience and self-sacrifice to others rather than taught how to assert her own needs. Her situation of subordination denies her the opportunities for individual achievement that are rightly hers.

> To every step of progress which she has made from slavery to the partial freedom she now enjoys, the church and the State alike have made the most cruel opposition, and yet, under all circumstances she has shown her love of individual freedom, her desire for self-government, while her achievements in practical affairs and her courage in the great emergencies of life have vindicated her capacity to exercise this right. . . .[27]

Men's notion of womanliness requires women's deference and submissiveness. 'It is to have a manner which pleases him – quiet, deferential, submissive, approaching him as a subject does a master. He wants no self-assertion on our part.'[28] The situation is appalling to Stanton. She agrees with John Stuart Mill; men cannot be virtuous unless women are their equals. 'Men will be wise and virtuous just in proportion as women are self-reliant and able to meet them on the highest planes of thought and of action.'[29] In contrast to Rousseau, Stanton argues that individual independence and freedom for men require that their partners be self-sufficient persons. The question remains whether either Stanton or Rousseau is correct. For although in Stanton's mind men can be independent and free alongside the emancipated woman, the question whether liberal-feminist citizen rights will emancipate women is left unresolved.

The demands of the women's rights movement emphasize the importance of individual merit. 'The right of suffrage is simply the right to govern one's self.'[30] The notion of woman's individuality also led some feminists, like Lucy Stone, to demand the right to keep her own name in marriage. Such a demand recognizes women's independence from men. 'A woman's dignity is equally involved in a life long name to mark her individuality. We cannot overestimate the demoralizing effect on woman herself, to say nothing of society at large, for her to consent thus to merge her existence so wholly in that of another.'[31] This concept of individuality also led Stanton to advise fathers to educate their daughters to 'self support, if they were to become happy and independent.'[32] They should not have to live at 'the bounty of another.'[33] The concern with woman's individuality presupposed Stanton's commitment to woman's freedom from the aristocracy of males and her equality with men. The resolution passed at the woman suffrage convention of 1885 stated that '. . . man was made in the image of God, male and female, and given dominion over the earth.'[34]

The above discussion elaborates the progressive import of the theory of liberal individualism for feminism. It is used to establish woman's rightful independence from men. This theory, however, makes for difficulties in Stanton's feminist thinking in much the same way it did for Harriet Taylor and John Stuart Mill. They confused woman's individuality and, hence, independence from men with the ideology of liberal individualism, the atomized individual, conceptualized as separate and apart from social life. Stanton articulates this conception of liberal individualism most clearly in her address 'Solitude of Self', delivered at the National Woman Suffrage Association in 1892.[35]

In this address she stresses woman's isolation and separation from others, men and women alike. In the end, when the crises of life hit one, the woman stands alone. Stanton therefore believes that women must learn to count on themselves, because ultimately this is all they have. Women must be self-reliant and self-sufficient because they are entities unto themselves.

> The isolation of every human soul and the necessity of self-dependency must give each individual the right to choose his own surroundings. The strongest reason for giving woman all the opportunities for higher education, for the full development of her faculties, her forces of mind and body; for giving her the most enlarged freedom of thought and action . . . is the solitude and personal responsibility of her own individual life.[36]

Stanton argues the isolation of each human soul[37] in order to establish what belongs to woman as an individual with a clear set of necessary rights. Woman is 'an imaginary Robinson Crusoe with her woman Friday on a solitary island'.[38]

The problem arises when one tries to sort through the meaning of woman as an independent self-contained individual. Much of the time Stanton uses the conception of liberal individualism to establish woman's independence from men. This is what she means when she criticizes the women in *Anna Karenina*, who are disappointed and unhappy; 'and well they may be, as they are made to look to men, and not to themselves for their chief joy.'[39]

Individualism posits the importance of self-sovereignty and independence as a universal claim and therefore can be used to justify women's independence from men. When the ideology of liberal individualism is used in this way, it lays the basis for recognizing women's economic, sexual, and political independence from men. Feminism uses the individualist stance against men because men inhibit women's self and collective development; it need not extend this vision to premise women's isolation from one another. In other words, the liberal conception of an individual with rights and of woman's independence from men are important contributions to feminist theory. These points must be distinguished from the ideology of liberal individualism that posits the isolated, competitive individual.

This brings us to the problem with Stanton's usage of the ideology of liberal individualism. Although she sometimes encourages this vision in her view of woman's separateness and distinctness from all others, she also is aware that in order for women to develop their capacities as individuals, they need connection to other women. My point is that Stanton often confuses the issue that women must be understood as independent from men with a view of atomized woman. And Stanton's theory of sex class, as we shall shortly see, rejects the atomized view of woman and instead recognizes woman as part of a social collectivity. For her, understanding woman's oppression requires a recognition of the social and individual nature of a woman's existence. Being a woman is not merely an individual experience because woman is always defined in relation to her sexual class. Stanton's radical-feminist vision allows her to use the ideology of liberal individualism for women. This claim, however, recognizes both the rights women have as individuals within the ideology of liberal individualism and their exclusion from these rights as part of a sexual class that recognizes women as a social collectivity. She therefore understood that women would not gain their rights without a social movement. This runs counter to her tendency to deal with women as 'atomized individuals.'

STANTON AS A RADICAL FEMINIST

When one reads the letters written between Stanton and Susan B. Anthony about the feminist struggle they were engaged in, it is clear that they believed they were engaged in revolution. 'We are in the midst of a social revolution, greater than any political or religious revolution that the world has ever seen, because it goes deep down to the very foundation of society.'[40] It was a moral revolution that Stanton knew could not be brought about in a day or even a year.[41] She was aware that many of the reforms she was fighting for were insufficient. They even appeared superficial in terms of what she understood needed to be changed. She writes: 'But above all this I am so full of dreams of the true associative life that all the reforms of the day beside that seem to be superficial and fragmentary.'[42]

Stanton and Anthony named their newspaper the *Revolution*. Stanton stood firm against criticism that the name for the newspaper was too radical, curtly replying to her critics that maybe they would be more pleased with a title like the 'Rosebud'. Stanton writes to Anthony:

> There could not be a better name than *Revolution*. The establishing of woman on her rightful throne is the greatest revolution the world has ever known or ever will know. To bring it about is no child's play. You and I have not forgotten the conflict of the last 20 years. . . . A journal called the *Rosebud* might answer for those who come with kid gloves . . . but for us . . . there is no name like the *Revolution*.[43]

Stanton spoke of revolution, and signed her letters to her father 'your affectionate and radical daughter', yet she was not a political revolutionary. Although much of her political analysis would seem to support revolutionary activity, she focused on the transformation of liberal law. She saw it as a necessary, though not a sufficient, step in women's struggle for emancipation. Because a significant contrast exists between Stanton's radical-feminist analysis of women's oppression and her liberal-political strategy demanding citizen rights and legal reform, we need to better understand both facets in order to understand the lost potential within liberal feminism. We can begin to do this by examining Stanton's radical-feminist analysis of woman's oppression in the family, in marriage, and in motherhood.

Woman as a Sex Class

Stanton sees woman's subjugation as a reflection of man's power over woman. Woman is forced to be who she is. There is nothing natural about her subordination. 'It has taken the whole power of the civil and canon law to hold woman in the subordinate position which it is said she willingly accepts.'[44] She parallels the position of woman and man with that of slave and slaveholder. She therefore opposes men being elected to the office of president of the woman's suffrage association. 'I would never vote for a man to any office in our societies, not, however, because I am "down on" men *per se*. Think of an association of black men officered by slaveholders.'[45]

All history reflects the sexual class struggle between man and woman for Stanton. The struggle is reflected in the laws, which are made by men and for men.

> All history shows that one class never did legislate with justice for another, and all philosophy shows they never can, as the relations of class grow out of either natural or artificial advantages which one has over the other and which it will maintain if possible. *It is folly to say that women are not a class, so long as there is any difference in the code of laws for men and women, any discrimination in the customs of society, giving advantages to men over women. . . .*[46]

Woman has been the great sufferer in history for so long that most people cannot[47] conceive of a future without her subjugation. 'Aristotle could not conceive of any form of government without slavery. Modern writers on social science cannot imagine any kind of civil or domestic government without the subjection of woman.'[48]

According to Stanton, woman's degradation stems from men's ideas of their sexual rights over women. 'Our religion, laws, customs, are all founded on the belief that woman was made for man.'[49] Men's rights to women's bodies are age-old. The feudal law know as Marchetta, or Marquette, which forced a newly married woman to have intercourse with the feudal lord from one to three days after her marriage,[50] is an example of this male sexual privilege. 'Women were taught by Church and State alike, that the Feudal lord or Seigneur had a right to them, not only as against themselves, but as against any claim of husband or father.'[51]

On Marriage

Stanton criticizes the inequalities between men and women in marriage from the vantage point of the liberal individual rights men enjoy as citizens. Woman's individual sovereignty and personal independence must be recognized within both the home and the state. 'This same law of equality that has revolutionized the State and the Church is now knocking at the doors of our homes, and sooner or later there too it must do its work.'[52] This is why men fight against woman's equality in the state and the church. They fear that once women are recognized as equal in the public realm of the state, women will demand equality within marriage and the home. She writes in agreement with John Stuart Mill that 'the generality of the male sex cannot yet tolerate the idea of living with an *equal* at the fireside, and here is the secret of the opposition to woman's equality in the state and the church; men are not ready to recognize it in the home.'[53]

According to Stanton, the marriage relation merely embodies the unequal power relations existing between the sexes. The marriage contract itself shows that these relations are ones of domination and subordination. 'If the contract be equal, whence comes the terms "marital power," "marital rights," "obedience and restraint," "dominion and control," "power and protection," etc. etc. . . .'[54] The marriage contract also reflects the fact that men and women have a different (and unequal) *relation* to marriage. The man gives up nothing and the woman gives up everything. As long as marriage remains the sole object in women's lives[55] and is only one among many choices for men, women will remain dependent on marriage in a way men are not. As long as this continues, alongside the impossibility of divorce, Stanton advises women not to marry. 'Verily, under such circumstances, it is better, as the apostle says, not to marry.'[56]

Women have no individual sovereignty in marriage. They are forced to live their lives through another. There is no personal freedom for a woman in the role of wife. 'Personal freedom is the first right to be proclaimed, and that does not and cannot now belong to the relation of wife, to the mistress of the isolated home, to the financial dependant.'[57] Wifehood and motherhood occupy too much of a woman's life when, in fact, they should be incidental relations that expand her horizons.[58] Women should share the responsibilities of the home with the man rather than be relegated to this 'sphere' by herself. 'It would be nearer the truth to say the difference indicates different duties in the same sphere, seeing that man and woman were evidently made for each other and have shown equal capacity in the ordinary range of human duties.'[59] Stanton tries to dismantle the notion of separate sexual spheres for men and women. She asks why women should accept the sphere assigned them by men when men make such serious mistakes about their own lives anyway.[60] 'There is no such thing as a sphere for sex.'[61] Only the individual herself can say what her sphere should be. 'If God has assigned a sphere to man, one to woman, we claim the right outselves to judge of His design in reference to us, and we accord to man the same privilege.'[62] Stanton uses Lucretia Mott as an example to prove her point. Mott is both a wonderful orator and a perfect domestic and mother: '. . . who shall tell us that this divinely inspired woman is out of her sphere in her public endeavors to rouse this wicked nation to a sense of its awful guilt, to its great sins of war, slavery, injustice to woman, and to the labouring poor?'[63]

Stanton also criticizes marriage as an institution of legalized prostitution. She states that no man suffers as a woman does in marriage, because the woman gives up control of her own body. 'A man in marriage gives up no right; but a woman, every right, even the most sacred of all – the right of her own person.'[64] Lucy Stone urged her to argue for the wife's right to her own body.[65] Before this could be argued in any sustained form, Stanton would have to first uncover the inequities existent in the marriage system that were cloaked in a language of mutual agreement. In reality, the emphasis on love in marriage covers up a particular form of slavery.

> They live the lives, these married couples, generally of mutual spies and tyrants over each other, and it is the most subtle form of slavery ever instituted because it is seemingly so fair, based as it is on mutual agreement and not incompatible with the full concession of the equality of the parties to this mutual treaty of self-stultification.[66]

Stanton also believes that woman is made into a drudge of the household in marriage. Woman's labor is stolen from her; she becomes an unpaid domestic. This rings particularly true for the married woman of the nineteenth century. 'Woman has been the great unpaid laborer of the world . . .'[67] in the home, and when she works in other employments she is not paid according to the value of her work, but instead, according to her sex.[68] Stanton uncovers the dependence of women in marriage in economic and sexual terms. Woman's role as a wife requires this dependence; the sexual class dependence that stands in stark contrast to the personal independence required by liberal individualism.

Stanton's discussion of woman as a part of a sexual class underlines her criticism of marriage: woman lacks power as a woman. There are sexual, economic, and legal components to woman's dependence on her husband. Stanton in the end focuses on the legal component of woman's oppression within marriage. She argues that because women give up their legal existence in marriage, they become nameless, purseless, and childless.[69] The husband and wife become one person legally – the husband. The man has custody of his wife's person. He is guardian of their children, owner of her property, and has rights to her industry.[70] Hence, the married woman has no legal status, and propertied single women are taxed without representation. If this is the problem, the solution in Stanton's mind was passage of the Married Woman's Property Act (1836–48). Beyond the Married Woman's Property Act, Stanton fought for changes in the divorce laws.

In the end, she argues that the problems in marriage can be dealt with by a change in the laws defining it. 'Again, I ask, is it possible to discuss all the laws of a relation, and not touch the relation itself!'[71] For Stanton, the law can regulate equality. Changes in the sphere of the law bring changes to the sexual and economic spheres. Hence, Stanton's belief that if one changes all the legal relations of the marriage contract, the relation itself must change. But this, of course, assumes that all the relations of marriage are embodied within the law. The point here is that the purpose of law in liberal and patriarchal society is to define certain relations of power outside the law. This mystifies these relations on two levels. First, it makes it seem as though the power does not exist. Second, if the relation of power does not exist within the law, but liberal analysis focuses on the law, one is trying to change the wrong thing. For instance, how does one try to restructure patriarchy through changing the law when there is no law that states that women shall be the mothers or the secondary wage earners? The question remains how the liberal-legal analysis will encompass the economic dependence of woman on her husband when there are no laws directly regarding woman as the unpaid laborer of the household. The control of woman's sexuality within marriage is also not completely embodied (directly) within the law. The patriarchal relations of marriage remain cloaked by an emphasis on liberal law.

On Motherhood

One might not be immediately aware of Stanton's criticisms of motherhood by merely studying her suggestions for the legal reform of marriage and divorce. Even though Stanton sees woman's inequality tied to motherhood, this discussion never takes a central place in her legal reform strategy. A partial reason for this is the idea, raised earlier, that many of Stanton's radical-feminist commitments could not be addressed by her liberal-legal political strategy. Most constraints on women in terms of the rearing of children were not embodied in the law, which applied to the public realm of social activity. Although Stanton did not accept the divorce of private and public life (as female and male spheres), she often adopted a politics that did. As such, it was difficult to directly address issues she herself was committed to.

Stanton, as a mother of seven children, could be highly critical of the organization of the isolated home from firsthand experience. Her work in her family and the responsibility for her children made it difficult for her to partake in activities and meetings outside the home. She was not free to partake fully in the feminist movement until after her own children had grown up. Susan B. Anthony, her beloved friend and colleague, often came to help Elizabeth with her domestic chores when all seemed hopeless. Stanton's husband, Henry, traveled a good deal in his abolitionist work and appears to have taken no responsibility for the care of the home or the children. Of course, if he had, he would have been a rare man indeed.

Stanton often writes to Anthony that she will be unable to attend conventions or meetings because of her competing responsibilities in the household.

> I have so much care with all these boys on my hands. But I will write a letter. How much I do long to be free from housekeeping and children, so as to have some time to read, and think, and write. But it may be well for me to understand all the trials of woman's lot, that I may more eloquently proclaim them when the time comes.[72]

She complains to Anthony that she does not have the time to search for the books she needs to write her speeches, and even when she does, she cannot find an hour of uninterrupted time in which to write: 'I seldom have one hour undisturbed in which to sit down and write . . . unlike men . . . when they wish to write a document, shut themselves up for days with their thoughts and their books.'[73]

There are times when Stanton longs for the pressures on her time to subside. In such moments, she writes to Susan B. Anthony and pleads with her not to ask her to make any trips or attend any conventions while she is still nursing her new baby. 'I am determined to make no effort to do anything beyond my imperative home duties until I can bring about the following conditions; first, Relieve myself of house-keeping altogether; second, Secure some capable teacher for my children; third, See my present baby on her feet.'[74] Anthony usually co-operates, although she sometimes pushes her friend to continue her suffrage work regardless: '. . . I beg you, with one baby on your knee and another at your feet, and four boys whistling, buzzing, hallooing, "Ma," "Ma," set yourself about the work.'[75]

Stanton's feminist criticism of motherhood is not a denial of its importance and value. Although she is critical of the arrangements of the isolated home, the difficulties of motherhood that arise from this, and longs for some peace and quiet from her children, she thinks motherhood is one of the most important activities of women. Her criticism is that motherhood at present defines and limits woman and relegates her to a separate sphere. But in and of itself, motherhood is important and necessary to reproduce the next generation. She therefore criticizes the practice of motherhood while noting its importance in women's lives. 'There is no such sacredness and responsibility in any human relaton as in that of the mother. . . . To this end we must learn how to live and how to marry, how to educate ourselves and children for the reproduction not only of the mortal but immortal part of our natures.'[76]

Stanton even believes that women's potential for motherhood should make them sacred. 'One would think that potential motherhood should make woman as a class as sacred as the priesthood.'[77] Woman's capacity for motherhood is a source of added power for women; bearing children is something men cannot do.

> There would be more sense in insisting on man's limitations because he can not be a mother, than on woman's because she can be. Surely maternity is an added power and development of some of the most tender sentiments of the human heart and not a 'limitation.' Yes, and it fits her for much of the world's work; a large share of human legislation would be better done by her because of this deep experience.[78]

Stanton notes, however, that instead of any recognition of the value of women as mothers, woman is usually dismissed from other privileges because she is a mother. Men always dwell on how maternity disqualifies women for civil and political rights. They take the unique capabilities of woman and turn them against her. Stanton begins to uncover the mystification of this reality within patriarchal ideology. She believes that women have a unique capacity to bear children and that men twist this to disqualify women from equality with men.

Stanton's discussion of marriage and motherhood is radical feminist in that she speaks to the unequal power relations of the sex–class system. She questions the dependent relations created between men and women as women are relegated to a separate sexual sphere. By doing so, Stanton begins to lay the foundation for attacking the patriarchal division of public and private life. She wants to ready women for participation in public life, rather than have them be exclusively directed toward the private duties of the family.

However, the division between public (citizen) and private (family) remains within the liberal-feminist political strategy to gain the franchise for women, even if these realms are no longer to be sexually defined. In this liberal-feminist vision, woman defined as a mother (private sphere) can *also* be a citizen. Instead of being relegated to the private world of the family, woman is to participate as *both* a mother and a citizen. Stanton's understanding of how motherhood and woman's domesticity *exclude* her from public (male) life appears to be forgotten here.

THE ENFRANCHISEMENT OF WOMEN AS LIBERAL-FEMINIST STRATEGY

The radical-feminist understanding of male sexual power stands outside the liberal theory of power and politics, defined as governmental activity. The sex–class theory of power actually contradicts the liberal differentiation of state and family rule. Liberal ideology, as we have seen, is in fact based in the differentiation of political and family life. Radical-feminist theory presumes their collaboration in the oppression of women. From this feminist base, Stanton demands the political enfranchisement of women. As Ellen Dubois has stated, 'It was a particularly feminist demand, because it exposed and challenged the assumption of male authority over women.'[79] Stanton sidesteps woman's place in the home and argues for her place in the public world. By doing so, Dubois argues that Stanton rejects the (patriarchal) notion that women's place is in the home.[80]

Although I agree with Dubois that women's demand for the franchise was a feminist one, I also think it was significantly liberal and republican in origin. The liberal-feminist problem stems from this fact: the political understanding behind women's claim for the vote was primarily feminist, and the adoption of a legal political strategy for citizenship rights is basically liberal. The contradiction derives from the patriarchal base of liberalism and republican theory and the antipatriarchal priorities of feminism. Another way of stating this is that although Stanton wished to break down the division between public and private life, nineteenth-century liberal politics was premised on this division. I argue that American feminism lost out as a result of this contradictory mix.

Stanton's republican roots help her focus on the importance of citizen activity for women. Republican theory defines the virtuous being as one who takes part in the public duties of society. The concept 'republican' stems from the term *res publica*, meaning 'things public'. The concept of a republic signifies the importance of the public realm over the concerns of private households. One becomes virtuous by contributing to the public sphere. Interestingly enough, the word virtue stems from *vir*, meaning 'man'.[81]

Of course, Stanton's purpose is to challenge the view that only men are capable of citizenry and, hence, that only men are capable of virtue. She rejects the ancient Greek and modern American view that public life should be open to men only. Stanton argues that no government should be called republican 'in which one-half the people are forever deprived of all participation in its affairs.'[82] The key to participation in government, of each and every citizen, is the key to a republic. Until women gain their citizen rights, liberal democracy is made a mockery of.

> The basic idea of a republic is the right of self-government, the right of every citizen to choose his own representatives and to have a voice in the laws under which he lives. As this right can be secured only by the exercise of the suffrage, the ballot in the hand of every qualified citizen constitutes the true political status of the people in a republic.[83]

The enfranchisement of women will equalize the opportunities between them and men in the *republic*. 'The right of suffrage in a republic means education, development, self-reliance, independence, courage in the hour of danger.'[84]

The liberal theory of politics is very much tied to the republican view of public life. The liberal ideology of the state – that the state represents the differing interests of society; that as such, it protects one's individuality and one's property; that it is the arena where decisions are made which affect and decide policy – focuses on the centrality of governmental politics and its separation from private life. Because politics is defined in relation to the governmental realm, political participation is defined as voting. Stanton wants women to be able to function as a part of this world. 'To refuse political equality is to rob the ostracized of all self-respect, of credit in the marketplace, of recompense in the world of work, of a voice in choosing those who make and administer the law. . . .'[85]

The problem is that the liberal state can grant equality of opportunity to women in the legal sense without creating the equality of conditions for them to participate. For there to be an equality of conditions, woman's sexual, economic, and racial equality have to be established. I have already argued that legal equality cannot in and of itself establish this. But Stanton sidesteps this issue and instead argues for woman's right to operate in *both* the public and private spheres. 'Why should representative American women be incapable of discharging similar public and private duties at the same time in an equally commendable manner?'[86]

Stanton is not always clear in her treatment of the relationship between public and private life. She answered those who fought the idea of women voting because women would have to face the 'vulgarities of public life'[87] at the polls, that women already face these abuses by drunkard husbands in the 'privacy' of the home. In this instance, Stanton, in effect, argues that the separation of these two worlds does not hold in actual fact. But she also believed that the family suffered from the separate 'sexual spheres' doctrine. To the degree men are schooled for the commercial life, they ignore their children; and to the degree women are prepared only for the family, they are unable to educate their children to be responsible members of the state.

> In a busy commercial life, fathers have but little time to guard their children against the temptations of life, or to prepare them for its struggles, and the mother educated to believe that she has not rights or duties in public affairs, can give no lessons on political morality from her standpoint. Hence, the home is in a condition of half orphanage for the want of fathers, and the State suffers for need of wise mothers.[88]

It is with this view to breaking down the separation between the family and public life, and between women and men, that Stanton, along with the feminist movement, demands the ballot. Woman's exclusion is based solely on the nature of her sex. This is no longer acceptable, given liberal 'rights' theory.

> Women are the only class of citizens still wholly unrepresented in the government, and yet we possess every requisite

qualification for voters in the United States. Women possess property, and education; we take out naturalization – papers and passports and register ships. . . . We are neither idiots, lunatics, nor criminals, and according to our state constitution lack but one qualification for voters, namely, sex, which is an insurmountable qualification, and therefore equivalent to a bill of attainder against one-half the people. . . .[89]

The National Woman Suffrage Association was formed to introduce an amendment to the federal constitution to ensure women's right to the vote. The Nineteenth Amendment stated women's right to the vote and disqualified sex as a basis for determining the right to the franchise. 'The right of suffrage in the United States shall be based on citizenship, and shall be regulated by Congress, and all citizens of the U.S., whether native or naturalized, shall enjoy this right equally, without any distinction or discrimination whatever founded on sex.'[90] Stanton thought that once women were put on par with men as citizens, they would be able to more easily continue the struggle for their equality. She knew the vote was only a first step. Woman's equality, expressed through the franchise, even if only an ideological cloaking of women's real economic dependence and sexual servitude, contradicted the patriarchal ideology of woman's inferiority. Stanton was forcing the liberal state, on the tenets of liberal individualism itself, to contradict openly patriarchal ideology's notion of woman's inequality.

At the same time Stanton fights for woman's recognition by the state, she knows the state oppresses women. There are moments when she understands that the problem is not merely the exclusion of women from participation in the state but actual oppression by it. She speaks of 'the hard iron rule we feel alike in the church, the state, and the home'.[91] She writes of the fourfold bondage of woman as including the state. 'To emancipate woman from the fourfold bondage she has so long suffered in the state, the church, the home and the world of work, harder battles than we have yet fought are still before us.'[92]

Stanton even discusses the self-interest of all classes in their own rule and the fact that rulers within the state fear woman's emancipation because they know women are superior to them. Men only fear that they will no longer be able to control women.

The narrow self-interest of all classes is opposed to the sovereignty of woman. The rulers in the State are not willing to share their power with a class equal if not superior to themselves, over which they could never hope for absolute control, and whose methods of government might in many respects differ from their own. The anointed leaders in the Church are equally hostile to freedom for a sex for wise purposes to have been subordinated by divine decree. The capitalist in the world of work holds the key to the trades and professions, and undermines the power of labor unions in their struggle for shorter hours and fairer wages, by substituting the cheap labor of a disenfranchised class, that cannot organize its forces, thus making wife and sister rivals of husband and brother in the industries, to the detriment of both classes . . . where then, can we rest the lever with which to lift one-half of humanity from these depths of degradation but on that columbiad of our political life – the ballot. . . .[93]

The patriarchal state and the capitalist class appear to be separate entities in the above discussion, although both manipulate women. Stanton speaks of the degradations of capitalism for the laboring poor. She asks: '. . . is it right that a large majority of the race should suffer all their days the cruel hardships of poverty that a small minority may enjoy all life's blessings and benefits?'[94] Women, like the laboring classes, are denied the fruits of their labor. 'The great motive for making a man a slave was to get his labor or its result for nothing.'[95] Women have been denied the product of their labor by denying them the right to property and the right to inheritance.

Property is a delicate test of the condition of a nation. It is a singular fact of history that the rights of property have everywhere been recognized before the rights of persons. . . . The enslavement of woman has been much increased from the denial of the rights of property to her, not merely to the fruits of her own labor, but to the right of inheritance.[96]

At the same time that capitalism degrades the worker and pits sister against brother, man against wife, it denies both men and women the fruits of their labor. The corruptness of politics, however, reflects more than the needs of the capitalist class. It reflects the patriarchal 'family of men' sharing the same interests. 'The family of men are amazingly like one another; Republicans and Democrats, saints and sinners, all act alike and talk each in his turn the same cant.'[97]

Given Stanton's critical analysis of the patriarchal state, capitalist-class relations, marriage, and the family, it is not surprising that she believed that gaining the vote for women was only the beginning of the long struggle toward true independence. The franchise would only lay the basis for woman's equality of opportunity with men in the public sphere. 'But the battle is not wholly fought until we stand equal in the church, the world of work, and have an equal code of morals for both sexes.'[98] Underlying this battle would be Stanton's attempt to change the way people think about women. She herself states the importance of this activity: '. . . when men and women think about a new question, the first step in progress is taken.'[99]

One needs to recognize the different theoretical strains within Stanton's feminist theory. Her sexual–class analysis of woman's oppression is not easily encompassed in the liberal feminist political strategy of the nineteenth-century American women's movement. Yet the roots of American feminism are found here, in Stanton's radical feminist criticism of marriage, the isolation of the family, and the oppressiveness of the patriarchal state. They are also to be found in the liberal demand for self-sovereignty, economic independence, and individuality, which can be distinguished from the ideology of liberal individualism that merely recognizes woman as a citizen with voting rights. However else one's feminism comes to be defined, its starting point is the notion of the separateness, distinctness, and independence of woman from man. This notion is as liberal as it is feminist.

NOTES

1 Stanton's writing was done in close collaboration with Susan B. Anthony and other women in the feminist movement. She wrote as a leader of a social movement, not in isolation or divorced from political activity. See the biographies, Alma Lutz, *Created Equal, A Biography of Elizabeth Cady Stanton, 1815–1902* (John Day, New York, 1940); Mary Ann Oakley, *Elizabeth Cady Stanton* (Feminist Press, New York, 1972); and the autobiography, Elizabeth Cady Stanton, *Eighty Years and More, Reminiscences 1815–1897* (Schocken, New York, 1971).

2 One of the major exceptions to this lack of theoretical analysis of Stanton's work is the writing of historian Ellen Dubois. The discussion provided in this chapter is very much indebted to Dubois's pioneering research and study of Stanton and the feminist movement of which she was a part. Although I present a somewhat different interpretation of Stanton from Dubois's, her excellent and groundbreaking work is used throughout my analysis. See Ellen Dubois, *Feminism and Suffrage, The Emergence of an Independent Women's Movement in America, 1848–1869* (Cornell University Press, Ithaca, 1978); and her *Elizabeth Cady Stanton–Susan B. Anthony: Correspondence, Writing, Speeches*

(Schocken, New York, 1981). Also see her 'The Nineteenth Century Woman Suffrage Movement and the Analysis of Women's Oppression', in *Capitalist Patriarchy and the Case for Socialist Feminism*, ed. Zillah Eisenstein (Monthly Review Press, New York, 1978); 'The Radicalism of the Woman Suffrage Movement', *Feminist Studies* 3. 1–2 (Fall 1975); and 'On Labor and Free Love: Two Unpublished Speeches of Elizabeth Cady Stanton', *Signs* 1. 1 (Autumn 1975), pp. 257–69. For a somewhat different yet interesting discussion of Stanton's work, see Gerda Lerner, *The Female Experience: An American Documentary* (Bobbs-Merrill, Indianapolis, 1977).

3 For a full discussion of republican theory, see J. G. A. Pocock, *The Machiavellian Moment, Florentine Political Thought and the Atlantic Republican Tradition* (Princeton University Press, Princeton, 1975).

4 Eleanor Flexner, *Century of Struggle, The Woman's Rights Movement in the United States* (Harvard University Press, Cambridge, Mass., 1975), p. 71.

5 Dubois, 'On Labor and Free Love', p. 258.

6 Theodore Stanton and Harriot Stanton Blatch (eds), *Elizabeth Cady Stanton* (Arno and The New York Times, New York, 1969), 2.105.

7 Ibid., p. 109.

8 Ibid., p. 110.

9 Elizabeth Cady Stanton, Susan B. Anthony, and Matilda Joslyn Gage (eds), *History of Woman Suffrage* (Source Book Press, New York, 1970), 3.81.

10 Ibid.

11 Stanton, Anthony, and Gage, *History of Woman Suffrage*, 2.273.

12 Susan B. Anthony and Ida Husted Hareper, *History of Woman Suffrage* (Source Book Press, New York, 1970), 4.42.

13 Stanton and Blatch, *Elizabeth Cady Stanton*, 2.237.

14 Stanton, Anthony, and Gage, *History of Woman Suffrage* (Fowler and Wells, New York, 1881), 1.26.

15 Ibid., p. 679.

16 Stanton and Blatch, *Elizabeth Cady Stanton*, 2.164.

17 Ibid.

18 Ibid., p. 130.

19 Elizabeth Cady Stanton, 'Address to the National Woman Suffrage Convention', in *The Concise History of Woman Suffrage*, Mari Jo and Paul Buhle (eds) (University of Illinois Press, Chicago, 1978), p. 252.

20 Stanton, Anthony, and Gage, *History of Suffrage*, 1.50 (italics mine).

21 Stanton, 'Address to Woman Suffrage Convention', p. 251.

22 Ibid., p. 30.

23 'Declaration of Sentiments and Resolutions, Seneca Falls', in *Feminism: The Essential Historical Writings*, ed. Miriam Schneir (Vintage, New York, 1972), p. 77.

24 Stanton and Blatch, *Elizabeth Cady Stanton*, 2.368.

25 Elizabeth Cady Stanton, '"Solitude of Self" Address before the U.S.

Senate Committee on Woman Suffrage, February 20, 1892', in Buhle and Buhle, *History of Woman Suffrage*, p. 327.
26 Stanton and Blatch, *Elizabeth Cady Stanton*, 2.335 (italics mine).
27 Anthony and Harper, *History of Woman Suffrage*, 4.41.
28 Elizabeth Cady Stanton, 'Womanliness', in Schneir, *Essential Writings*, p. 155.
29 Elizabeth Cady Stanton, *The Woman's Bible, Parts I and II* (New York: Arno, 1972), p. 57.
30 Anthony and Harper, *History of Woman Suffrage*, 4.41.
31 Stanton, Anthony, and Gage, *History of Woman Suffrage*, 1.80.
32 Paulina Davis, comp. *A History of the National Woman's Rights Movement, For Twenty Years, with the proceedings of the decade meeting held at Apollo Hall, October 20, 1870, from 1850 to 1870* (Journeymen Printers', New York, 1871), p. 63.
33 Ibid.
34 Stanton and Blatch, *Elizabeth Cady Stanton*, 2.223.
35 Stanton was seventy-seven years old at the time of this address. One can argue that this address reflects the fact that she was an aging woman, and was concerned with the situation of older women. Ellen DuBois thinks that this speech also reflects the political isolation of Stanton after she had been pushed out of her leadership role in the feminist movement. My point is that it is particularly in such moments that one's view of life is stated most straightforwardly. I therefore think one gains a real insight into Stanton's view of 'liberal individualism' from this speech. Stanton writes in Blatch and Stanton, *Elizabeth Cady Stanton*, of this speech, that 'I am much inclined myself to think it is the best thing I have ever written at least in my declining years' (2.281–2).
36 Stanton, 'Solitude of Self', p. 326.
37 Ibid., p. 325.
38 Ibid.
39 Stanton and Blatch, *Elizabeth Cady Stanton*, 2.237.
40 Davis, *History of Woman's Rights*, p. 60.
41 Stanton and Blatch, *Elizabeth Cady Stanton*, 2.67.
42 Ibid., p. 51.
43 Ibid., p. 124.
44 Anthony and Harper, *History of Woman Suffrage*, 4.41.
45 Stanton and Blatch, *Elizabeth Cady Stanton*, 2.253.
46 Anthony and Harper, *History of Woman Suffrage*, 4.42 (italics mine).
47 Stanton and Blatch, *Elizabeth Cady Stanton*, 2.171.
48 Ibid., p. 145.
49 Ibid., p. 82.
50 Stanton, Anthony, and Gage, *History of Woman Suffrage*, 1.762.
51 Ibid.
52 Davis, *History of Woman's Rights*, p. 62.
53 Ibid., p. 60. Stanton thought Mill understood the situation of women better than any man before him. She wrote in Blatch and Stanton, *Elizabeth Cady Stanton*, 'To my mind, no thinker has so calmly,

truthfully, and logically revealed the causes and hidden depths of woman's degradation. . . . it is the first response from any man to show that he is capable of seeing and feeling . . . degrees of woman's wrongs' (2.122).

54 Stanton, *Eighty Years and More*, p. 222.
55 Elizabeth C. Stanton, 'Debates on Marriage and Divorce, 1860', in Buhle and Buhle, *History of Woman Suffrage*, p. 175.
56 Davis, *History of Woman's Rights*, p. 76.
57 Stanton and Blatch, *Elizabeth Cady Stanton*, 2.70.
58 Stanton, Anthony, and Gage, *History of Woman Suffrage*, 1.22.
59 Ibid., p. 18.
60 Stanton and Blatch, *Elizabeth Cady Stanton*, 2.19.
61 Ibid.
62 Ibid.
63 Ibid., p. 20.
64 Ibid., p. 70.
65 Ibid., p. 68.
66 DuBois, 'On Labor and Free Love', p. 266.
67 Ibid.
68 Harriet Stanton Blatch wrote at greater length than her mother did on the economic value of women's domestic work. She agreed with Charlotte Perkins Gilman that women's work as mothers remained unpaid labor to keep women economically dependent on men. In Blatch and Lutz, *Challenging Years*, Blatch recommended a motherhood endowment (p. 333). She corresponded with Theodore Roosevelt about the idea of a motherhood pension, which, according to Blatch, he appears to have greeted with some enthusiasm (p. 332). Also see Charlotte Perkins Gilman, *Women and Economics* (Harper and Row, New York, 1966); and *The Home: Its Work and Influence* (University of Illinois Press, Urbana, 1972).
69 Elizabeth C. Stanton, 'Address to the New York State Legislature, 1854', in Schneir, *Essential Writings*, p. 113.
70 Stanton, Anthony, and Gage, *History of Woman Suffrage*, 1.261.
71 Stanton, *Eighty Years and More*, p. 225.
72 Stanton and Blatch, *Elizabeth Cady Stanton*, 2.41–42.
73 Ibid., p. 55.
74 Ibid., pp. 51–2.
75 Ibid., p. 64.
76 Davis, *History of Woman's Rights*, p. 82.
77 Stanton, *The Woman's Bible, Part I*, p. 102.
78 Anthony and Harper, *History of Woman Suffrage*, 4.58.
79 DuBois, *Feminism and Suffrage*, p. 46. For other interpretations of the nineteenth-century feminist movement, see Barbara Berg, *The Remembered Gate: Origins of American Feminism, The Woman and the City 1800–1860* (Oxford University Press, New York, 1978); Flexner, *Century of Struggle*; Alan Grimes, *The Puritan Ethic and Woman Suffrage* (Oxford University Press, New York, 1967); Aileen Kraditor,

The Ideas of the Woman Suffrage Movement, 1890–1920 (Columbia University Press, New York, 1965); William O'Neill, *Everyone Was Brave, A History of Feminism in America* (Quadrangle, Chicago, 1969); and Ross Evans Paulson, *Women's Suffrage and Prohibition: A Comparative Study of Equality and Social Control* (Scott, Foresman, Illinois, 1973).

80 DuBois, *Feminism and Suffrage*, p. 46.

81 Pocock, *The Machiavellian Moment*, p. 37. By focusing on these particular strains within Stanton's thought, I do not mean to deny the importance of other forces like the Protestant Reformation in changing the way women thought about themselves. See Stanton's *The Woman's Bible*; and Ann Douglas, *The Feminization of American Culture* (Knopf, New York, 1977).

82 Stanton, Anthony, and Gage, *History of Woman Suffrage*, 3.81.

83 Anthony and Harper, *History of Woman Suffrage*, 4.41.

84 Ibid.

85 Stanton, 'Solitude of Self', p. 326.

86 Stanton, *The Woman's Bible, Part I*, p. 78.

87 Stanton, Anthony, and Gage, *History of Woman Suffrage*, 1.682.

88 Stanton, *The Woman's Bible, Part I*, p. 137.

89 Stanton, Anthony, and Gage, *History of Woman Suffrage*, 3.85.

90 Ibid., p. 83.

91 Stanton, 'Address to Woman Suffrage Convention', p. 253.

92 Anthony and Harper, *History of Woman Suffrage*, 4.114.

93 Stanton, Anthony, and Gage, *History of Woman Suffrage*, 3.vi.

94 DuBois, 'On Labor and Free Love', p. 261.

95 Ibid.

96 Stanton, Anthony, and Gage, *History of Woman Suffrage*, 1.770.

97 Stanton and Blatch, *Elizabeth Cady Stanton*, 2.101.

98 Ibid., 2.338.

99 Ibid., 2.20.

5

Feminist Critiques of the Public/Private Dichotomy

CAROLE PATEMAN

The dichotomy between the private and the public is central to almost two centuries of feminist writing and political struggle; it is, ultimately, what the feminist movement is about. Although some feminists treat the dichotomy as a universal, trans-historical and trans-cultural feature of human existence, feminist criticism is primarily directed at the separation and opposition between the public and private spheres in liberal theory and practice.

The relationship between feminism and liberalism is extremely close but also exceedingly complex. The roots of both doctrines lie in the emergence of individualism as a general theory of social life; neither liberalism nor feminism is conceivable without some conception of individuals as free and equal beings, emancipated from the ascribed, hierarchical bonds of traditional society. But if liberalism and feminism share a common origin, their adherents have often been opposed over the past 200 years. The direction and scope of feminist criticism of liberal conceptions of the public and the private have varied greatly in different phases of the feminist movement. An analysis of this criticism is made more complicated because liberalism is inherently ambiguous about the 'public' and the 'private', and feminists and liberals disagree about where and why the dividing line is to be drawn between the two spheres, or, according to certain contemporary feminist arguments, whether it should be drawn at all.

Feminism is often seen as nothing more than the completion of the liberal or bourgeois revolution, as an extension of liberal principles and rights to women as well as men. The demand for equal rights has, of course, always been an important part of feminism. However, the attempt to universalize liberalism has more

Reprinted with permission from *Public and Private in Social Life*, edited by S. I. Benn and G. F. Gaus (Croom Helm, Kent, 1983), pp. 281–303.

far-reaching consequences than is often appreciated because, in the end, it inevitably challenges liberalism itself.[1] Liberal feminism has radical implications, not least in challenging the separation and opposition between the private and public spheres that is fundamental to liberal theory and practice. The liberal contrast between private and public is more than a distinction between two kinds of social activities. The public sphere, and the principles that govern it, are seen as separate from, or independent of, the relationships in the private sphere. A familiar illustration of this claim is the long controversy between liberal and radical political scientists about participation, the radicals denying the liberal claim that the social inequalities of the private sphere are irrelevant to questions about the political equality, universal suffrage and associated civil liberties of the public realm.

Not all feminists, however, are liberals; 'feminism' goes far beyond liberal-feminism. Other feminists explicitly reject liberal conceptions of the private and public and see the social structure of liberalism as the political problem, not a starting point from which equal rights can be claimed. They have much in common with the radical and socialist critics of liberalism who rely on 'organic' theories but they differ sharply in their analysis of the liberal state. In short, feminists, unlike other radicals, raise the generally neglected problem of the patriarchal character of liberalism.

I   LIBERALISM AND PATRIARCHALISM

Benn and Gaus's account of the liberal conception of the public and the private illustrates very nicely some major problems in liberal theory.[2] They accept that the private and the public are central categories of liberalism, but they do not explain why these two terms are crucial or why the private sphere is contrasted with and opposed to the 'public' rather than the 'political' realm. Similarly, they note that liberal arguments leave it unclear whether civil society is private or public but, although they state that in both of their liberal models the family is paradigmatically private, they fail to pursue the question why, in this case, liberals usually also see civil society as private. Benn and Gaus's account of liberalism also illustrates its abstract, ahistorical character and, in what is omitted and taken for granted, provides a good example of the theoretical discussions that feminists are now sharply criticizing. The account bears out Eisenstein's claim that 'the ideology of public and private life' invariably presents 'the division between public and private life

. . . as reflecting the development of the bourgeois liberal state, not the patriarchal ordering of the bourgeois state.'[3]

The term 'ideology' is appropriate here because the profound ambiguity of the liberal conception of the private and public obscures and mystifies the social reality it helps constitute. Feminists argue that liberalism is structured by patriarchal as well as class relations, and that the dichotomy between the private and the public obscures the subjection of women to men within an apparently universal, egalitarian and individualist order. Benn and Gaus's account assumes that the reality of our social life is more or less adequately captured in liberal conceptions. They do not recognize that 'liberalism' is patriarchal liberalism and that the separation and opposition of the public and private spheres is an unequal opposition between women and men. They thus take the talk of 'individuals' in liberal theory at face value although, from the period when the social contract theorists attacked the patriarchalists, liberal theorists have excluded women from the scope of their apparently universal arguments.[4] One reason why the exclusion goes unnoticed is that the separation of the private and public is presented in liberal theory as if it applied to all individuals in the same way. It is often claimed – by anti-feminists today, but by feminists in the nineteenth century, most of whom accepted the doctrine of 'separate spheres' – that the two spheres are separate, but equally important and valuable. The way in which women and men are differentially located within private life and the public world is, as I shall indicate, a complex matter, but underlying a complicated reality is the belief that women's natures are such that they are properly subject to men and their proper place is in the private, domestic sphere. Men properly inhabit, and rule within, both spheres. The essential feminist argument is that the doctrine of 'separate but equal', and the ostensible individualism and egalitarianism of liberal theory, obscure the patriarchal reality of a social structure of inequality and the domination of women by men.

In theory, liberalism and patriarchalism stand irrevocably opposed to each other. Liberalism is an individualist, egalitarian, conventionalist doctrine; patriarchalism claims that hierarchical relations of subordination necessarily follow from the natural characteristics of men and women. In fact, the two doctrines were successfully reconciled through the answer given by the contract theorists in the seventeenth century to the subversive question of who counted as free and equal individuals. The conflict with the patriarchalists did not extend to women or conjugal relations; the latter were excluded from individualist arguments and the battle was fought out over the relation of adult sons to their fathers.

The theoretical basis for the liberal separation of the public and the private was provided in Locke's *Second Treatise*. He argued against Filmer that political power is conventional and can justifiably be exercised over free and equal adult individuals only with their consent. Political power must not be confused with paternal power over children in the private, family sphere, which is a natural relationship that ends at the maturity, and hence freedom and equality, of (male) children. Commentators usually fail to notice that Locke's separation of the family and the political is also a sexual division. Although he argued that natural differences between men, such as age or talents, are irrelevant to their political equality, he agrees with Filmer's patriarchal claim that the natural differences between men and women entail the subjection of women to men or, more specifically, wives to husbands. Indeed, in Locke's statement at the beginning of the *Second Treatise* that he will show why political power is distinctive, he takes it for granted that the rule of husbands over wives is included in other (non-political) forms of power. He explicitly agrees with Filmer that a wife's subordination to her husband has a 'Foundation in Nature' and that the husband's will must prevail in the household as he is naturally 'the abler and the stronger'.[5] But a natural subordinate cannot at the same time be free and equal. Thus women (wives) are excluded from the status of 'individual' and so from participating in the public world of equality, consent and convention.

It may appear that Locke's separation of paternal from political power can also be characterized as a separation of the private from the public. In one sense this is so; the public sphere can be seen as encompassing all social life apart from domestic life. Locke's theory also shows how the private and public spheres are grounded in opposing principles of association which are exemplified in the conflicting status of women and men; natural subordination stands opposed to free individualism. The family is based on natural ties of sentiment and blood and on the sexually ascribed status of wife and husband (mother and father). Participation in the public sphere is governed by universal, impersonal and conventional criteria of achievement, interests, rights, equality and property – liberal criteria, applicable only to men. An important consequence of this conception of private and public is that the public world, or civil society, is conceptualized and discussed in liberal theory (indeed, in almost all political theory) in abstraction from, or as separate from, the private domestic sphere.

It is important to emphasize at this point that the contemporary feminist critique of the public–private dichotomy is based on the same Lockean view of the two categories; domestic life is as paradigmatically private for feminists as it is in (this interpretation of) Locke's theory. However, feminists reject the claim that the separation of the private and the public follows inevitably from the natural characteristics of the sexes. They argue that a proper understanding of liberal social life is possible only when it is accepted that the two spheres, the domestic (private) and civil society (public), held to be separate and opposed, are inextricably interrelated; they are the two sides of the single coin of liberal-patriarchalism.

If, at one theoretical level, feminists and liberals are in conflict over a shared conception of the public and the private, at another level they are at odds about these very categories. There is another sense in which the private and public are far from synonymous with Locke's paternal and political power. Precisely because liberalism conceptualizes civil society in abstraction from ascriptive domestic life, the latter remains 'forgotten' in theoretical discussion. The separation between private and public is thus re-established as a division *within* civil society itself, within the world of men. The separation is then expressed in a number of different ways, not only private and public but also, for example, 'society' and 'state'; or 'economy' and 'politics'; or 'freedom' and 'coercion'; or 'social' and 'political'.[6] Moreover, in *this* version of the separation of private and public, one category, the private, begins to wear the trousers (to adapt J. L. Austin's patriarchal metaphor for once in an appropriate context). The public or political aspect of civil society tends to get lost, as, for example, Wolin points out in *Politics and Vision*.[7]

The uncertain position of the public sphere develops for very good reason; the apparently universal criteria governing civil society are actually those associated with the liberal conception of the male individual, a conception which is presented as that of *the* individual. The individual is the owner of the property in his person, that is to say, he is seen in abstraction from his ascribed familial relations and those with his fellow men. He is a 'private' individual, but he needs a sphere in which he can exercise his rights and opportunities, pursue his (private) interests and protect and increase his (private) property. If all men ('individuals') are so to act in an orderly fashion, then, as Locke is aware, a public 'umpire' (rather than a hidden – private? – hand), or a representative, liberal state, is required to make and enforce publicly known, equitable laws. Because individualism is, as Benn and Gaus remark, 'the dominant mode of liberal theory and discourse', it is not surprising either that the private and the public appear as the 'obvious' pair of liberal categories, or that the public gets stripped of its trousers and civil society is seen, above all else, as the sphere of private interest, private enterprise and private individuals.[8]

In the late twentieth century the relation between the capitalist economy and the state no longer looks like that between Locke's umpire and civil society and confusion abounds about the boundary between the private and public. But the confusion is unlikely to be remedied from within a theory which 'forgets' that it includes another boundary between private and public. One solution is to reinstate the political in public life. This is the response of Wolin or of Habermas in his rather opaque discussion of the 'principle' of the public sphere, where citizens can form reasoned political judgements.[9] Unlike these theorists, feminist critiques insist that an alternative to the liberal conception must also encompass the relationship between public and domestic life. The question that feminists raise is why the patriarchal character of the separation of a depoliticized public sphere from private life is so easily 'forgotten'; why is the separation of the two worlds located within civil society so that public life is implicitly conceptualized as the sphere of men?

The answer to this question can be found only by examining the history of the connection between the separation of production from the household and the emergence of the family as paradigmatically private. When Locke attacked (one aspect of) patriarchalism, husbands were heads of households but their wives played an active, independent part in numerous areas of production. As capitalism and its specific form of sexual as well as class division of labour developed, however, wives were pushed into a few, low-status areas of employment or kept out of economic life altogether, relegated to their 'natural', dependent, place in the private, familial sphere.[10] Today, despite a large measure of civil equality, it appears natural that wives are subordinate just because they are dependent on their husbands for subsistence, and it is taken for granted that liberal social life can be understood without reference to the sphere of subordination, natural relations and women. The old patriarchal argument from nature and women's nature was thus transformed as it was modernized and incorporated into liberal capitalism. Theoretical and practical attention became fixed exclusively on the public area, on civil society – on 'the social' or on 'the economy' – and domestic life was assumed irrelevant to social and political theory or the concerns of men of affairs. The fact that patriarchalism is an essential, indeed constitutive, part of the theory and practice of liberalism remains obscured by the apparently impersonal, universal dichotomy between private and public within civil society itself. The intimate relation between the private and the natural is obscured when the private and the public are discussed in abstraction from their historical development and also from other ways of expressing this fundamental structural separation within liberalism. I have already observed that, when the separation is located within civil society, the dichotomy between private and public is referred to in a variety of ways (and a full account of liberalism would have to explain these variations). Similarly, the feminist understanding of the private and the public, and the feminist critique of their separation and opposition, are sometimes presented in these terms, but the argument is also formulated using the categories of nature and culture, or personal and political, or morality and power, and, of course, women and men and female and male. In popular (and academic) consciousness the duality of female and male often serves to encapsulate or represent the series (or circle) of liberal separations and oppositions: female, or – nature, personal, emotional, love, private, intuition, morality, ascription, particular, subjection; male, or – culture, political, reason, justice, public, philosophy, power, achievement, universal, freedom. The most fundamental and general of these oppositions associates women with nature and men with culture, and several contemporary feminists have framed their critiques in these terms.

II   NATURE AND CULTURE

Patriarchalism rests on the appeal to nature and the claim that women's natural function of childbearing prescribes their domestic and subordinate place in the order of things. J. S. Mill wrote in the nineteenth century that the depth of the feelings surrounding the appeal to nature was 'the most intense and most deeply-rooted of all those which gather round and protect old institutions and customs'.[11] In the 1980s, when women in the liberal democracies have won citizenship and a large measure of legal equality with men, the arguments of the organized anti-feminist movement illustrate that the appeal to nature has lost none of its resonance. From the seventeenth century a question has been persistently asked by a few female voices: 'If all men are born free, how is it that all women are born slaves?'[12] The usual answer, vigorously presented by Mary Wollstonecraft in the *Vindication of the Rights of Women* in 1792, and today by feminist critics of the sexism of children's books, schooling and the media, is that what are called women's natural characteristics are actually, in Wollstonecraft's phrase, 'artificial', a product of women's education or lack of it. However, even the most radical changes in educational practice will not affect women's natural, biological capacity to bear children. This difference between the sexes is independent of history and culture, and so it is perhaps not surprising that the natural difference, and the opposition between (women's) nature and (men's) culture, has been central to some well-known feminist attempts to explain the apparently universal subordination of women. Arguments focusing on nature/culture fall into two broad categories, the anthropological and the radical feminist.[13]

In one of the most influential anthropological discussions, Ortner argues that the only way to explain why the value universally assigned to women and their activities is lower than that assigned to men and their pursuits is that women are 'a symbol' of all 'that every culture defines as being of a lower order of existence than itself'.[14] That is, women and domestic life symbolize nature. Humankind attempts to transcend a merely natural existence so that nature is always seen as of a lower order than culture. Culture becomes identified as the creation and the world of men because women's biology and bodies place them closer to nature than men, and because their child-rearing and domestic tasks, dealing with unsocialized infants and with raw materials, bring them into closer contact with nature. Women and the domestic sphere thus appear inferior to the cultural sphere and male activities, and women are seen as necessarily subordinate to men.

It is unclear whether Ortner is arguing that women's domestic activities symbolize nature, are part of nature or, rather, place women in a mediating position between nature and culture. She argues that the opposition between women/nature and men/culture is itself a cultural construct and not given in nature; 'Woman is not "in reality" any closer to (or further from) nature than man — both have consciousness, both are mortal. But there are certainly reasons why she appears that way.'[15] However, Ortner fails to give sufficient weight to the fundamental fact that men and women are social and cultural beings, or to its corollary that 'nature' always has a social meaning, a meaning that, moreover, varies widely in different societies and in different historical periods. Even if women and their tasks have been universally devalued, it does not follow that we can understand this important fact of human existence by asking questions in universal terms and looking for general answers formulated in terms of universal dichotomies. The distinction between domestic, private women's life and the public world of men does not have the same meaning in pre-modern European society as in present liberal capitalism, and to see both the latter and hunter–gatherer societies from the perspective of a general opposition between nature and culture, or public and private, can lead only to an emphasis on biology or 'nature'. Rosaldo recently criticized arguments about women's subordination that, like Ortner's, implicitly rest on the question, 'How did it begin?' She points out that to seek a universally applicable answer inevitably opposes 'woman' to 'man', and gives rise to a separation of domestic life from 'culture' or 'society' because of the 'presumably panhuman functions' thus attributed to women.[16]

The most thorough attempt to find a universal answer to the question of why it is that women are in subjection to men, and the most stark opposition between nature and culture, can be found in the writings of the radical feminists who argue that nature is the single cause of men's domination. The best known version of this argument is Firestone's *The Dialectic of Sex*, which also provides an example of how one form of feminist argument, while attacking the liberal separation of private and public, remains within the abstractly individualist framework which helps constitute this division of social life. Firestone reduces the history of the relation between nature and culture or private and public to an opposition between female and male. She argues that the origin of the dualism lies in 'biology itself – procreation',[17] a natural or original inequality that is the basis of the oppression of women and the source of male power. Men, by confining women to reproduction (nature), have freed themselves 'for the business of the world'[18] and so have created and controlled culture. The proposed solution is to eliminate natural differences (inequalities) between the sexes by introducing artificial reproduction. 'Nature' and the private sphere of the family will then be abolished and individuals, of all ages, will interact as equals in an undifferentiated cultural (or public) order.

The popular success of *The Dialectic of Sex* owes more to the need for women to continue to fight for control of their bodies and reproductive capacity than to its philosphical argument. The key assumption of the book is that women necessarily suffer from 'a fundamentally oppressive biological condition',[19] but biology, in itself, is neither oppressive nor liberating; biology, or nature, becomes either a source of subjection or free creativity for women only because it has meaning within specific social relationships.

Firestone's argument reduces the social conceptions of 'women' and 'men' to the biological categories of 'female' and 'male', and thus denies any significance to the complex history of the relationship between men and women or between the private and public spheres. She relies on an abstract conception of a natural, biological female individual with a reproductive capacity which puts her at the mercy of a male individual, who is assumed to have a natural drive to subjugate her.[20] This contemporary version of a thorough Hobbesian reduction of individuals to their natural state leads to a theoretical dead end, not perhaps a surprising conclusion to an argument that implicitly accepts the patriarchal claim that women's subordination is decreed by nature. The way forward will not be found in a universal dichotomy between nature and culture, or between female and male individuals. Rather, as Rosaldo argues, it is necessary to develop a feminist theoretical perspective that takes account of the social relationships between women and men in historically specific structures of domination and subordination; and, it might be added, within the context of specific interpretations of the 'public' and 'private'.

III   MORALITY AND POWER

The long struggle to enfranchise women is one of the most important theoretical and practical examples of feminist attacks on the dichotomy between the private and public. Suffragist arguments show how the attempt to universalize liberal principles leads to a challenge to liberalism itself, and this is particularly well, if implicitly, illustrated in the writing of J. S. Mill. Despite the enormous amount of attention given to voting over the past thirty years, remarkably little attention has been paid by either theoretical or empirical students of politics to the political meaning and consequences of manhood and womanhood suffrage. In recent feminist literature, however, two different views can be found about the implications of the enfranchisement of women for the separation between the public and the private. There is disagreement whether the suffrage movement served to reinforce the sexual separation in social life or whether, rather despite itself, it was one means of undermining it. In the mid-nineteenth century, when feminism emerged as an organized social and political movement, the argument from nature had been elaborated into the doctrine of separate spheres; men and women, it was claimed, each naturally had a separate, but complementary and equally valuable, social place. The most striking difference between the early feminists and suffragists and contemporary feminists is that almost everyone in the nineteenth century accepted the doctrine of separate spheres.

The early feminists bitterly opposed the grossly unequal position of women but the reforms they struggled to achieve, such as an end to the legal powers of husbands that made their wives into private property and civil non-persons, and the opportunity to obtain an education so that single women could support themselves, were usually seen as means to equality for women who would remain within their own private sphere. The implicit assumption was that the suffrage, too, meant different things to men and women. This comes out clearly in one of the most passionately sentimental, and anti-feminist, statements of the doctrine of separate spheres. In 'Of Queens' Gardens', Ruskin argues that, 'the man's duty, as a member of the commonwealth, is to assist in the maintenance, in the advance, in the defence of the state. The woman's duty, as a member of the commonwealth, is to assist in the ordering, in the comforting, and in the beautiful adornment of the state.'[21] Citizenship for women could thus be seen as an elaboration of their private, domestic tasks and one of the suffragists' main arguments was that the vote was a necessary means to protect and strengthen women's special sphere (an argument that gained weight at the end of the century as legislatures increasingly interested themselves in social issues related to women's sphere). Moreover, both the most ardent anti-suffragists and vehement suffragists agreed that women were weaker, but more moral and virtuous, than men. The anti-suffragists argued that, therefore, enfranchisement would fatally weaken the state because women could not bear arms or use force; the suffragists countered by claiming that women's superior morality and rectitude would transform the state and usher in a reign of peace. All this has led Elshtain to argue that it was precisely because the suffragists accepted the assumptions of the doctrine of separate spheres that they 'failed, even on their own terms.' Far from raising a challenge to the separation of the public and private, they merely 'perpetuated the very mystifications and unexamined presumptions which serve to rig the system against them.'[22]

Much of Elshtain's argument is conducted in terms of the duality of morality and power, one way of formulating the separation of private and public when this is located within civil society. Liberal theorists often contrast the political sphere (the state), the sphere of power, force and violence, with the society (the private realm), the sphere of voluntarism, freedom and spontaneous regulation.[23] However, the argument about the implications of women's moral superiority, and Elshtain's use of the duality of morality and power, refer rather to the more fundamental separation of the private, domestic sphere from public life or civil society. The opposition between morality and power then counterposes physical force and aggression, the natural attributes of manliness, which are seen as exemplified in the military force of the state, against love and altruism, the natural attributes of womanhood, which are, paradigmatically, displayed in domestic life where the wife and mother stands as the guardian of morality.[24] Was the struggle for womanhood suffrage locked in the separation and dichotomies of patriarchal liberalism, within the duality of morality and power (which, again, is one way of expressing the doctrine of separate spheres), to the extent suggested by Elshtain? To vote is, after all, a political act. Indeed, it has come to be seen as *the* political act of a liberal-democratic citizen, and citizenship is a status of formal civil or public equality.

A different assessment of the suffrage movement is presented in recent work by DuBois, who argues that the reason that both sides of the struggle for enfranchisement saw the vote as the key feminist demand was that the vote gave women 'a connection with the social order not based on the institution of the family and their subordination within it . . . As citizens and voters, women would participate directly in society as individuals, not indirectly through their subordinate position as wives and mothers.'[25] DuBois emphasizes that the suffragists did not question women's 'peculiar suitability' for domestic life, but the demand for the vote constituted a denial that women were naturally fit *only* for private life. The demand for the suffrage thus reached to the heart of the mutual accommodation between patriarchalism and liberalism since to win the vote meant that, in one respect at least, women must be admitted as 'individuals'. This is why DuBois can argue that women's claim for a public, equal status with men, 'exposed and challenged the assumption of male authority over women'.[26] An important long-term consequence of women's enfranchisement, and the other reforms that have led to women's present position of (almost) formal political and legal equality with men, is that the contradiction between civil equality and social, especially familial, subjection, including the beliefs that help constitute it, is now starkly revealed. The liberal-patriarchal separation of the public and private spheres has become a political problem.

The dimensions of the problem are set out – very clearly, with the benefit of hindsight – in John Stuart Mill's feminist essay *The Subjection of Women* and his arguments for womanhood suffrage.

Mill's essay shows that the assumption that an individual political status can be added to women's ascribed place in the private sphere and leave the latter intact, or even strengthened, is ultimately untenable. Or, to make this point another way, liberal principles cannot simply be universalized to extend to women in the public sphere without raising an acute problem about the patriarchal structure of private life. Mill shows theoretically, as the feminist movement has revealed in practice, that the spheres are integrally related and that women's full and equal membership in public life is impossible without changes in the domestic sphere.

In the *Subjection*, Mill argues that the relation between men and women, or more specifically between husbands and wives, forms an unjustified and unjustifiable exception to the liberal principles of individual freedom and equality, free choice, equality of opportunity and allocation of occupations by merit that (he believes) govern other social and political institutions in nineteenth-century Britain. The social subordination of women is 'a single relic of an old world of thought and practice exploded in everything else'.[27] At the beginning of the essay Mill attacks the appeal to nature and argues that nothing can be known about the natural differences, if any, between women and men until evidence is available about their respective attributes within relationships and institutions where they interact as equals instead of as superiors and inferiors. Much of Mill's argument is directed against the legally sanctioned powers of husbands which placed them in the position of slave-masters over their wives. Legal reform should turn the family from a 'school of despotism' into a 'school of sympathy in equality' and a 'real school of the virtues of freedom'.[28] However, as recent feminist critics have pointed out, in the end he falls back on the same argument from nature that he criticizes. Although Mill argues that in the prevailing circumstances of women's upbringing, lack of education and occupational opportunities, and legal and social pressures, they do not have a free choice whether or not to marry, he also assumes that, even after social reform, most women will still choose marital dependence. He states that it will generally be understood that when a woman marries she has chosen her 'career', just like a man entering a profession: 'she makes choice of the management of a household, and the bringing up of a family, as the first call upon her exertions . . . She renounces [all occupations] not consistent with the requirements of this.'[29] The question why, if marriage is a 'career', liberal arguments about (public) equality of opportunity have any relevance to women, is thus neatly begged.

Mill introduced the first measure for womanhood suffrage into the House of Commons in 1867. He advocated votes for women for the same two reasons that he supported manhood suffrage; because it was necessary for self-protection or the protection of interests and because political participation would enlarge the capacities of women. However, it is not usually appreciated that Mill's acceptance of a sexually ascribed division of labour, or the separation of domestic from public life, cuts the ground from under his argument for enfranchisement. The obvious difficulty for his argument is that women as wives will be largely confined to the small circle of the family so they will find it hard to use their votes to protect their interests. Women will not be able to learn what their interests are without experience outside domestic life. This point is even more crucial for Mill's argument about individual development and education through political participation. Mill, in what Benn and Gaus call his 'representative liberal text', refers to the development of a 'public spirit' by citizens.[30] In the *Subjection* he writes of the elevation of the individual 'as a moral, spiritual and social being' that occurs under 'the ennobling influence' of free government.[31] This is a large claim to make for the periodic casting of a ballot and Mill did not think that such consequences would arise from the suffrage alone. He writes that 'citizenship', and here I take him to be referring to universal suffrage, 'fills only a small place in modern life, and does not come near the daily habits or inmost sentiments'.[32] He goes on to argue that the (reformed) family is the real school of freedom. However, this is no more plausible than the claim about liberal democratic voting. A despotic, patriarchal family is no school for democratic citizenship; but neither can the egalitarian family, on its own, substitute for participation in a wide variety of social institutions (especially the workplace) that Mill, in his other social and political writings, argues is the necessary education for citizenship. How can wives who have 'chosen' private life develop a public spirit? Women will thus exemplify the selfish, private beings, lacking a sense of justice, who result, according to Mill, when individuals have no experience of public life.

   Mill's ultimate failure to question the 'natural' sexual division of labour undermines his argument for an equal public status for women. His argument in the *Subjection* rests on an extension of liberal principles to the domestic sphere – which immediately brings the separation of the private and public, and the opposition between the principles of association in the two spheres into question. He would not have remained Benn and Gaus's 'exemplary' liberal theorist if he had not, at least in part, upheld the patriarchal-liberal ideology of the separation between public and private. On the other hand, by throwing doubt on the original Lockean separation of paternal and political power, and by arguing that the same political principles apply to the structure of family life as to political life, Mill also raises a large question about the status of the family. The language of 'slaves', 'masters', 'equality', 'freedom' and 'justice' implies that the family is a conventional not a natural association. Mill would not want to draw the conclusion that the family is political, but many contemporary feminists have done so. The most popular slogan of today's feminist movement is 'the personal is the political', which not only explicitly rejects the liberal separation of the private and public, but also implies that no distinction can or should be drawn between the two spheres.

IV   'THE PERSONAL IS THE POLITICAL'

The slogan 'the personal is the political' provides a useful point from which to comment on some of the ambiguities of the public and private in liberal patriarchalism and also, in the light of some of its more literal feminist interpretations, to comment further on an alternative feminist conception of the political. Its major impact has been to unmask the ideological character of liberal claims about the private and public. 'The personal is the political' has drawn women's attention to the way in which we are encouraged to see social life in personal terms, as a matter of individual ability or luck in finding a decent man to marry or an appropriate place to live. Feminists have emphasized how personal circumstances are structured by public factors, by laws about rape and abortion, by the status of 'wife', by policies on childcare and the allocation of welfare benefits and the sexual division of labour in the home and workplace. 'Personal' problems can thus be solved only through political means and political action.

  The popularity of the slogan and its strength for feminists arises from the complexity of women's position in contemporary liberal-patriarchal societies. The private or personal and the public or political are held to be separate from and irrelevant to each other; women's everyday experience confirms this separation yet, simultaneously, it denies and it affirms the integral connection between the two spheres. The separation of the private and public is both part of our actual lives and an ideological mystification of liberal-patriarchal reality.

  The separation of the private domestic life of women from the public world of men has been constitutive of patriarchal liberalism from its origins and, since the mid-nineteenth century, the economically dependent wife has been presented as the ideal for all respectable classes of society. The identification of women and the domestic sphere is now also being reinforced by the revival of anti-feminist organizations and the 'scientific' reformulation of the argument from nature by the socio-biologists.[33] Women have never been completely excluded, of course, from public life; but the way in which women are included is grounded, as firmly as their position in the domestic sphere, in patriarchal beliefs and practices. For example, even many anti-suffragists were willing for women to be educated, so that they could be good mothers, and for them to engage in local politics and philanthropy because these activities could be seen, as voting could not, as a direct extension of their domestic tasks. Today, women still have, at best, merely token representation in authoritative public bodies; public life, while not entirely empty of women, is still the world of men and dominated by them.

Again, large numbers of working-class wives have always had to enter the public world of paid employment to ensure the survival of their families, and one of the most striking features of post-war capitalism has been the employment of a steadily increasing number of married women. However, their presence serves to highlight the patriarchal continuity that exists between the sexual division of labour in the family and the sexual division of labour in the workplace. Feminist research has shown how women workers are concentrated into a few occupational areas ('women's work') in low-paid, low-status and non-supervisory jobs.[34] Feminists have also drawn attention to the fact that discussions of worklife, whether by *laissez-faire* liberals or Marxists, always assume that it is possible to understand economic activity in abstraction from domestic life. It is 'forgotten' that the worker, invariably taken to be a man, can appear ready for work and concentrate on his work free from the everyday demands of providing food, washing and cleaning, and care of children, only because these tasks are performed unpaid by his wife. And if she is also a paid worker she works a further shift at these 'natural' activities. A complete analysis and explanation of the structure and operation of capitalism will be forthcoming only when the figure of the worker is accompanied by that of the housewife.

Feminists conclude that the 'separate' liberal worlds of private and public life are actually interrelated, connected by a patriarchal structure. This conclusion again highlights the problem of the status of the 'natural' sphere of the family, which is presupposed by, yet seen as separate from and irrelevant to, the conventional relations of civil society. The sphere of domestic life is at the heart of civil society rather than apart or separate from it. A widespread conviction that this is so is revealed by contemporary concern about the crisis, the decline, the disintegration of the nuclear family that is seen as the bulwark of civilized moral life. That the family is a major 'social problem' is significant, for the 'social' is a category that belongs in civil society, not outside it, or, more accurately, it is one of the two sides into which civil society can be divided; the social (private) and the political (public). Donzelot has recently explored how the emergence of the social is also the emergence of 'social work' and a wide variety of ways of (politically) 'policing' the family, giving mothers a social status, and controlling children.[35] Feminists, too, have been investigating how personal and family life is politically regulated, an investigation which denies the conventional liberal claim that the writ of the state runs out at the gate to the family home. They have shown how the family is a major concern of the state and how, through legislation concerning marriage and sexuality and the policies of the welfare state, the subordinate status of women is presupposed by and maintained by the power of the state.[36]

These feminist critiques of the dichotomy between private and public stress that the categories refer to two interrelated dimensions of the structure of liberal patriarchalism; they do not necessarily suggest that no distinction can or should be drawn between the personal and political aspects of social life. The slogan 'the personal is the political' can, however, be taken literally. For example, Millett, in *Sexual Politics*, implicitly rejects Locke's distinction between paternal and political power. In political science the political is frequently defined in terms of power, but political scientists invariably fail to take their definition to its logical conclusion. Millett agrees with the definition but, in contrast, argues that all power is political so that, because men exercise power over women in a multitude of ways in personal life, it makes sense to talk of 'sexual politics' and 'sexual dominion . . . provides [the] most fundamental concept of power'.[37] The personal becomes the political. This approach illuminates many unpalatable aspects of sexual and domestic life, in particular its violence, that too frequently remain hidden, but it does not greatly advance the critique of patriarchal liberalism. As the radical feminist attempts to eliminate nature, as one side of the dichotomy, so Millett seeks to eliminate power, thus echoing the suffragist vision of a moral transformation of politics. But this does nothing to question the liberal association (or identification) of the political with power, or to question the association of women with the 'moral' side of the duality. Other feminists have also rejected the identification of the political with power. Sometimes, by standing liberal patriarchalism on its head, it is merely claimed that, properly understood, political life is thus intrinsically feminine.[38] More fruitfully, the feminist rejection of 'masculine' power also rests on an alternative conception of the political. It is argued that the political is the 'area of shared values and citizenship',[39] or that it 'includes shared values and civic concerns in which power is only one aspect'.[40] These conceptions remain undeveloped in feminist writings, but they are closely related to the arguments of the critics of liberalism who deplore the depoliticization of civil society or liberalism's loss of distinctive sense of the political. For instance, Habermas argues for public, shared communication so that substantive political problems can be rationally evaluated, and Wolin states that the 'public' and the 'common' are 'synonyms for what is political', so that 'one of the essential qualities of what is political . . . is its relationship to what is "public"'.[41] These critics and some feminists agree that what is not personal is public – and that what is public is political. The implication is that there is no division within civil society, which is the realm of the public, collective, common political life of the community. The argument is usually developed, however, without any consideration of how this conception of the public-political sphere is related to domestic life, or any indication that such a problem arises. The feminists have posed, but have not yet answered, this fundamental question. What can be said is that although the personal is not the political, the two spheres are interrelated, necessary dimensions of a future, democratic feminist social order.

V CONDITIONS FOR A FEMINIST ALTERNATIVE TO LIBERAL PATRIARCHALISM

Feminist critiques of the liberal-patriarchal opposition of private and public raise fundamental theoretical questions, as well as the complex practical problems of creating a radical social transformation. But one objection to feminist arguments denies that our project is even sensible. Wolff has recently claimed, from a position sympathetic to feminism, that overcoming the separation of the two spheres presents an inherently insoluble problem. To 'struggle against the split' is pointless; the best that can be achieved is ad hoc adjustments to the existing order. The separation of public and private derives from two 'equally plausible and totally incompatible conceptions of human nature'. One is that of 'man [*sic*] as essentially rational, atemporal, ahistorical', and the second is of 'man as essentially time bound, historically, culturally and biologically conditioned'.[42] To argue that everyone should be treated in the public world as if the facts of sex, class, colour, age and religion do not count, is to insist that we should deny the most basic human facts about ourselves and thus accentuate the inhumanity and alienation of the present. But Wolff's two conceptions are not of a single 'human' nature, and they are far from equally plausible; they represent the liberal-patriarchal view of the true natures of (private) women and (public) men. Human beings *are* time bound, biological and culturally specific creatures. Only from a liberal individualist perspective (one failing to see itself as a patriarchalist perspective) that abstracts the male individual from the sphere where his wife remains in natural subjection, then generalizes this abstraction as public man, can such an opposition of 'human' nature, of women and men, private and public, appear philosophically or sociologically plausible.

Feminists are trying to develop a theory of a social practice that, for the first time in the western world, would be a truly general theory – including women and men equally – grounded in the inter-relationship of the individual to collective life, or personal to political life, instead of their separation and opposition. At the immediately practical level, this demand is expressed in what is perhaps the most clear conclusion of feminist critiques; that if women are to participate fully, as equals, in social life, men have to share equally in childrearing and other domestic tasks. While women are identified with this 'private' work, their public status is always undermined. This conclusion does not, as is often alleged, deny the natural biological fact that women, not men, *bear* children; it does deny the patriarchal assertion that this natural fact entails that only women can *rear* children. Equal parenting and equal participation in the other activities of domestic life presuppose some radical changes in the public sphere, in the organization of production, in what we mean by 'work', and in the practice of citizenship. The feminist critique of the sexual division of labour in the workplace and in political organizations of all ideological persuasions, and its rejection of the liberal-patriarchal conception of the political, extends and deepens the challenge to liberal capitalism¹ posed by the participatory democratic and Marxist criticism of the past two decades, but also goes well beyond it.

The temptation, as Wolff's argument shows, is to suppose that if women are to take their place as public 'individuals', then the conflict is about the universalization of liberalism. But that is to ignore the feminist achievement in bringing to light the patriarchal character of liberalism and the ambiguities and contradictions of its conception of the private and public. A full analysis of the various expressions of the dichotomy between the private and the public has yet to be provided, together with a deeper exploration than is possible in this essay of the implications of the double separation of domestic life from civil society and the separation of the private from public within civil society itself. Feminist critiques imply a dialectical perspective upon social life as an alternative to the dichotomies and oppositions of patriarchal liberalism. It is tempting, as shown by feminists themselves, either to replace opposition by negation (to deny that nature has any place in a feminist order) or to assume that the alternative to opposition is harmony and identification (the personal is the political; the family is political). The assumptions of patriarchal liberalism allow only these two alternatives, but feminist critiques assume that there is a third.

Feminism looks toward a differentiated social order within which the various dimensions are distinct but not separate or opposed, and which rests on a social conception of individuality, which includes both women and men as biologically differentiated but not unequal creatures. Nevertheless, women and men, and the private and the public, are not necessarily in harmony. Given the social implications of women's reproductive capacities,[43] it is surely Utopian to suppose that tension between the personal and the political, between love and justice, between individuality and communality will disappear with patriarchal liberalism.

The range of philosophical and political problems that are encompassed, implicitly or explicitly, in feminist critiques indicates that a fully developed feminist alternative to patriarchal liberalism would provide its first truly 'total critique'.[44] Three great male critics of abstractly individualist liberalism already claim to have offered such a critique, but their claim must be rejected. Rousseau, Hegel and Marx each argued that they had left behind the abstractions and dichotomies of liberalism and retained individuality within communality. Rousseau and Hegel explicitly excluded women from this endeavour, confining these politically dangerous beings to the obscurity of the natural world of the family; Marx also failed to free himself and his philosophy from patriarchal assumptions. The feminist total critique of the liberal opposition of private and public still awaits its philosopher.

ACKNOWLEDGEMENTS

I am grateful to Stanley Benn and Jerry Gaus for the care with which they read and criticized my arguments.

NOTES

1 The subversive character of liberal feminism has recently been uncovered by Z. Eisenstein, *The Radical Future of Liberal Feminism* (Longman, New York, 1981).
2 S. Benn and J. Gaus (eds), *Public and Private in Social Life*, ch. 2 (Croom Helm, Kent, 1983).
3 Eisenstein, *The Radical Future*, p. 223.
4 J. S. Mill is an exception to this generalization, but Benn and Gaus do not mention *The Subjection of Women*. It might be objected that B. Bosanquet, for example, refers in *The Philosophical Theory of the State* (ch. X, p. 6), to 'the two persons who are [the] head' of the family. However, Bosanquet is discussing Hegel, and he shows no understanding that Hegel's philosophy rests on the explicit, and philosophically justified, exclusion of women from headship of a family or from participating in civil society or the state. Bosanquet's reference to 'two persons' thus requires a major critique of Hegel, not mere exposition. Liberal arguments cannot be universalized by a token reference to 'women and men' instead of 'men'. On Hegel see P. Mills, 'Hegel and "The Woman Question": Recognition and Intersubjectivity', in L. Clark and L. Lange (eds), *The Sexism of Social and Political Theory* (University of Toronto Press, Toronto, 1979). (I am grateful to Jerry Gaus for drawing my attention to Bosanquet's remarks.)
5 J. Locke, *Two Treatises of Government*, 2nd edn, P. Laslett (ed.) (Cambridge University Press, Cambridge, 1967), Bk. I, ch. 47; Bk. II, ch. 82. The conflict between the social contract theorists and the patriarchalists is more fully discussed in T. Brennan and C. Pateman, '"Mere Auxiliaries to the Commonwealth": Women and the Origins of Liberalism', *Political Studies*, XXVII (1979), pp. 183–200.
6 Rawls's two principles of justice provide an example of this division. He states that the principles 'presuppose that the social structure can be divided into two more or less distinct parts.' He does not call these private and public, but the 'equal liberties of citizenship' are usually called 'political' liberties and the 'social and economic inequalities' of the second part are usually seen as part of the 'private' sphere. In Rawls's final formulation it is clear that the principles refer to civil society and

society and that the family is outside their scope. Part (b) of the second principle, equality of opportunity, cannot apply to the family, and part (a), the difference principle, may not apply. A clever son, say, may be sent to university at the expense of other family members. (I owe this last point to my student Deborah Kearns.) John Rawls, *A Theory of Justice* (The Belknap Press of Harvard University Press, Cambridge, Mass., 1971), pp. 61, 302.

7 S. Wolin, *Politics and Vision* (Little, Brown, Boston, 1960).
8 It is also the sphere of privacy. J. Reiman, 'Privacy, Intimacy, and Personhood', *Philosophy and Public Affairs*, 6 (1976), p. 39, links 'owning' one's body to the idea of a 'self' and argues this is why privacy is needed. My comments in the text do not explain why liberal theorists typically write of the private and the public rather than the political. An explanation could only be found in a full examination of liberal ambiguities about the public and the political, which takes us far from the purpose of this essay, although the problem arises again below in the context of the feminist slogan 'the personal is the political.'
9 J. Habermas, 'The Public Sphere', *New German Critique*, VI. 3 (1974), pp. 49–55. However, Habermas, like other writers, ignores the fact that women are conventionally held to be deficient in reason and so unfit to participate in a public body.
10 In the present context these remarks must be very condensed. For amplification see Brennan and Pateman, '"Mere Auxiliaries to the Commonwealth": Women and the Origins of Liberalism'; R. Hamilton, *The Liberation of Women: A Study of Patriarchy and Capitalism* (Allen and Unwin, London, 1978); H. Hartmann, 'Capitalism, Patriarchy and Job Segregation by Sex', *Signs*, 1. 3, Pt. 2 (Supp. Spring 1976), pp. 137–70; A. Oakley, *Housewife* (A. Lane, London, 1974), chs. 2 and 3.
11 J. S. Mill, *The Subjection of Women*, in A. Rossi (ed.), *Essays on Sex Equality* (University of Chicago Press, Chicago, 1970), pp. 125–242, at p. 126.
12 M. Astell, 'Reflections on Marriage' (published 1706), cited in L. Stone, *The Family, Sex and Marriage in England: 1500–1800* (Weidenfeld and Nicolson, London, 1977), p. 240.
13 'Radical feminists' is the term used to distinguish the feminists who argue that the male–female opposition is the cause of women's oppression from 'liberal feminists' and 'socialist feminists'.
14 S. B. Ortner, 'Is Female to Male as Nature is to Culture?', in M. Z. Rosaldo and L. Lamphere (eds), *Women, Culture and Society* (Stanford University Press, Stanford, 1974), p. 72. Ortner says nothing about the writers over the past two centuries who have glorified nature and seen culture as the cause of vice and inequality. However, the meaning of 'nature' in these arguments is extremely complex and the relationship of women to nature is far from clear. Rousseau, for instance, segregates women and men even in domestic life because women's natures are seen as a threat to civil life (culture). For some

Critiques of the Public/Private Dichotomy 125

comments on this question see my '"The Disorder of Women":
Women, Love and the Sense of Justice', *Ethics*, 91 (1980), pp. 20–34.
15 Ortner, 'Is Female to Male as Nature is to Culture?', p. 87.
16 M. Z. Rosaldo, 'The Use and Abuse of Anthropology: Reflections on
 Feminism, and Cross-Cultural Understanding', *Signs*, 5. 3 (1980),
 p. 409. D. Haraway, 'Animal Sociology and a Natural Economy of the
 Body Politic, Part I: A Political Physiology of Dominance', *Signs*, 4. 1
 (1978), esp. pp. 24–5.
17 S. Firestone, *The Dialectic of Sex* (W. Morrow, New York, 1970), p. 8.
18 Ibid., p. 232. She also fails to distinguish 'culture' as art, technology,
 etc. from 'culture' as the general form of life of humankind.
19 Ibid., p. 255.
20 I owe the last point to J. B. Elshtain, 'Liberal Heresies: Existentialism
 and Repressive Feminism', in M. McGrath (ed.), *Liberalism and the
 Modern Polity* (Marcel Dekker, New York, 1978), p. 53.
21 J. Ruskin, 'Of Queens' Gardens', in C. Bauer and L. Pitt (eds), *Free and
 Ennobled* (Pergamon Press, Oxford, 1979), p. 17.
22 J. B. Elshtain, 'Moral Woman and Immoral Man: A Consideration of
 the Public-Private Split and its Political Ramifications', *Politics and
 Society*, 4 (1974), pp. 453–61.
23 A recent argument that relies on this contrast is J. Steinberg, *Locke,
 Rousseau and the Idea of Consent* (Greenwood Press, Westport,
 Conn., 1978), esp. chs. 5–7. Emphasis on consent gives an appearance
 of morality to the private sphere, which is far less evident when, as is
 usually the case, self-interest is seen as the governing principle of
 (private) civil society. If the division within civil society is seen as
 freedom (as self-interest) opposing power, the location of morality
 within domestic life is more pointed but poses a serious problem of
 order for liberal public or civil society.
24 An acute problem about 'nature' and women's 'nature' now emerges
 because women are seen both as natural guardians of morality and as
 naturally politically subversive: see my '"Disorder of Women"'.
25 E. DuBois, 'The Radicalism of the Woman Suffrage Movement',
 Feminist Studies, 3. 1/2 (1975), pp. 64, 66.
26 E. DuBois, *Feminism and Suffrage* (Cornell University Press, Ithaca,
 N.Y., 1978), p. 46.
27 Mill, *Subjection*, p. 146.
28 Ibid., pp. 174–5.
29 Ibid., p. 179.
30 See Benn and Gaus (eds), *Public and Private*, ch. 2, p. 303 above,
 referring to Mill's *Considerations on Representative Government*.
31 Mill, *Subjection*, p. 237.
32 Ibid., p. 174.
33 On sociobiology see, e.g., E. O. Wilson, *Sociobiology: The New
 Synthesis* (Harvard University Press, Cambridge, Mass., 1975), and
 S. Goldberg, *The Inevitability of Patriarchy*, 2nd edn (W. Morrow,
 New York, 1974). For a critique, see, e.g., P. Green, *The Pursuit of*

Inequality (Martin Robertson, Oxford, 1981), ch. 5.

34 See, e.g., for Australia, K. Hargreaves, *Women at Work* (Penguin Books, Harmondsworth, 1982); for England, J. West (ed.), *Women, Work and the Labour Market* (Routledge and Kegan Paul, London, 1982); for America, Eisenstein, *The Radical Future of Liberal Feminism*, ch. 9.

35 J. Donzelot, *The Policing of Families* (Pantheon Books, New York, 1979). 'The most surprising thing is the status "the social" has won in our heads, as something we take for granted' (p. xxvi).

36 On marriage see, e.g., D. L. Barker, 'The Regulation of Marriage: Repressive Benevolence', in G. Littlejohn et al. (eds), *Power and the State* (Croom Helm, London, 1978); on rape see my 'Women and Consent', *Political Theory*, 8 (1980), pp. 149–68, and A. G. Johnson, 'On the Prevalence of Rape in the United States', *Signs*, 6, no. 1 (1980), pp. 136–46; on the welfare state see, e.g., E. Wilson, *Women and the Welfare State* (Tavistock, London, 1977).

37 K. Millett, *Sexual Politics* (Hart-Davis, London, 1971), pp. 25, 26.

38 N. McWilliams, 'Contemporary Feminism, Consciousness Raising and Changing Views of the Political', in J. Jaquette (ed.), *Women in Politics* (Wiley, New York, 1974), p. 161.

39 Ibid.

40 L. B. Iglitzin, 'The Making of the Apolitical Woman: Femininity and Sex-Stereotyping in Girls', in Jaquette, *Women in Politics*, p. 34.

41 J. Habermas, 'The Public Sphere', and Wolin, *Politics and Vision*, pp. 9, 2.

42 R. P. Wolff, 'There's Nobody Here but Us Persons', in C. Gould and M. Wartofsky (eds), *Women and Philosophy* (Putnam's, New York, 1976), pp. 137, 142–3. Wolff also objects to the feminist struggle against the separation of private and public because it builds normative assumptions about human nature into the advocacy of new forms of social institutions – an oddly misplaced objection in the light of the assumption about women's and men's nature embodied in patriarchal liberalism.

43 See R. P. Petchesky, 'Reproductive Freedom: Beyond "A Woman's Right to Choose"', *Signs*, 5. 4 (1980), pp. 661–85.

44 I have taken the phrase from R. M. Unger, *Knowledge and Politics* (Free Press, New York, 1975). Unger's claim to have provided a total critique of liberalism must also be rejected. He fails to see that the antinomies of theory and fact, reason and desire, and rules and values are, at the same time, expressions of the patriarchal antinomy between man and woman. He states (p. 59) that 'the political form of the opposition of formal reason to arbitrary desire is the contrast between public and private existence' – but it is also the opposition between the 'nature' of men and women.

6

The Radicalism of the Woman Suffrage Movement: Notes Toward the Reconstruction of Nineteenth-Century Feminism

ELLEN DUBOIS

The major theoretical contribution of contemporary feminism has been the identification of the family as a central institution of women's oppression.[1] On the basis of this understanding we are seeing the beginnings of a revisionist history of American feminism which challenges the significance that has traditionally been attributed to the woman suffrage movement. Aileen Kraditor and William O'Neill have suggested that the woman suffrage movement did not lead to female emancipation because it accepted women's traditional position within the home.[2] While attacking this 'what-went-wrong' approach, Daniel Scott Smith has contended that suffragism should yield its claim to the central place in the history of nineteenth-century feminism to a phenomenon he calls 'domestic feminism.'[3] Similarly, in her study of the female moral reform movement of the 1830s, Carroll Smith-Rosenberg argues that 'it can hardly be assumed that the demand for votes for women was more radical than' the moral reform movement's attack on the sexual double standard.[4]

These revisionist efforts are commendable in that they expand our sense of nineteenth-century feminism to include a much larger and more diverse group of women's activities than merely suffrage. On the other hand, I think they do an historical disservice to the woman suffrage movement. Nineteenth-century feminists and anti-feminists alike perceived the demand for the vote as the most radical element in women's protest against their oppression and we

Reprinted with permission from *Feminist Studies*, vol. 3, no. 1/2 (Fall 1975), pp. 63–71. Copyright © *Feminist Studies*, c/o Women's Studies Program, University of Maryland, College Park, MD 20742.

are obligated to honor the perceptions of the historical actors in question. When considering nineteenth-century feminism, not as an intellectual tradition but as a social movement, as a politics that motivated people to action, twentieth-century historians are in no position to redefine what was its most radical aspect. What we can do is analyze the position of nineteenth-century women and the nature of suffragism in order to understand why the demand for the vote was the most radical program for women's emancipation possible in the nineteenth century.

I would like to suggest an interpretation of nineteenth-century suffragism that reconciles the perceived radicalism of the woman suffrage movement with the historical centrality of the family to women's condition. My hypothesis is that the significance of the woman suffrage movement rested precisely on the fact that it bypassed women's oppression within the family, or private sphere, and demanded instead her admission to citizenship, and through it admission to the public arena. By focusing on the public sphere, and particularly on citizenship, suffragists demanded for women a kind of power and a connection with the social order not based on the institution of the family and their subordination within it.

Recent scholarship has suggested that the sharp distinction between public and private activities is a relatively modern historical phenomenon. In his work on the evolution of the idea of childhood in Western Europe, Phillipe Aries demonstrates that there was considerable overlap between family life and community life in the premodern period. He traces a gradual separation of public and private life from the sixteenth century to the nineteenth century, when 'family' and 'society' came finally to be viewed as distinct, even hostile institutions.[5] This development seems to have been clear and compact in American history. In seventeenth-century New England, all community functions – production, socialization, civil government, religious life – presumed the family as the basic unit of social organization.[6] The whole range of social roles drew on familial roles. The adult male's position as producer, as citizen, as member of the church, all flowed from his position as head of the family. Similarly, women's exclusion from church and civil government and their secondary but necessary role in production coincided with their subordinate position within the family.[7] A few women enjoyed unusual economic or social privileges by virtue of their family connections, but, as Gerda Lerner has pointed out, this further demonstrated women's dependence on their domestic positions for the definition of their roles in community life.[8]

By the nineteenth century, this relationship between family and society had undergone considerable change. Although the family continued to perform many important social functions, it was no longer the sole unit around which the community was organized. The concept of the 'individual' had emerged to rival it. In the nineteenth century, we can distinguish two forms of social organization – one based on this new creature, the individual, the other based on the family. These overlapping, but distinct, structures became identified respectively as the public sphere and the private sphere. The emergence of a form of social organization not based on the family meant the emergence of social roles not defined by familial roles. This was equally true for women and men. But because women and men had different positions *within* the family, the existence of nonfamilial roles had different implications for the sexes. For women, the emergence of a public sphere held out the revolutionary possibility of a new way to relate to society not defined by their subordinate position within the family.

However, only men emerged from their familial roles to enjoy participation in the public sphere. Women on the whole did not. Women were of course among the first industrial workers, but it is important to remember that these were overwhelmingly unmarried women, for whom factory work was a brief episode before marriage. Adult women remained almost entirely within the private sphere, defined politically, economically, and socially by their familial roles. Thus, the public sphere became man's arena; the private, woman's. This gave the public/private distinction a clearly sexual character. This phenomenon, canonized as the nineteenth-century doctrine of sexual spheres, is somewhat difficult for us to grasp. We are fond of pointing out the historical durability of sexual roles into our own time and miss the enormous difference between the twentieth-century notion of sexual roles and the nineteenth-century idea of sexual spheres. The difference is a measure of the achievements of nineteenth-century feminism.

The contradiction between the alternative to familial roles that activity in the public sphere offered and the exclusion of women from such activity was particularly sharp with respect to civil government. In seventeenth-century New England, citizenship was justified on the basis of familial position; the freeholder was at once the head of the household and a citizen. By contrast, nineteenth-century citizenship was posed as a direct relationship between the individual and his government. In other words, patriarchy was no longer the official basis of civil government in modern industrial democracy. However, in reality only men were permitted to become citizens. The exclusion of women from participation in political life in the early nineteenth century was so absolute and unchallenged that it did not require explicit proscription. It was simply assumed that political 'persons' were male. The US Constitution did not specify the sex of citizens until the Fourteenth Amendment was ratified in 1869, after women had begun actively to demand the vote. Prior to that, the equation between 'male' and 'person', the term used in the Constitution, was implicit. The same by the way was true of the founding charter of the American Anti-Slavery Society. Written in 1833, it defined the society's membership as 'persons,' but for six years admitted only men into that category.

The doctrine of separate sexual spheres was supreme in the nineteenth century and even suffragists were unable to challenge certain basic aspects of it. Most notably, they accepted the particular suitability of women to domestic activities and therefore their special responsibility for the private sphere, and did not project a reorganization of the division of labor within the home. Antoinette Brown Blackwell, pioneer suffragist and minister, asserted, 'The paramount social duties of women are household duties, avocations arising from their relations as wives and mothers. . . . The work nearest and dearest before the eyes of average womanhood is work within family boundaries – work within a sphere which men cannot enter.'⁹ No suffragist of whom I am aware, including the otherwise iconoclastic Elizabeth Cady Stanton, seriously suggested that men take equal responsibilities with women for domestic activities. 'Sharing housework' may be a more uniquely twentieth-century feminist demand than 'smashing monogamy.' To nineteenth-century feminists, domestic activities seemed as 'naturally' female as childbearing, and as little subject to social manipulation.

Although suffragists accepted the peculiarly feminine character of the private sphere, their demand for the vote challenged the male monopoly on the public arena. This is what gave suffragism much of its feminist meaning. Suffragists accepted women's 'special responsibility' for domestic activity, but refused to concede that it prohibited them from participation in the public sphere. Moreover, unlike the demand that women be admitted to trades, professions, and education, the demand for citizenship applied to all women and it applied to them all of the time – to the housewife as much as to the single, self-supporting woman. By demanding a permanent, public role for all women, suffragists began to demolish the absolute, sexually defined barrier marking the public world of men off from the private world of women. Even though they did not develop a critical analysis of domestic life, the dialectical relationship between public and private spheres transformed their demand for admission to the public sphere into a basic challenge to the entire sexual structure. Thus, although she never criticized women's role in the family, Stanton was still able to write: 'One may as well talk of separate spheres for the two ends of the magnet as for man and woman; they may have separate duties in the same sphere, but their true place is together everywhere.'[10]

Suffragists' demand for a permanent, public role for all women allowed them to project a vision of female experience and action that went beyond the family and the subordination of women which the family upheld. Citizenship represented a relationship to the larger society that was entirely and explicitly outside the boundaries of women's familial relations. As citizens and voters, women would participate directly in society as individuals, not indirectly through their subordinate positions as wives and mothers. Mary Putnam Jacobi identified this as the revolutionary core of suffragism. The American state, she explained, is based on 'individual cells,' not households. She went on: 'Confessedly, in embracing in this conception women, we do introduce a change which, though in itself purely ideal, underlies all the practical issues now in dispute. In this essentially modern conception, women also are brought into direct relations with the State, independent of their "mate" or "brood".'[11] Without directly attacking women's position within the private sphere, suffragists touched the nerve of women's subordinate status by contending that women might be something other than wives and mothers. 'Womanhood is the great fact in her life,' Stanton was fond of saying; 'wifehood and motherhood are but incidental relations.'[12]

On one level, the logic behind the demand for woman suffrage in a country professing republican principles is obvious, and suffragists made liberal use of the tradition and rhetoric of the Revolution. Yet this is not sufficient to explain why suffrage became the core of a *feminist* program, why enfranchisement was perceived as the key to female liberation. I hypothesize that because enfranchisement involved a way for women to relate to society independent of their familial relations, it was the key demand of nineteenth-century feminists. It was the cornerstone of a social movement that did not simply catalogue and protest women's wrongs in the existing social movement that did not simply catalogue and protest women's wrongs in the existing sexual order, but revealed the possibility of an alternative sexual order. Unlike the tradition of female protest, from the moral reformers of the 1830s to the temperance women of the 1880s, which was based in the private sphere and sought to reinterpret women's place within it, suffragism focused squarely on the public sphere.

In part, the feminist, liberating promise of enfranchisement rested on the concrete power that suffragists expected to obtain with the vote. Suffragists expected women to use the ballot to protect themselves and to impose their viewpoint on political issues. They anticipated that by strategic use of their political power women would break open new occupations, raise the level of their wage scales to that of men, win strikes, and force reforms in marriage and family law in order to protect themselves from sexual abuse, the loss of their children, and the unchecked tyranny of their husbands. The demand for suffrage drew together protest against all these abuses in a single demand for the right to shape the social order by way of the public sphere. No longer content either with maternal influence over the future voter's character or an endless series of petitions from women to law makers, suffragists proposed that women participate directly in the political decisions that affected their lives. 'Like all disfranchised classes, they began by asking to have certain wrongs redressed,' Stanton wrote. But suffragism went beyond what she called 'special grievances' to give women's protest 'a larger scope.'[13]

In evaluating suffragists' expectations of the power that the vote would bring women, it is important to keep in mind the structure of political power in the nineteenth century. Political decisions were less centralized in the federal government and more significant at the local level than they are now. Herbert Gutman's analysis of the assistance which local politicians gave labor activists in nineteenth-century Patterson, New Jersey suggests that Susan B. Anthony's prediction that woman suffrage would win women's strikes had some basis in reality.[14]

Even granted the greater power of the individual voter over political decisions that would affect her or his life, suffragists did not understand the ballot as merely a weapon with which to protect their interests in the political process. They also expected enfranchisement to transform woman's consciousness, to reanchor her self-image, not in the subordination of her familial role, but in the individuality and self-determination that they saw in citizenship. This was a particularly important aspect of the political thought of Elizabeth Cady Stanton, the chief ideologue of nineteenth-century suffragism. It is developed most fully in 'Solitude of Self,' the speech she thought her best. She wrote there: 'Nothing strengthens the judgment and quickens the conscience like individual responsibility.

Nothing adds such dignity to character as the recognition of one's self-sovereignty.'[15] Elsewhere, she wrote that, from the 'higher stand-point' of enfranchisement, woman would become sensitive to the daily indignities which, without due appreciation for her own individuality, she ignored and accepted.[16] She developed the theme of the impact of enfranchisement on women's self-concept most fully in a speech simply titled, 'Self-Government the Best Means of Self-Development.'[17]

Given the impact on consciousness that suffragists expected from the vote, they generally refused to redirect their efforts toward such partial enfranchisements as municipal or school suffrage. Although these limited suffrages would give women certain political powers, they were suffrages designed especially for women and justified on the basis of women's maternal responsibilities. Their achievement would not necessarily prove women's right to full and equal participation in the public sphere. Suffragists did not simply want political power; they wanted to be citizens, to stand in the same relation to civil government as men did. As a result, it was primarily clubwomen who worked for school and municipal suffrage, while those who identified themselves as suffragists continued to concentrate on the admission of women to full citizenship.[18]

An important index to the nature and degree of suffragism's challenge to the nineteenth-century sexual order was the kind and amount of opposition that it inspired. Antisuffragists focused on the family, its position *vis-à-vis* the state, and the revolutionary impact of female citizenship on that relation. In response to suffragists' demand that modern democracy include women, antisuffragists tried to reinstate a patriarchal theory of society and the state.[19] The family, they contended, was the virtual, if not the official unit of civil government, and men represented and protected the women of their families in political affairs. Antisuffragists regularly charged that the enfranchisement of women would revolutionize the relations of the sexes and, in turn, the character and structure of the home and women's role within it. The 1867 New York Constitutional Convention expressed this fear for the future of the family when it rejected suffrage because it was an innovation 'so revolutionary and sweeping, so openly at war with a distribution of duties and functions between the sexes as venerable and pervading as government itself, and involving transformations so radical in social and domestic life.'[20]

Most suffragists were much more modest about the implications of enfranchisement for women's position within the family. They expected reform of family law, particularly the marriage contract, and the abolition of such inequities as the husband's legal right to his wife's sexual services. They also anticipated that the transformation in woman's consciousness which enfranchisement would bring would improve the quality of family relations, particularly between wife and husband. Stanton argued that once women were enfranchised they would demand that democracy be the law of the family, as well as of the state.[21] Her comment suggests that, by introducing women into a form of social organization not based on patriarchal structures, she expected enfranchisement to permit women a much more critical perspective on the family itself. However, suffragists regularly denied the antisuffragists' charge that woman suffrage meant a revolution in the family. Most would have agreed with Jacobi that, if antisuffragists wanted to argue that familial bonds were mere 'political contrivances', requiring the disfranchisement of women to sustain them, suffragists had considerably more faith in the family as a 'natural institution,' able to survive women's entry into the public sphere.[22]

Suffragists worked hard to attract large numbers of women to the demand for the vote. They went beyond the methods of agitational propaganda which they had learned as abolitionists, and beyond the skills of lobbying which they had developed during Radical Reconstruction, to become organizers. As suffragists' efforts at outreach intensified, the family-bound realities of most women's lives forced more and more domestic imagery into their rhetoric and their arguments. Yet suffrage remained a distinctly minority movement in the nineteenth century. The very thing that made suffragism the most radical aspect of nineteenth-century feminism – its focus on the public sphere and on a nonfamilial role for women – was the cause of its failure to establish a mass base. It was not that nineteenth-century women were content, or had no grievances, but that they understood their grievances in the context of the private sphere. The lives of most nineteenth-century women were overwhelmingly limited to the private realities of wifehood and motherhood, and they experienced their discontent in the context of those relations. The enormous success of the Women's Christian Temperance Union, particularly as contrasted with the nineteenth-century suffrage movement, indicates the capacity for protest and activism among nineteenth-century women, and the fact that this mass feminism was based in the private sphere. The WCTU commanded an army in the nineteenth century, while woman suffrage remained a guerilla force.

Unlike the woman suffrage movement, the WCTU took as its

starting point woman's position within the home; it catalogued the abuses she suffered there and it proposed reforms necessary to ameliorate her domestic situation. As the WCTU developed, its concerns went beyond the family to include the quality of community life, but its standard for nonfamilial relations remained the family and the moral values women had developed within it. The WCTU spoke to women in the language of their domestic realities, and they joined in the 1870s and 1880s in enormous numbers. Anchored in the private realm, the WCTU became the mass movement that nineteenth-century suffragism could not.

The WCTU's program reflected the same social reality that lay beyond suffragism – that the family was losing its central place in social organization to nondomestic institutions, from the saloon to the school to the legislature, and that woman's social power was accordingly weakened. Yet the WCTU, Luddite-like, defended the family and women's traditional but fast-fading authority within it. Its mottos reflected this defensive goal: 'For God and Home and Native Land'; 'Home Protection'. In 1883, the WCTU formally endorsed the demand for female enfranchisement, but justified its action as necessary to protect the home and women within it, thus retaining its family-based analysis and its defensive character. The first resolutions introduced by Frances Willard in support of suffrage asked for the vote for women in their roles as wives and mothers, to enable them to protect their homes from the influence of the saloon.[23] This was the woman suffrage movement's approach to female oppression and the problem of spheres stood on its head – women entering the public arena to protect the primacy of the private sphere, and women's position within it. Yet, the very fact that the WCTU had to come to terms with suffrage and eventually supported it indicates that the woman suffrage movement had succeeded in becoming the defining focus of nineteenth-century feminism, with respect to which all organized female protest had to orient itself. Even though the WCTU organized and commanded the forces, the woman suffrage movement had defined the territory.

Suffrage became a mass movement in the twentieth century under quite different conditions, when women's position *vis-à-vis* the public and private spheres had shifted considerably. Despite, or perhaps because of, the home-based ideology with which they operated, the WCTU, women's clubs, and other branches of nineteenth-century feminism had introduced significant numbers of women to extradomestic concerns.[24] Charlotte Perkins Gilman noted the change among women in 1903: 'The socialising of this hitherto subsocial, wholly domestic class, is a marked and marvellous event, now taking place with astonishing rapidity.'[25] Similarly, Susan B. Anthony commented at the 1888 International Council of Women: 'Forty years ago women had no place anywhere except in their homes, no pecuniary independence, no purpose in life save that which came through marriage. . . . [I]n later years the way has been opened to every avenue of industry – to every profession. . . . What is true in the world of work is true in education, is true everywhere.'[26] At the point that it could attract a mass base, suffragism no longer opened up such revolutionary vistas for women; they were already operating in the public world of work and politics. The scope and meaning of twentieth-century suffragism requires its own analysis, but the achievement of nineteenth-century suffragists was that they identified, however haltingly, a fundamental transformation of the family and the new possibilities for women's emancipation that this revealed.

ACKNOWLEDGEMENTS

I wish to thank Amy Bridges, Mari Jo Buhle, Ann D. Gordon, Linda Gordon, Carolyn Korsemeyer, and Rochell Ruthchild for their comments and suggestions on earlier versions of this article.

NOTES

1 The clearest exposition of this is Juliet Mitchell, *Women's Estate* (Penguin Books, Baltimore, 1971).
2 Aileen Kraditor, *Up From the Pedestal* (Quadrangle Books, Chicago, 1968), pp. 21–4. William L. O'Neill, 'Feminism as a Radical Ideology', in *Dissent: Explorations in the History of American Radicalism*, ed. Alfred F. Young (Northern Illinois University Press, De Kalb, Ill., 1968), p. 284.
3 Daniel Scott Smith, 'Family Limitation, Sexual Control and Domestic Feminism in Victorian America', *Feminist Studies* 1, no. 3/4 (1973): 40–57; reprinted in *Clio's Consciousness Raised*, eds., Mary Hartman and Lois W. Banner (Harper Torchbooks, New York, 1974).
4 Carroll Smith-Rosenberg, 'Beauty, the Beast, and the Militant Woman: Sex Roles and Social Stress in Jacksonian America', *American Quarterly* 23 (1971), p. 584.
5 Philippe Ariès, *Centuries of Childhood: A Social History of Family Life* (Vintage Books, New York, 1962), especially pp. 365–407.
6 Edmund Morgan, *The Puritan Family: Religion and Domestic Relations in Seventeenth-Century New England* (Harper and Row, New York,

1966), especially ch. 6. John Demos, *A Little Commonwealth: Family Life in Plymouth Colony* (Oxford University Press, New York, 1970), pp. 2–11.

7 Morgan, *The Puritan Family*, ch. 2. Demos, *A Little Commonwealth*, pp. 82–4.

8 Gerda Lerner, 'The Lady and the Mill Girl: Changes in the Status of Women in the Age of Jackson', *Midcontinent American Studies Journal* 10 (1969), p. 6.

9 Antoinette Brown Blackwell, 'Relation of Woman's Work in the Household to the Work Outside', repr. in Kraditor, *Up From the Pedestal*, p. 151.

10 Elizabeth Cady Stanton, 'Speech to the 1885 National Suffrage Convention', in *History of Woman Suffrage*, Elizabeth Cady Stanton, Susan B. Anthony, and Matilda Joslyn Gage (eds) (Susan B. Anthony, Rochester, N.Y., 1889), 4. 58.

11 Mary Putnam Jacobi, *'Common Sense' Applied to Woman Suffrage* (Putnam, New York, 1894), p. 138.

12 Stanton, 'Introduction', *History of Woman Suffrage*, 1. 22.

13 Ibid., 1. 15.

14 Herbert Gutman, 'Class, Status, and Community Power in Nineteenth Century American Industrial Cities – Paterson, New Jersey: A Case Study', in *The Age of Industrialism in America*, ed. Frederic C. Jaher (Free Press, New York, 1968), pp. 263–87. For Anthony's prediction on the impact of woman suffrage on women's strikes, see 'Woman Wants Bread, not the Ballot', repr. in *The Life and Work of Susan B. Anthony*, ed. Ida Husted Harper (Bower-Merrill Co., Indianapolis and Kansas City, 1898), 2. 996–1003.

15 Elizabeth Cady Stanton, 'Solitude of Self', repr. in *History of Woman Suffrage*, 4. 189–91.

16 Stanton, 'Introduction', *History of Woman Suffrage*, 1. 18.

17 Stanton, 'Self-Government the Best Means of Self-Development', repr. in *History of Woman Suffrage*, 4. 40–2.

18 See Lois B. Merk, 'Boston's Historical Public School Crisis', *New England Quarterly* 31 (1958), pp. 196–202.

19 See, e.g., Orestes Brownson, 'The Woman Question', in Kraditor, *Up From the Pedestal*, pp. 192–4.

20 'Report on the Committee on Suffrage', repr. in *History of Woman Suffrage*, 2. 285.

21 Elizabeth Cady Stanton, 'The Family, the State, and the Church', unpublished manuscript speech, Elizabeth Cady Stanton Papers, Library of Congress, Manuscript Division.

22 Jacobi, *'Common Sense'*, p. 108.

23 Mary Earhart, *Frances Willard: From Prayers to Politics* (University of Chicago Press, Chicago, 1944), ch. 10.

24 This process is described in Anne Firor Scott, *The Southern Lady: From Pedestal to Politics 1830–1930* (University of Chicago Press, Chicago, 1970), ch. 6.

25 Charlotte Perkins Gilman, *The Home: Its Work and Influence* (McClure, Phillips, and Co., New York, 1903), p. 325.
26 Susan B. Anthony, 'Introductory Remarks', *Report of the International Council of Women* assembled by the National Woman Suffrage Association (Rufus H. Darby, Printer, Washington, DC, 1888), p. 31.

7

Against Androgyny

JEAN BETHKE ELSHTAIN

Although androgyny has become a pervasive feature in contemporary feminist discourse and is widely accepted as a model for a rational reordering of our presently inegalitarian sexual and social arrangements, the notion itself has rarely come in for systematic criticism.[1] It promises a shiny new world where human beings no longer exhibit 'negative and distorted personality characteristics', where the 'ideal androgynous being . . . could have no internal blocks to attaining self-esteem.'[2] Yet, its near irresistibility requires explanation. Why is it that to be against androgyny leads one to being immediately branded as a 'naturalist,' an 'essentialist,' or even worse, a 'sociobiologist,' a 'biological reductionist,' or the representative of other obnoxious and reactionary viewpoints? The implication is that if one truly understood androgynist claims one would stop thrashing about in the darkness of gendered distortions and join up with the chorus of the future: Androgyny Now! If one refuses to join the chorus and rejects the various ready-made labels androgynists use to ignore their opponents, one must be prepared to make a case for an alternative vision of human psycho-sexual and social identity as one feature of a potentially emancipatory politics. Repudiating the ellide into degendered homogeneity, does not necessarily mean to reproduce our current, unacceptable sexual *division* and our structured sexual inequality.

Androgyny is an old term to which feminist discourse has given new life. In mythology, androgyny was the fusion of male and female, including secondary sexual characteristics, into a single being. This fusion was believed to exert an effeminizing influence, i.e. the female characteristics tended to 'swamp' the male. The original androgyne, Hermaphrodite, son of Hermes and Aphrodite, is forced, against his will, into union with a female nymph. The nymph, overcome with desire, snares and literally insinuates herself

Reprinted, with permission, from *Telos* 47 (Spring 1981), pp. 5–21.

into the unwilling Hermaphrodite until they are one flesh. According to May, 'This vision of female power is one of the persistent threads in the idea of androgyny, at least as seen through male eyes.'[3] In the myth's original meaning, the concrete physical intermingling of male and female ushered into a re-union between these formerly separate, sexed beings, and this myth is part of a continuing tradition whose vagaries can be traced through diverse modes of historic representation.

The resurgence of the image of the androgyne throughout history is evocative and suggests that human beings have always been vexed with the existence of two clearly distinct sorts of being within the broader generic frame, human being. For some this differentness has been an occasion for celebration. For others, it is a concern and for a few a calamity. But human beings generally have fantasies, at one time or another, of sexual fusion, of 'becoming' the 'other,' of wrenching free from the physical 'constraint' or 'limit' of being only one sex in one body. The seeds of envy are here, along with the seed-bed of narcissistic fantasies of grandiose limitlessness – of attaining what Freud called the 'oceanic feeling,' if necessary by eradicating the stubborn 'other' embodied (quite literally) within the 'opposite sex.' Androgyny, then, is an ancient myth reflecting and refracting those human yearnings, urging fears and fantasies surrounding human embodiment.

But something happened to androgyny on its way to becoming feminist dogma. Human bodies disappeared – they were dismantled, dismembered or, at least, dis-remembered. Androgyny was dusted off, stripped of its deeply sensual and sexed roots and its previous mythic meaning. In place of the body, contemporary androgynists put 'free will' or 'flexible sex roles' or the 'union of positively valued traits.' Reaching back to androgyny's Greek roots, one feminist philosopher neatly disentangles the term from its mythological foundation and comes up with a tidy etymological derivation, as if the notion originated in a Greek version of Webster's New Abridged Dictionary. 'The term "androgyny,"' she writes, 'has Greek roots: *andros* means man, and *gyne*, woman. An androgynous person would combine some of each of the characteristic traits, skills, and interests that we now associate with stereotypes of masculinity and femininity.'[4] Hermaphrodite and his lusting nymph give way to 'the ideal androgynous being,' one 'who transcends those old categories in such a way as to be able to develop positive human potentialities . . . he or she would have no internal blocks to attaining self-esteem.' 'It is the flexibility and union of positively valued traits that is critical,' writes another feminist literary critic.[5]

For some androgynists, androgyny is deployed to knock down what they see as a conceptual prop for systemic sexual inequality in traditionalist presumptions that sexual differences have pre-determined social outcomes. For most androgynists, however, androgyny is put forth primarily as a portrait of the ideal human being, one who has, along with the concrete physicality imbedded in the androgyne myth, sloughed off *all* 'limiting' sexed definitions, biological and social: '. . . only androgynous people can attain the full human potential possible given our present level of material and social resources. . . . Androgynous women would be just as assertive as men about their own needs in a love relationship. . . . Androgynous men would be more sensitive and aware. . . . They would be more concerned with the feelings of all people.'⁶ Human beings in the here and now can partially succeed in transcending sexual gender. But the full achievement of an androgynous world is possible only with the total elimination of sex roles and the 'disappearance . . . of any biological need for sex to be associated with procreation.' At that fateful moment, 'there would be no reason why such a society could not transcend sexual gender.'⁷

A vision of pure positivity emerges: an ideal, all-purpose, abstract person with all nastiness expunged, bodilyness removed, and differences (which might be points of fruitful tension, debate, or just interest) eliminated. The androgyne is non-specific with reference to social location: he or she is 'at home' anywhere, is free-floating with reference to all traditional loci of human identity. A feminist sociologist, writing on 'The Androgynous Life,' suggests as her ideal person one who 'combines characteristics usually attributed to men with characteristics usually attributed to women.'⁸ The road to positive androgyny requires the elimination by fiat of any negative irritants in the image. Feminist psychologist Judith M. Bardwick sees the androgyne as the next mental health 'ideal.' In the feminist future, the 'healthy' individual will be the androgynous man or woman. 'We would then expect both nurturance and competence, openness and objectivity, compassion and competitiveness from both women and men, as individuals, according to what they are doing.'⁹

A second feminist psychologist, working within a behavior modification framework, reports that androgyny 'does not lie in some far-off feminist future. Androgyny is here. The research findings tell us so.'¹⁰ Androgyny is already with us, it turns out, because 'sex is an easy and obvious independent variable.' Abstractly predefining sex as the '*assignment*' an obstetrician makes at birth 'on the basis of genitalia' (as if this were a contingent and arbitrary matter), the voice of behaviorism finds it clear that sex 'is primarily . . . a social fact not a biological fact.'[11] We exhibit sex differences, or there are sex differences, she claims, because people *believe* there are sex differences and act accordingly. Were it not for this stubborn belief, and the sexist practices it shores up or that rise on the basis of it, 'It seems clear that given the same social situation, the same reinforcement contingencies, the same expectancies, both sexes will react similarly.' Finally, she notes 'it is always satisfying to strike down another sex difference.'[12] Having struck them all down by fiat, she proclaims us to be in the androgynist future though it is a pity most of us seem unaware of it yet.

Feminist literary scholars seem to find the androgynous myth particularly compelling as the depiction of the ideal artist and the perfect creative mind. As Virginia Woolf writes: 'If one is a man, still the woman part of the brain must have effect; and a woman also must have intercourse with the man in her. Coleridge perhaps meant this when he said that a great mind is androgynous. It is when this fusion takes place that the mind is fully fertilized and uses all its faculties.'[13] Some critics who celebrate the Bloomsbury group, of which Woolf was a member, as uniquely creative, attribute 'this enormous intellectual and artistic productivity' to living the androgynous life.[14]

Androgyny advocates agree that the achievement of a fully androgynous society requires major reconstruction of the human subject. For some, an enlightened androgynous vanguard can move ahead right now to lead androgynous lives. But for society to become truly androgynous, for a world in which one's sexuality is as 'innocuous as current reactions to hair color,' some sort of social revolution which will bring forth reconstructed androgynous human subjects is required.

A fairly innocuous, simplistic version of the thesis of androgyny as the goal of feminist political ideology is featured in Yates's 'androgynous paradigm' which 'represents a women- and men-equal-to-each-other view. . . . It holds that tasks, values, and behavior traditionally assigned to one sex or the other should be shared by them both.'[15] Yates claims the 'androgynous mode' as 'the operating paradigm' is 'the most revolutionary of the concepts informing the new wave of feminism. . . . It suggests that men should be equal to women as well as women equal to men. . . . The androgynous position offers a model of cooperation and of rationality.'[16] Firestone, on the other hand, offers the extreme androgynous apocalypse as cultural revolution with:

the reintegration of the Male (Technological Mode) with the Female (Aesthetic Mode), to create an androgynous culture surpassing the highs of either cultural stream, or even of the sum of their integrations. More than a marriage, rather an abolition of the cultural categories themselves, a mutual cancellation – a matter–antimatter explosion, ending with a poof! culture itself. We shall not miss it. We shall no longer need it.[17]

Though not all feminists explicitly adopt visions of an androgynous world, many embrace milder, implicit versions of the androgyny agenda with arguments for the total elimination of all 'sex roles' (as if every activity in which a male or female engaged could be pared down to a 'role,' an abstract sociological construct, and thereby readily eliminated by socio-political fiat) and the achievement of a society in which all 'roles' are freely exchanged and no one is tied, in any way, to a role that reflects gender identity or definition (if indeed such persists at all).

What androgyny offers – or seems to – to its feminist adherents is, first, an ideal of what human beings can become once they break the bonds of overly restrictive sexed definitions and, second, a vision of an egalitarian future in which all forms of sexual domination and inequality, now buttressed, they argue, by beliefs concerning 'natural' sex differences will have been quite overcome and, finally, a vision of the artist and the creative individual as one who has transcended the muck of matter and attained a purity of thought and expression within the rarified ideal of androgyny. All this – and more – is pegged on a term that falls wholly outside the frame of political discourse as the stock of common, if not wholly agreed-upon, notions available to social participants when they act politically. Androgyny does not arouse political debate and public challenge in the way calls for social justice of equality can, and do. Indeed, part of androgyny's appeal must be the promise it holds forth for a brave new world attained, somehow, through human beings rationally and freely willing to have done with the sexed old and to embrace the degendered new, with the androgynous vanguard, through the force of example and a superior 'lifestyle,' leading the way.

Beyond androgynists' explicit commitments there are a number of unacknowledged presumptions imbedded within androgynous discourse which help to account, first, for why this 'new' notion of androgyny 'caught on' and remains a standard feature in much feminist thought and, second, for where the androgynists ought to be 'located' within a wider frame of discursive practices and theoretical traditions. There are two broad features that move implicitly through various androgynist evocations. Both locate androgynist discourse securely within the boundaries of classical liberal thought. First, all androgynists propound as an article of faith, an example of right reason, and an instance of scientific truth that human nature is more or less plastic. Writes an androgynist philosopher, 'it seems . . . plausible to assume that human nature is plastic and moldable.'[18] More correctly, she should have observed this 'seems plausible' if one operates within a framework of liberal environmentalism. That this is where the androgynists implicitly locate themselves becomes clear when this plasticity is questioned, for the interlocutor is slotted into a fixed, static 'essentialist' posture that reflects perfectly one of the received antinomies of liberal discourse. A picture of the human being as Silly Putty or a Blank Slate goes under the contemporary name 'sex-role socialization theory' or, sometimes, 'social learning theory.' The view is that children acquire their patterns of behavior through a process of external reinforcements. Sex-role behavior is maintained by these same external forces. As these forces change, or reinforcements alter, different 'behaviors' will be reinforced and called forth.[19]

Even feminist critics of some versions of the androgynist thesis call upon environmental determinism to buttress the case for their own alternative. For example: a philosopher who questions what she calls 'monoandrogynism' (the adoption of a single, uniform androgynist standard for all, though even that is preferable, she says, to what we now have) and opts for an alternative she dubs 'polyandrogynism' (in which more options would be open to individuals along masculine-feminine boundaries or markers) reaffirms that human beings are totally products of their external environment. This means the only question for her is: which version of androgynism, given that each alternative androgynous society will socialize people either to make everyone androgynous in one way or to help everyone make themselves androgynous in a number of ways, 'is preferable for a hypothetical future society.'[20]

The thesis that people are blank slates, totally molded by external pressures, makes the androgynous project sound feasible. One creates the androgynous society and gets the ideal androgynous 'product.' (Of course it is not easy to square the commitment to a prescriptive environmentalism with the robust androgynist voluntarism also embraced by some, an elite who have reconstructed themselves showing others the way.) The presumption is that males and females are, 'for all reasonable intents and purposes alike.

Differences between them . . . are chiefly due to culture and conditioning.'[21] This means that by eliminating the force of present social conditioning what will be liberated is not diverse human potentialities but human homogeneities! Millett declares that '. . . the sexes are inherently in everything alike, *save* reproductive systems, secondary sexual characteristics, orgasmic capacity, and genetic and morphological structure.'[22] Her argument that we treat sexual reproduction, male and female sexual responsivity, the entire complex structure of our genetic inheritance together with our morphological characteristics as trivial, uninteresting and unimportant facts about ourselves is an apt instance of one of the androgynists opening moves: to cancel out the significance of human sexual differences, in advance of launching any inquiry or making sustained arguments, by treating sexual identity as an arbitrary, external and contingent phenomena.

This leads to the second major fulcrum which 'moves' within androgynist thinking, i.e. the expressed conviction that the body is a prison, a constraint, an unacceptable limitation from which human beings must be liberated and which they will eventually 'transcend.' If the body is a prison for androgynists, the female body is life imprisonment with torture to boot. One finds repeated expressions of contempt for the female body.[23] Those who are not contemptuous are often merely dismissive of the body or they reduce its complex richness as a human standpoint in the world with statements about 'biological disadvantages,' for the female, her 'role in biological reproduction.'[24] Steps must be taken to erase all these biological disadvantages, all the limitations which inhere in sexual identity. The need to hold the body at arm's length and to view embodiment as a trap and a straightjacket is clear.[25]

Androgynists, then, adopt two tacit presuppositions: (1) They treat the human body reductionistically as 'nothing but . . .' or 'no more than . . .' and *must* see, within the iron cage of their liberal dualism, those who question their rigidity as themselves rigid 'essentialists' or 'naïve naturalists'; thus they evade the possibility that human beings may have a 'nature' of some sort that is not exhausted with reference to the social forces that have impinged upon it. This feature of the androgynist perspective places its proponents squarely within classical liberal discourse. For androgynists, the world revolves around a series of pure opposites: pure freedom vs. total determinism, nature vs. nurture, reason vs. passion, mind vs. body, and so on. (2) They embrace a thoroughgoing environmentalist determinism as the only sure and secure avenue to human 'reconstruction' along androgynist lines. In the androgynist new world, because the right kinds of reinforcers will be present, human beings will exhibit all and only the positive traits of the other.Given their dualist starting point, in which other minds can exist only by inference or analogy, one is presented with the image of an aggregate of androgynes, complete unto themselves and, like *homo economicus* in liberal contract theory, the androgyne is a being fundamentally unchanged by any human relation. For when one reaches the stage of pure androgynous positivity, where no negative intrudes to create friction ('no internal blocks'), and where one lives in a world populated only by other positivities, there can be nothing like a determinate negation anytime, anywhere. At this fateful juncture, social being and social consciousness will have become one. There will be nothing for the dialectic to work on or work through: no rough edges, no unseemly spots, no lines or ruptures, nor points of friction through which doubt, questioning, negation might erupt.

A case against androgyny can be made in terms of what is required for human beings to locate themselves spatially and temporally within a natural and social world. When we take the human body as a starting point we locate a corporeal entity of a particular kind within a complex world. From birth this entity is implicated in relations with others. What Freud once called the 'momentous and fateful' prolonged dependency of human infants on adult others is assumed embodiment, for children are born as helpless and totally dependent embodied beings. The human body is part of the material reality of nature: we experience that world Schutz calls 'paramount reality' (both 'inner' and 'outer') in and through our bodies. Within the sphere of daily human life, 'the individual locates himself as a body, as operating physically in the world, and as meeting the resistance of fellow men as well as of things.'[26] The starting-point of each and every human being is his or her particular location in space and time; this is, inescapably, the body.

That a social theorist must defend the universally true proposition that human beings can experience the world only in and through their bodies attests to the continued sway of the dualisms inherent in the psychological principles which flow from classical liberal thought.[27] If the androgynists' implicit denials or explicit repudiations of human embodiment were spelled out, the claims would go something like this: (1) personal identity (that which I am) is entirely distinct from my body, (2) the body cannot be said to 'know,' nor can it serve as a vehicle for, or mediator of, knowledge, (3) the only genuine 'I' is a rational ego which is analytically distinct from that embodiment to which it enjoys a contingent relation. The implication would be that to specify biological features of human existence, and to draw these into the frame of an over-all account of human identity is to slide, irrevocably, into some sort of universalist, totalist, or ontological trap. In this way, through such evasions, debate on these matters is quashed. Those who argue 'my body, my self,' and insist upon incorporating biological imperatives into a comprehensive account of the human subject are labeled, within the androgynist frame, as embracing the notion that there are rigid, fixed 'innate' givens in human nature that appear invariantly and identically in all times and in all places.[28] This is palpable nonsense but it is understandable and convenient nonsense. It enables androgynists to avoid engaging their strongest opponents and it reaffirms various antinomies – freedom vs. determinism, innate vs. social, heredity vs. environment, biological explanation vs. social explanation – as mutually exclusive alternatives.

To break down and through the rigidities implicit in androgynism one can begin by asking, simply, what having a relationship which persists over time requires. In order for a relationship to persist for a single day, or even one hour, each party to that relationship must have a continuing identity, must perceive herself as acting and speaking in and through a body which situates her and from which she moves, sees, acts, and can be held accountable for her actions.[29] She must also perceive of the other as a being with similar temporal continuity, one with whom she shares a common humanity for he, like she, occupies space in the temporal world. The solipsism implicit in classical-liberal personality theory cannot account for real relations between persons, for it is not able to recognize others as beings like oneself save by analogy and inference. The recognition of the humanity of the other is not, in itself, sufficient to constitute a persisting relationship. For that to happen personal identity over time must hold.

There could be no social relations if each person began each day as if it were their first: if individuals lacked memories tied to a sense of self as persisting over time and in space. Memory requires a *particular* history of having lived, as a body, in a social world. Human action turns on such considerations as well. These dimensions of personal identity are part of a human, and thus social, context of which a human, and bodily, subject is the basis. The only way we can know that the same person is in the body, whether our own or some other's, at different times is if we grasp persistence over time.[30] Another essential feature which makes human relationship possible is language. It allows us to differentiate and to classify reality so that we can identify more or less constant subjects and objects of reference. Through language we may single out a particular so-and-so as the same so-and-so, one who may share certain properties in common with some larger, generic grouping but he is, as well, a unique individual with such-and-such properties.[31]

If bodily identity as one feature of spatio-temporal persistence is an inescapable feature of the human condition, is the division of humanity into two distinct sexes an essential and important, or a contingent and relatively trivial aspect of this identity? Males and females, of course, are beings who share in the most basic general characteristics; yet they differ along recognizable and distinctive lines. To introduce the sex distinction is not to surreptitiously inject considerations of gender at this point in the argument. To insist that 'my body, myself' are temporally and spatially defined, and that this body will either be a male or female body, says nothing in itself about what we call 'masculine' or 'feminine' identities or psychologies. In androgynous discourse, remember, the presumption is that the sex distinction *itself* can and must be transcended or eliminated (at least in maximalist statements of androgyny); that human beings can somehow 'return to a state of nature and to an innocent eye' and start to build up language and culture all over again, junking all inherited forms, particularly those grounded in the differentiation between the sexes. This is problematic because important distinctions, like male and female, are not only imbedded in language, they are constitutive of a way of life. To see basic notions as simply or purely arbitrary and contingent is to trash centuries of human concern, fear, desire, denial, passion, rage, joy, longing, hope and despair in a fit of ahistorical hubris. For human beings do not make distinctions nor draw visions about the most basic things – sexuality, birth, life, death – in wholly capricious ways, but to certain vital ends and purposes. To presume one can simply blur or obliterate even the most fundamental distinction between human beings presumes a great deal.

If one agrees that the sex distinction is ineliminable and important, does this mean one simply acquiesces in received notions of 'masculinity' and 'femininity'? Clearly not. To determine whether or not the claim that bodily identity is a feature of personal identity implies that a sexed identity, maleness or femaleness, is also necessarily linked with bodily identity, we must turn to a developmental account of the human subject. The human subject is a creation, an emergent from a developmental process over time, in history. Androgynous arguments, notoriously, omit *any* coherent developmental account of the human subject. This is explainable in part by the indebtedness of androgynists to liberal notions of abstract individuals. But there is another reason: androgyny is primarily, in most instances exclusively, focused on adult males and females. Children, save as so much raw material to be molded into future androgynes, are missing from the picture. It is far easier to speak of 'mere biology' or 'transcending sex roles' if one ignores birth, infancy, and childhood development.

The developmental account owes much to Freud's theory of human development as a dynamic, ineluctably biological and social process. For Freud the human body 'registers itself' through a complex inner–outer dialectic in which the human infant makes internal representations to itself of its own body. This account is a powerful theoretical alternative to dualist, solipsistic, environmentally deterministic, and exclusively ontological notions of the subject.[32] The argument goes roughly like this: from its first moments the infant experiences its own body as a source of pleasure and unpleasure. This goes beyond the registering of sensations of hunger, pain, or pleasure. It implicates the infant as an active not a merely passive being, in the construction of an inner world through the literal 'taking in' of its own body's surface as part of a wider 'external' reality. Given this process, the human 'I,' the self, is always, importantly, an embodied 'I.' The infant simply does not have the cognitive or neurological structure and organization to make clear distinctions between inner and outer, internal and external. But the infant does 'take in' with eyes, ear, mouth, and touch that 'external' world. Slowly, the 'I' is built up in part through complex representations of the child's body, 'inner' and 'outer,' and the bodies of others with whom the child is implicated in exquisitely social relations from the start. The surface of the child's body is from the first 'a place from which both external and internal perceptions may spring. It is *seen* like any other object, but to the *touch* it yields two sorts of sensations, one of which may be equivalent to an internal perception.' The 'I,' then, is 'first and foremost a *bodily ego*: it is not merely a surface entity, but is itself the projection of a surface.'[33]

Our corporeality bears powerful imperatives for how we come to know. The fact that our knowing is essentially tied to our experiences of ourselves as bodies means that the mind and its activities must be conceived in a manner that is 'tinged with spatiality.' 'We are at home in our mind somewhat as in a body,' argues Wollheim.[34] The corporeal ego plays a vital role in the child's epistemic constitution of his or her identity. A child can neither physically negate nor conceptually transcend the manner in which his or her body 'registers itself,' and that body must be understood within the terms of each successive stage of psycho-sexual maturation. The particular meeting of mind–body which emerges from this developmental theory is no chance encounter but involves powerful imperatives. The child evokes the body and its processes as he or she learns. The body involves and mediates ways of knowing. It is neither a substanceless structure, nor a hollow shell, nor inert matter to which no meaning can be imputed or applied. Our most original experiences must be understood with reference to an embodied engagement with the world.

Nothing so far demands that the 'I' conceive of itself as belonging to one gender or another from the start; indeed, no such differentiation is possible until the child begins what Freud calls its early 'sexual researches.'[35] Certainly, by the time the child is five or six, if not before, he or she will have distinguished two 'types' of bodily sexed beings, though the child often remains uncertain as to the meaning of this distinction and confused on how to make determinations in specific cases. To live in a sexed, social universe is not, necessarily, to inhabit a world in which differential evaluations are placed on 'maleness' or 'femaleness.'[36]

Gender identity, a notion of masculinity and femininity or maleness and femaleness, is one feature in the child's identity formation as he or she enters puberty and young adulthood and, simultaneously, a more complex social world. Children locate themselves in that world on the basis of gender; children seek some measure of security in these matters for they are of pre-eminent concern and urgency to them. Rosenthal observes that when Dante wishes to imagine persons in hell he imagines them as deprived of the security of the knowledge that 'one is a man, if one is one, or that one is a woman, if one is one.' She continues: 'To have outlines and insides that – for oneself and others – *fluctuate dangerously* is to be in hell.'[37] For androgynists, the child's concerns are construed as a behavioral response to environmental stimuli exclusively, thus denying the child his or her own integrity as a self-constituting, embodied subject. Androgynists claim that it is possible to achieve *psychological* androgyny or non-differentiation along markers of maleness and femaleness, as well as 'masculinity' and 'femininity,' without positing bodily identity as a prior condition. This surely begs the issue. For what androgynists must figure out is how to prevent the child from becoming intensely interested in his or her own body and the bodies of others similar to yet different from himself or herself. The child lives out a deep sense of urgency in and through his or her body – is it whole? is it strong? is it attractive? will it grow? am I sick? am I the 'right' kind of boy–girl? – will be unmoved by appeals to transcend or eliminate the importance of gender for that is precisely what he or she is trying to figure out, work on, and work through.

In the final analysis, however, even the urge to eliminate concerns with gender, to try to institute a human condition in which human beings do not care what 'biological sex' they or anybody else may be, in which the distinction between males and females has ceased to be a central and interesting feature of human life is incoherent and impossible short of the mutation of human beings.

What would a world in which sex distinctions were ignored or denied look like? First, it would be an inchoate muddle for maleness and femaleness (that is, our corporeal sexed selves) are our ways of experiencing the world. In Winch's words: '. . . masculinity or femininity are not just *components* in . . . life, they are its *mode*.'[38] (Winch here refers to male and female as human sexed identity, not to social and cultural notions of the masculine and the feminine.) Second, it would be a hypocritical world of lies and denials. Repression of infantile sexuality would have to go far beyond anything we have known. Children would have to be surveilled night and day in order that any moves to touch, look at, sniff, or play with their bodies could be prohibited and deflected. Only in this way could one forestall the child's inner representations of the surface of its body. Of course, psychic representations of inner drives and states would continue, but the child would be forbidden to see or touch its own or other bodies. Children would be barraged with the insistence that any differences they discovered, despite efforts to preclude childish sexual researches, did not matter, were of no interest, and were inessential aspects of human life. Not only would this be a cruel deception, it would hamper the development of the self which is grounded in the child's ability to differentiate objects, things, and events along lines of what is important. For a child such distinctions include big–small, family–not family, pleasure–unpleasure, my body–other bodies, male bodies–female bodies.[39] The first great problem which exercises the child concerns his or her body and the bodies of others. Should parents suppress these 'burning question(s)' they will damage the child's 'genuine instinct of research' and 'begin to erode his confidence in his parents.'[40]

The rigid suppression of knowledge of sex distinctions or the denial of their importance would undermine the moral order and erode social life. The category of the serious and the less serious is, as Bernard Williams points out, 'itself a moral category, and that it is itself a moral criticism to say of somebody that he is regarding a serious issue as trivial or a trivial issue as serious.'[41] Those who regard the serious issue of the real, not fantasized, distinctions between the sexes as a trivial issue which the androgynist revolution will eliminate are engaged in a form of abstracted and wishful thinking that posits free-floating pictures as genuine human alternatives. Such pictures ignore social forms and the many-layered complexity of the persons who live in and through them, who must live in and through them. History is in some sense both a physical and a psychological category for, as Hegel insisted, historical accounts by human beings are 'about claims to operate with one's body in definite relations.'[42] In Showalter's words: 'the androgynous mind is . . . a utopian projection of the ideal artist: calm, stable, unimpeded by consciousness of sex . . . like other utopian projections, her vision is inhuman. Whatever else one may say of androgyny, it represents an escape from the confrontation with femaleness and maleness.'[43]

The androgynist might respond to these charges by insisting that a notion of psychological androgyny need not ignore distinctions between the sexes; it simply holds forth the possibility that these distinctions, assimilated to sex roles, a sexual division of labor, and inequality between the sexes, can be muted, disregarded, or become irrelevant insofar as the social world is concerned and insofar as the development of a psychologically androgynous individual is concerned. These are separate and distinct claims. Consider the notion of the 'psychologically androgynous' individual. The claim goes like this: without forcing children to ignore their bodies, or the differences between male and female bodies, it is possible through intensive, overt intervention on the part of 'socializers' to downplay sex-differences as an important distinction between persons. It is, in other words, possible to resist gender identification without deploying the repressive measures previously indicated as needed in order to create children who view sex distinctions as inessential and not terribly interesting characteristics of self and others.

The problem with this claim is that it is grounded in no explanatory account of child development which incorporates both theoretical and empirical dimensions, offers no historic examples, has no base in ordinary language, is buttressed by no clinical evidence: it is a purely abstract claim, repeated rhetorically and pronounced *a priori* without reference to actual, historically situated human beings. The motive force behind this utopian ideal appears to be a fantasy of the indistinguishability or interchangeability of selves, a wish to return to an undifferentiated state of symbiotic oneness with others or with *an* other. In Secor's terms, the notion of androgyny is that of a person 'devoid of context.'[44] The process of growing up involves breaking away from such a symbiotic fusion. Only then does the child begin his or her own psychic life. Urges to return to a condition of non-individuation are the 'projection into the future of a totally regressive urge.'[45] This makes of androgyny a 'limiting and probably reactionary concept.'[46] Visions that require that we abandon the distinctions, differences, separations and divisions essential to any coherent identity and existence are portraits of epistemic confusion and abstract ahistoricity.

Nothing has been claimed thus far – that bodily identity is a necessary feature of personal identity and that personal identity is necessarily a sexual or sexed identity – that either presupposes, entails, or buttresses the continued social and political inequality between the sexes. The sex distinctions of a biological or psychological nature which have been linked historically to inequality between the sexes are not necessarily thus linked. Will inequality always turn on, or require, positing alleged differences between the sexes which then serve both as the 'reason for' and the 'justification of' inegalitarian outcomes? Although sex distinctions have served as a justification for sex inequality in the past, these differences, to the extent that they are not relevant to the distinctions being made, need not serve this function in the future. That is a matter for political struggle. Indeed, the argument that some putative 'sameness' or blending of identities between males and females is the *only* safe and secure foundation for social equality has the precise effect of displacing a political focus upon structures of inequality in favor of advancing abstract rhetorical claims about the personalities of persons.

Androgyny as a social and political ideal is confused. Its proponents offer no coherent account of the androgynous society nor how we are to achieve one. More importantly, when androgyny touches upon or alludes to certain worthy political ideals and principles, these ideals and principles are more coherently and powerfully couched in a political language which is already a feature of political debate and life. Androgyny as a social imperative tends to get conflated with 'role sharing' and with the simplistic notion of each sex exhibiting characteristics stereotypically held of the other. Thus women would compete in the marketplace for the rewards of the society, men would do household tasks, etc. But androgyny as a social category ultimately fails to come to grips with the realities of a world which denies to a majority of its men and women those social goods which characterize the lives of the privileged. Androgyny forces attention back on the blurring or merging of sexual characteristics and diverts attention away from the cateories of *class* and *race* as determinants of the social positions of large numbers of male and female participants within American society.[47] Androgyny can neither help to forge, nor even identify, collective movements for social change. Finally, androgynism rests on the proposition that the 'problem' for women lies in the relations which pertain between men and women.

Androgyny, like any term of discourse with a long history, is located in the web of its traditional mythic and symbolic meanings; thus it cannot serve, not now and not in the future, as a politically resonant cry for social change in the way, say, 'liberation' or 'equality,' two powerful terms of *political* discourse imbedded within a net of political meanings, can. No movement for social change will be fought under the banner 'androgyny' but many have been and will be waged under the banners 'freedom,' 'equality,' 'liberty,' 'peace.' The feminist thinker who would articulate a theory of social change which may also serve as concrete historical analysis recognizes that equality, unlike androgyny, is a concept with common, shared social and political meanings. It can serve as a weapon to put pressure upon social practices and institutions in a way that androgyny, lacking this critical 'purchase' cannot.[48] Arguments for equality of respect and treatment are more securely lodged in the insistence by the political thinker that there are characteristics and qualities all persons *qua* persons share. To state this does not require denying that there are important and vital differences between persons, as groups and individuals, as well. To assert equality as a statement about persons can be deployed as a powerful wedge to press for more egalitarian arrangements. This presumption forces the analyst, if he or she contends that all persons are equal to one another in the most important respects with reference to their shared social universe, but finds that inequality in treatment exists, to look to those structures implicated in such differences in treatment. The qualities we all share as sentient creatures who have a capacity to suffer, to feel pain, to experience joy, to possess moral capacities, and so on, override, for purposes of pressing for social equality, those other characteristics not shared by all.[49] There is a dignity, as well as a political resonance to this argument; on both scores, androgynism will forever fall short.

This tour through the inner workings of androgyny and its implications suggest some modest conclusions. The first is that we would all be better off, as well as much closer to creating a world to our heart's desiring, if we accepted our bodies, in better grace and recognized that a *sexual difference* is neither an affront, nor an outrage, nor a narcissistic injury. A *sexual division*, on the other hand, one that separates the sexes and locks each into a vector of isolated, alienated activity *is* both a deep wound to the psychosexual identity of the human subject as well as a specific damage of an overly rigidified system of stratification and specialization. In order to fight the destructiveness of the system of sexual division, one must be able to say that the body is good and that a recognition and acceptance of sex differences makes us all richer, not poorer; that these differences enhance rather than constrict our world. The androgynist assault on human sexed identities bespeaks, at base, a contempt for the body and this contempt will invariably manifest itself in other ways and spheres.

To offer an account of the human being as a subject operating within a body, in a socio-historic context within which she launches claims, against and towards which she defines herself in determinate relations, is to repudiate abstracted androgynes. Yet the vexing question remains: *Why* androgyny? Why did this notion catch fire? There is yet another, unacknowledged imperative at work within the androgyny debate that may help to explain why the notion is so tenacious. This is an urge located on the level of discourse itself. Androgynism is an instance of what Hegel calls thought which 'pacifies itself.' Having come face to face with daunting philosophical questions, vexing debates over meaning and purposes, moral dilemmas and political puzzles, androgynists turned in upon themselves. Given their indebtedness to classical liberal thought, one way out of the difficulties presented by the antinomies of that discourse is to leap-frog over them. This can look like a solution but it is, in fact, a conceptual cop-out and a theoretical dead-end. Androgyny is sometimes over-used in the way 'dialectical' is: whenever a thinker bumps up against a stubborn theoretical, analytic, or moral dilemma and seeks a tidy way out that has the additional advantage of being politically 'correct,' he may sprinkle on a 'dialectic' here or an 'androgyny' there like so many conceptual croutons.

Androgyny, at base, is a very bizarre idea. As featured in feminist discourse it is a discursive artifact having no essential connection to anything other than itself. It is tied to no real (natural or social) object. Androgynists lodge rhetorical claims involving wholly unreal characterizations of abstract futures rather than struggling to create a set of reflective possibilities for human emancipation within the historic and social world. Androgyny *imposes* a rationalistic external standard upon human subjects and finds them wanting (unenlightened, irrational, living in bad faith, clinging to old superstitions, or wallowing in false consciousness). The androgynous faith is endlessly self-confirming. Not making contact with reality, it need never bump up against opposition, binds, tensions, paradoxes, ironies. A strange purity enters and the end-point is silence: the silence of the human subject who cannot, by definition, speak as an *androgynous* subject. In this way androgynism helps to 'bury the problems which have gathered behind the contradictory desires and refusals of contemporary heterosexuality.'[50] It proffers no ideal toward which people may reasonably aspire. In its dream of the fusion of social being with social consciousness it depoliticizes by eliminating all lines of fault through which critical ruptures might be possible. Androgynists offer up only a politics of displacement which leaves human subjects stuck, once again, in a sexual politics that aims to desexualize the subject. The androgynist impulse is in league, not at odds with, the social world in its primary force. If the androgynist project were activated it would speed up processes of rationaliz-ation; it would further homogenize human subjects. As Kristeva put it: 'Feminism can be but one of capitalism's more advanced needs to rationalize.'[51] Having first reduced the richness and mystery of the human body as a point of reference, a locus for action, a foundation for identity, and a way of knowing, androgynists point to their one-dimensional creation and go on to confuse real human beings with their impoverished vision. Androgynists are the bland leading the bland.

NOTES

1 There have been some doubters and critics but they have most often concentrated on but one feature or dimension of the androgynist argument. See, e.g., Cynthia Secor, 'Androgyny: An Early Reappraisal', *Women's Studies*, 2 (2) (1974), pp. 161–9; Daniel A. Harris, 'Androgyny: The Sexist Myth in Disguise,' ibid., pp. 171–84; Elaine Showalter, *A Literature of Their Own. British Women Novelists from the Brontës to Lessing* (Princeton University Press, Princeton, 1977), pp. 263–89; most recently, Robert May, *Sex and Fantasy. Patterns of Male and Female Development* (W. W. Norton, New York, 1980). Radical feminism's leading theologian, Mary Daly, also rejects androgyny, but for this

reason: she wants her woman to be altogether free from any taint by the old man. See her essay, 'The Qualitative Leap Beyond Patriarchal Religion,' *Quest*, 1. 4 (Spring, 1975), pp. 229ff.

2 Ann Ferguson, 'Androgyny as an Ideal for Human Development', in Mary Vetterling-Braggin, Frederick A. Elliston and Jane English, *Feminism and Philosophy* (Littlefield, Adam and Co., Totowa, New Jersey, 1977), pp. 45–69.

3 May, *Sex and Fantasy*, p. 165.

4 Ferguson, 'Androgyny as an Ideal', pp. 45–6.

5 Carolyn Heilbrun, *Toward a Recognition of Androgyny* (Knopf, New York, 1973).

6 Ferguson, 'Androgyny as Ideal', pp. 62–3.

7 Ibid., p. 65.

8 Caroline Bird, *Born Female* (Pocket Books, New York, 1968), p. xi.

9 Judith M. Bardwick, 'Androgyny and Humanistic Goods, or Goodbye, Cardboard People', in *The American Woman: Who Will She Be?*, Mary Louise McBee and Kathryn N. Blake (eds) (Glencoe Press, Beverly Hills, California, 1974), p. 61. Bardwick's formulation is an open invitation to a new and terrible form of social engineering. There are dangers implicit in any normative ideal of mental health but hers, couched as it is, as the most perfect, most rational, most healthy possible would exert terrible pressure on real, unrecalcitrant human 'material.' For a discussion of American feminism's long links with, among others, the social engineering impulse, see William Leach, *True Love and Perfect Union. The Feminist Reform of Sex and Society* (Basic Books, New York, 1980).

10 Kathleen E. Grady, 'Androgyny Reconsidered', in Juanita H. Williams (ed.), *Psychology of Women. Selected Readings* (W. W. Norton, New York, 1979), pp. 172–7.

11 Ibid., p. 174.

12 Ibid., p. 176.

13 Quoted in Showalter, *A Literature of Their Own*, p. 287.

14 Gayle Graham Yates, *What do Women Want. The Ideas of the Movement* (Harvard University Press, Cambridge, Mass., 1975), p. 122. Of course, Woolf, finally, didn't live it, she died it, and Elaine Showalter argues that androgyny was Woolf's way of dealing with feelings that were 'too hot to handle' that, finally, androgyny became a form of repression, 'an escape from the confrontation with femaleness and maleness'. Showalter, *A Literature of Their Own*, pp. 286, 289.

15 Yates, *What do Women Want*, p. 19.

16 Ibid., p. 117.

17 Shulamith Firestone, *The Dialectic of Sex* (Bantam Books, New York, 1972), p. 190.

18 Ferguson, 'Androgyny as an Ideal', p. 62.

19 See ch. 6, 'Classic Theories of Sex-Role Socialization', in *Women and Sex Roles: A Social-Psychological Perspective* (W. W. Norton, New York, 1978), pp. 95–113.

20 Joyce Trebilcot, 'Two Forms of Androgynism', in *Feminism and Philosophy*, p. 74.

21 Elizabeth H. Wolgast, *Equality and the Rights of Women* (Cornell University Press, Ithaca, New York, 1980), p. 125.

22 Kate Millett, *Sexual Politics* (Doubleday, New York, 1969), p. 93. Emphasis added.

23 See, e.g., Firestone's 'pregnancy is barbaric' with cruel children pointing fingers and sneering, 'Who's the fat lady?' Or, alas, even Simone de Beauvoir who, following Sartre, launches volleys against the female body as being 'wanting in significance by itself' though the male body has its own integrity and 'makes sense.' Woman is portrayed as 'the victim of the species.' Pregnancy is described as 'alienation' and, with no apparent awareness of what she is up to, de Beauvoir calls a woman's breasts 'mammary glands' that 'play no role in woman's individual economy: they can be excised at any time of life.' See Simone de Beauvoir, *The Second Sex*, trans. H. M. Parshley (Bantam Books, New York, 1968), pp. xvi, 24.

24 Ferguson, 'Androgyny as Ideal', p. 52.

25 The most straightforward creation of a utopian society based upon contempt for the body and an urge to transcend it remains Plato's *Republic*.

26 Alfred Schutz, *Collected Papers*, vol. 1 (Martinus Nijhoff, The Hague, 1962), p. xlii.

27 Roberto Mangabeira Unger, *Knowledge and Politics* (Free Press, New York, 1972), p. 55.

28 May, *Sex and Fantasy*, p. 80.

29 Stuart Hampshire, *Thought and Action* (Viking Press, New York, 1959), pp. 54–85.

30 Unger, *Knowledge and Politics*, p. 57.

31 Hampshire, *Thought and Action*, pp. 11–12, 20, 31.

32 See Freud's discussion over the confusion between biological, psychological, and social meanings of 'masculinity' and 'femininity.' From the beginning, Freud adhered to a theory of biological and psychological bisexuality. See Sigmund Freud, 'Hysterical Phantasies and Their Relation to Bisexuality', *Three Essays on the Theory of Sexuality* (1980), particularly the long footnote added in 1915; the elegant and powerful essay, 'A Child is Being Beaten' (1919) in which Freud demonstrates the internal connection between children's beating fantasies and the 'bisexual constitution of human beings.'

33 Sigmund Freud, *The Ego and the Id* (W. W. Norton, New York, 1970), p. 16.

34 Richard Wollheim, 'The Mind and the Mind's Image of itself', in *On Art and the Mind* (Harvard University Press, Cambridge, Mass., 1974), p. 53.

35 Whether Freud is correct that the distinction between male and female does not become fully entrenched until the genital stage of development or some of his critics are correct that the 'certainty' of one's gender

occurs earlier is not important in order to make the point that boys and girls experience the surfaces of their bodies as a feature of 'external' reality which is taken in and represented intrapsychically in somewhat different ways.

36 Richard Wollheim, 'Psychoanalysis and Feminism', *New Left Review*, 93 (1975), p. 64. Wollheim argues that gender identification begins earlier than Freud's account would indicate. But this gender identification still occurs before any full-blown notions of 'masculine' and 'feminine' develop.
37 Abigail Rosenthal, 'Feminism without Contradictions', *Monist*, 57. 1, p. 29.
38 Peter Winch, 'Understanding a Primitive Society', in Bryan R. Wilson, ed., *Rationality* (Harper Torchbooks, New York, 1970), p. 110.
39 Sigmund Freud, 'Analysis of a Phobia in a Five Year Old Boy', *Standard Edition*, X (1909), p. 7.
40 Sigmund Freud, 'The Sexual Enlightenment of Children', *Standard Edition*, IX (1907), p. 136.
41 Bryan Magee, ed., *Modern British Philosophy*, 'Conversation with Bernard Williams: Philosophy and Morals' (St. Martin's Press, New York, 1971), p. 154.
42 Rosenthal, 'Feminism Without Contradictions', p. 40.
43 Showalter, *A Literature of Their Own*, p. 289.
44 Secor, 'Androgyny', p. 163.
45 Tony Tanner, 'Julie and "La Maison Paternelle": Another Look at Rousseau's La Nouvelle Heloise', *Daedalus* (Winter, 1976), p. 40.
46 Secor, 'Androgyny', p. 163.
47 Barbara Charlesworth Gelpi, 'The Politics of Androgyny', *Women's Studies*, 2 (1974), pp. 151–60.
48 'Equality' is an intersubjective notion; 'androgyny' is not. Intersubjective meanings are ways of experiencing action in society which are expressed in common language, rooted in social institutions, practices, and relations and which serve to constitute those very institutions, practices and relations.
49 Certain immediate questions arise which, for the most part political theorists and moral philosophers have ignored, namely, what about those human beings of whom one cannot assert the full range of what constitutes humans-as-such, provided one adopts the notion. I think of the severely retarded, for example. One could build a case for their having moral claims on others by virtue of the fact that, although they may not be capable of rational thought, dear to the heart of Western philosophers, they certainly can feel pain and experience affection.
50 Rosenthal, 'Feminism Without Contradictions', p. 42.
51 Julia Kristeva, 'Woman Can Never Be Defined', in Elaine Marks and Isabelle de Courtivron (eds), *New French Feminisms; an Anthology* (University of Massachusetts Press, Amherst, 1980), p. 141.

8

Women, Class and Sexual Differences

SALLY ALEXANDER

. . . it is impossible ever to govern subjects rightly, without knowing as well what they really are as what they only seem; which the *Men* can never be supposed to do, while they labour to force *Women* to live in constant masquerade.

Sophia,
Woman not Inferior to Man

This desire of being always woman is the very consciousness that degrades the sex. Excepting with a lover, I must repeat with emphasis, a former observation, – it would be well if they were only agreeable or rational companions.

Mary Wollstonecraft,
A Vindication of the Rights of Woman

Throughout history, people have knocked their heads against the riddle of the nature of femininity . . . Nor will you have escaped worrying over this problem – those of you who are men; to those of you who are women this will not apply – you are yourselves the problem.

Sigmund Freud,
Lecture on Femininity

For a long time I have hesitated to write a book on woman. The subject is irritating, especially to women; and it is not new. . . . The voluminous nonsense uttered during the last century seems to have done little to illuminate the problem.

Reprinted, with permission, from 'Women, Class and Sexual Differences in the 1830s and 1840s: Some Reflections on the Writing of a Feminist History', *History Workshop Journal* 17 (Spring 1984), pp. 125–49. This version is an extract, edited with the author's permission.

After all, is there a problem? And if so, what is it? Are there women really? . . . One wonders if women still exist, if they will always exist, whether or not it is desirable that they should, what place they occupy in this world, what their place should be.

Simone de Beauvoir,
The Second Sex

I THE PROBLEM: WOMAN, A HISTORICAL AND POLITICAL CATEGORY

The problem: woman, the riddle: femininity have a capricious but nevertheless political history. Capricious because they surface at different moments among different social milieus, within diverse political movements; and a history in the sense that the social conditions and political status of women have undergone changes which may be traced, and with them some of the shifts in the meanings of femininity. As we become acquainted with the historical range and diversity of women's political status and social roles, the enigma itself occupies a different place. It is removed outside history to some other realm beyond the reach of social analysis or political theory. Since there can be no aspect of the human condition which is not social where could that other place be?

If the meaning of femininity, the political implications of Womanhood have at moments in the past 300 years been contested, then it must be that what they represent is not some external and universal essence of woman, but the difficulty of the sexual relation itself between women and men; which is always a social ordering, and one where the unconscious and its conflicting drives and desires presses most urgently on conscious behaviour, where political thought, though most capable of producing principles of equality and justice in its delineations of the proper relations between the sexes, nevertheless cannot always anticipate or circumscribe the urgency of those conflicts as they are lived.

Feminism, the conscious political movement of women, has been since the seventeenth century the principal contender in the struggles for the reorganization of sexual difference and division, and hence the social meaning of womanhood. If feminism's underlying demand is for women's full inclusion in humanity (whether that inclusion is strategically posed in terms of equal rights, socialism or millenarianism), then the dilemma for a feminist political strategy may be summed up in the tension between the plea for equality and the assertion of sexual difference. If the sexes are different, then how may that difference (and all that it implies for the relative needs and desires of women and men) be represented throughout culture, without the sex that is different becoming subordinated.

History offers many symptoms of this difficulty; from the sixteenth-century Royal Edicts which prohibited women's public gossip, to the nineteenth-century House of Commons references to women as 'the sex' or feminism as the 'shrieking sisterhood'. Whether dismissed as a 'monstrous regiment', 'set of devils' or a 'menace to the Labour movement',[1] feminism both arouses sexual antagonisms and invokes a threat which cannot be explained with reference to the demands of the women's movements – nothing if not reasonable in themselves. By suggesting that what both feminism and femininity stand for is not Woman – who like Man is no more nor less than human – but the social organization of sexual difference and division, I am refusing to abandon femininity to an enigma/mystery beyond history. But then the problem becomes how to write a history of women and feminism which engages with those issues.

II 'A HISTORY OF OUR OWN'

It is difficult to remember now how there could have been such a gust of masculine laughter at the 1969 Ruskin History Workshop when a number of us women asked for a meeting of those present who might be interested in working on 'Women's History'. I do remember the bewilderment and indignation we felt as we walked away from the conference to plan another of our own. It seemed to be the word – Woman – which produced the laughter. Why? Those plans became the first National Women's Liberation conference held at Ruskin College, Oxford in early 1970 (an event which wiped the smile off the male students' faces). The television room had been taken over by the crèche (run by men), and the college was swarming with women, women and women. Student Union meetings for weeks afterwards rang with incoherent, but passionate, antagonism to the Women's Conference, focusing on the violation of students' freedoms that it had imposed. The different implications, it seems, of women's liberation were lived vividly, though differently, for some men and hundreds of women that weekend. So my interest in women's history coincided with the beginning of my own education as an intellectual at a trade-union college (I was a student at Ruskin from 1968 to 1970) and the emergence of the Women's Liberation Movement from the late 1960s. The dichotomies – Women and Labour, Sex and Class, Feminism and Socialism have been the intimate inhabitants of both my psyche and my intellectual work (if the two can be separated) as they have been for many women of my political generation.

Intellectual Feminism

In the early 1970s socialist feminists struggled to transform those dichotomies into political and theoretical relationships through campaigns and study groups. We diligently appraised and attempted to secure for our own purposes some of the traditions of Marxist thought, appropriating the concepts of political economy, historical and dialectical materialism and assessing their revolutionary practices through a feminist lens. If I ask what was/is the relationship between class struggle and the sexual division of labour, then historical materialism's focus on the mode of production is illuminating and suggestive. It imaginatively speculates on labour both as a form of activity which involves a relationship between Man and Nature, and as a system of social relations between women and men. But if the categories of political economy can sometimes reveal the operations of the labour market convincingly, the political traditions of Marxism have had little to say about feminism or the needs and aspirations of women; while historical materialism, by identifying class struggle as the motor of history pushes the questions of sexual divisions and difference to the periphery of the historical process. Whether posited as objects of analysis, or included as part of the narrative, they can be present in Marxist – and most labour – history, only as digressions from the real subject of history – class struggle; and their theoretical status is subservient to the study of modes of production.

If feminism has been only one of the detonators of 'crisis' in Marxist thought and practice it has been the most insistently subversive because it will not give up its wish to speak in the name of women; of women's experience, subjectivity and sexuality. 'A history of our own', 'a language of our own', 'the right to determine our own sexuality', these were the distinctive themes of rebellion for the Women's Liberation Movement in the early 1970s. We were asking the impossible perhaps. As a feminist I was (and still am) under the spell of those wishes, while as a historian writing and thinking in the shadow of a labour history which silences them. How can women speak and think creatively within Marxism when they can neither enter the narrative flow as fully as they wish, nor imagine that there might be other subjectivities present in history than those of class (for to imagine that is to transgress the laws of historical materialism)? This is a difficulty to which I shall return.

Other intellectual traditions and ways of thinking about women, sexual divisions and feminism pushed the categories Woman and Labour, Sex and Class, Feminism and Socialism apart in my mind, refusing any analogy between them, or any mutual set of determinations and effects. The discovery of histories of women written by earlier generations of feminists showed how women's experience has to be remembered anew with each resurgence of feminist consciousness; between times it leaves scarcely a trace. Why this recurring amnesia, and why the attenuated feminist voice?

Radical feminism (from the United States: British radical-feminist history surfaced later in the decade), offered a breath-takingly audacious understanding of relations between the sexes in history. Sexual divisions prefigure those of class was the message that Shulamith Firestone and Kate Millett flung at a male-dominated intellectual world; patriarchy the concept which they restored to the centre of debates around social formations and social relations between the sexes.[2]

Since the seventeenth century feminists have rallied against the tyranny of men, male power, male domination and in the idiom of the 1970s, sexism. But those categories, while retaining a polemical conviction, I believe, have to be transcended too in any full history of women or feminism. Ironically, radical feminism writes women's subjectivity and active agency out of history as effectively as any Marxism. Little girls become women because of what male-dominated institutions tell and compel them to do. History is simply one long death-knell of women's independent activity and consciousness. There were witches, but men killed them; women were sensual, erotic and adventurous, but men used and abused them; women loved each other, but men forbade that love to be spoken; women were workers, but men seized their skills, etc., etc. Men have much to answer for, but the envy and fears and desires of one sex can't carry all the determinations of history. If they can, then we are again in a world where women's identity, action, speech and desires are all explained in terms of something else, in this case, the male psyche. Women are subordinated and silenced because they live in a world shaped in the interests of and dominated by men. Only a political revolution of women could ever destroy male power if it is conceived as so absolute in its effects. But the writings and campaigns of previous feminism exhibit contradictions and difficulties internal to the thoughts of both individual feminists, and the movements for which they claimed to speak, that cannot be reduced to the tyranny of men. As the vindicator of women's rights, Mary Wollstonecraft, for instance, did not absolve women from culpability in their own history: she castigated the coquetry of women of the leisured classes, condemned their feeble development of reason and virtue, their excess of sensibility, their false modesty. All this she attributed to an education which fitted women exclusively for marriage and the pleasures of men. But reading her letters and novels brings the irresistible recognition that she could diatribe so thoroughly against the thrall of men's authority and desires over women's lives, because she herself fell so violently and seemingly arbitrarily a prey to them herself. Do we reject the authenticity of those conflicting desires because men have placed them there for us? And then, how do we explain divisions within the women's movement itself in the mid-nineteenth century?

Just two examples: in the 1870s the suffrage campaign refused to endorse publicly the Ladies' National Association's Campaign against the Contagious Diseases Acts. Josephine Butler and the 'grave and educated ladies' who reached out to their 'fallen sisters' acquiesced in this suffragist silence, a denial as profound as any repudiation of a common sisterhood of women that came from outside the women's movement.[3] The suffragists' decision was made for reasons of political expediency. The second example indicates deeper tensions and divisions within the women's movement on the same questions: the identity or nature of woman, and the political representation of sexual difference.

The coalescence of feminist organizations broke up with the partial achievement of 'Votes for Women' in 1918. From 1917 the largest suffragist organization, The National Union of Societies for Equal Citizenship (formerly named the National Union of Suffrage Societies), had been debating political priorities, culminating in Eleanor Rathbone's attempt to place the endowment of motherhood and birth-control as the new unifying aims in 1924. Eleanor Rathbone argued that what distinguished women from men was motherhood; from maternity the natural feminine dispositions flowed and should be acknowledged in the economic policies and social provisions demanded by the women's movement.[4] We must', she argued in a Presidential speech to NUSEC early in the 1920s, 'demand what we want for women, not because it is what men have got, but because it is what women need to fulfil the potentialities of their own natures and to adjust themselves to the circumstances of their own lives.'

But any projection of motherhood into the political arena had always been strongly opposed by those who, led by Millicent Garrett Fawcett, had always maintained that to emphasize sexual difference, or women's 'maternal function', would jeopardize their claims for equality. The theme of this disagreement was insistent: equality or difference, and if difference, then how could that difference be represented within politics without it being used to submerge women in domesticity, to deny them the full fruits of equality – by justifying their economic dependence and political subjection? The extent of sisterhood, the political implications of womanhood have proved as elusive and divisive within the women's movement as within the government, political parties or the male-dominated Labour Movement in the past 150 years.

Every moment of dissonance and disagreement within feminism, as well as between women and men, demands recovering and disentangling – demands a historical reading. Neither Marxism nor radical feminism yet offers a history which can grasp the issues that feminism both stands for and raises. If Marxism persistently avoids sexual antagonism by relegating sexual difference to a natural world, then radical feminism conceives of women as shaped literally by men's desires. Histories of femininity and feminism have temporalities of their own – apart from those of class or men. The political narratives of feminism are as diverse and fractured as the vocabulary of individual rights and egalitarian aspiration itself is, when it surfaces now among the ascendent bourgeoisie in eighteenth-century Britain, now among the English Jacobins in the 1790s, among the Owenites and Unitarians in the 1820s and 1840s, and in Victorian Britain, accumulating an intensity of grievance and yearning among women from very different social and political milieus.

The emergence of a mass-feminist politics is most often attributed to the effects of the industrial revolution and the ideological hegemony of the bourgeoisie.[5] The former, by separating work and home, the latter by instilling ideas of domesticity among the working classes, allocated women and men to the private and public domains respectively. But we come closer to the terrain of feminist grievance and capture a decisive moment in its political temporality if we examine the forms of working-class politics themselves in the 1830s and 1840s, and their language of demand and aspiration. If the working class emerged as a political category in those years (remembering its long history of gestation), then Woman emerged as a social problem. The emergence was simultaneous, the roots of grievance and their political representation different.

Feminist Consciousness and Class Struggle

Feminism, as a self-conscious political movement appears when women, or some women in the name of their sex, distinguish themselves and their needs, from those of their male kin within families, communities and class. Feminism's protest is always posed in terms of women's perceptions of themselves and their status in relation to men. From a litany of their discontents feminism gathers an identity of women, and formulates the demands and aspirations that will transform the social relations/conditions in which women and men will live. Whatever the starting-point of its dissatisfactions – lack of education, men's property over women in marriage, 'domestic drudgery', the prohibitions on female labour, the double standard of sexual morality, exclusion from the franchise – feminists from the seventeenth century have refused to concede that relationships between the sexes belong outside history in any conception of the natural world, which is where philosophers, poets or Marxist historians, until provoked, have been content to abandon or place them. Feminism looks outward at the social forms of sexual division and the uneven destinies that claim the two sexes, but the critical look becomes an enquiry into the self and sexual difference and asks 'what am I, a woman, and how am I different from a man?' No social relationship is left unturned, if only by implication, in this endeavour.

Feminism's return to the individual subject in its attempt to distinguish woman as a social category from man is one clue to some of its moments of emergence. There must be available a language of the individual political subject – a language which articulates the dissemination of a political order through the individual's identification with (and subjection to) its law. Some seventeenth-century protestant sects which proposed the unmediated communion between the Soul and God and dissolved the family in the community of all believers enabled women to claim an equal right with men to 'preach and prophesy', for the 'soul knows no distinction of sex';[6] and in the eighteenth and nineteenth centuries feminism seized on the language of democratic rights within both liberal and utopian political discourse. But for the individual voice of a 'Sophia' or Mary Wollstonecraft to become a movement there had to be not only feminine discontent, but also a widespread yearning for another way of life. Before a language of rebellion can pass into general speech it must appeal to the imagination of a wide social group. Thus feminism appears at moments of industrial and political dislocation when disparate social groups are struggling to 'find a voice' in the new emerging order, when seemingly stable forms of social organization are tumbling down, as in the English and French revolutions and in the 1830s and 1840s.[7]

In speaking of the self and sexual difference feminism is at its most disturbing. Sexuality, intimacy, divergent conceptions of need are evoked and haunt the Marxist historian with the spectres of bourgeois individualism, gossip, and the crumbling of working-class unity. Ten years of women's history has calmed immediate fears. Few labour historians now hesitate to write of women's work, to mention the family or note the absence of women from some forms of political life. Working-class 'experience' has been stretched – though the political significance of those worlds beyond the workplace, ale-house, clubroom, union branch meeting are still argued about.[8] But if we are to pursue the history of women's experience and of feminism there can be no retreat from a closer enquiry into subjectivity and sexual identity. For if feminism insists on the political significance of the female subject and on the urgent need to reorganize sexual difference and division, it is to convey a more generous conception of human consciousness and its effects at the levels of popular resistance, collective identifications, and forms of political address and organization.

Social Being: Consciousness or Subjectivity?

The focus on the self and sexual difference throws into disarray the smooth elision assumed within Marxist thought between social being, consciousness and politics. Two distinctions are drawn: between material and mental life and true and false consciousness. Mental life flows from material conditions. Social being is determined above all by class position – location within the relations of production. Consciousness and politics, all mental conceptions spring from the material forces and relations of production and so reflect those class origins.[9] Collective class-consciousness is the recognition of the shared experience of exploitation, and working-class politics its expression, which in its most advanced form is revolutionary socialism. Thus there are graduated levels of consciousness (from spontaneous to political) before the historic destiny of the working class can be realized.[10]

When historical materialism is compressed in this way in
of laws, they are abandoned only at the risk of jetti
dynamics of history.

Let a more skilled philosopher unravel the polaritie..
mental; true/false; cause/effect. Here I only want to point to the
absence of the individual sexually differentiated subject in Marxism.
The question-marks hover over social being, and how it is
experienced – by women and by men.

'Experience' of class, even if shared and fully recognized, does
not, as Edward Thompson and others have suggested, produce a
shared and even consciousness.[11] Class is not only a diverse
(geographically, from industry to industry, etc.) and divisive
(skilled/unskilled; male/female labour, etc.) 'experience', but that
experience itself is given different meaning. For Marxists, meaning
is produced through ideologies. The bourgeoisie as the dominant
class has control over the relations and the forces of production and
therefore the production of ideologies, which mask the reality of
social being to the working class. Thus ideologies serve the interests
of antagonistic classes.

Debates within Marxism which attempt to release ideology from
its economic/material base are inexhaustible. Engels and Lenin have
been perhaps the sternest advocates of the grip of the base on the
superstructure; Gramsci and Mao Tse-Tung elaborating on the
continuum and flux of ideas among the people, the tenacity of
traditions, and the irrepressible capacity of human consciousness
to produce forms of communal order and ways of thinking
independent of the sway of hegemonic ideologies. But if we step
aside from these debates to ask not how are ideologies produced,
but how, in Juliet Mitchell's phrase, do 'we live as ideas', then we
enter the realm of social being and experience along another path –
the path of subjectivity and sexual identity.[12] Against Marxism's
claims that the determining social relationship is between wage
labour and capital, exploiter and exploited, proletarian and
capitalist, feminism insists on the recognition that subjective
identity is also constructed as masculine or feminine, placing the
individual as husband or wife, mother or father, son or daughter,
and so on. And these subjectivities travel both into political
language and forms of political action, here they may be severed
from class or class interests, indeed may be at odds with them.

In order to place subjectivity and sexual difference firmly at the
centre of my research and historical writing I draw on the psycho-
analytic account of the unconscious and sexuality. Psycho-analysis
offers a reading of sexual difference rooted not in the sexual

division of labour (which nevertheless organizes that difference), nor within nature, but through the unconscious and language. This poses the issue of psychic reality – a reality which like Marx's concepts of commodity fetishism and exploitation, will not be encountered through empirical observation. Psycho-analysis allows for a rich elaboration of subjectivity, identification and desire – essentially psychic processes which give a political movement its emotional power.

Subjectivity, Sexual Difference and Language

The French psycho-analyst Jacques Lacan's re-emphasis on the part played by language – the symbolic order – in the production of meaning, and unconscious fantasy in the construction of subjectivity has been taken up by some feminists because it retrieves sexual difference from the seemingly obvious 'anatomy is destiny'. Perhaps this needs further elaboration.

For Lacan the acquisition of subjectivity and sexual identity are a simultaneous and always precarious process which occurs as the human infant enters language; that is, as s/he is spoken to and about and as s/he learns to speak. The human animal is born into language and comes into being through its terms.[13] Or, to put it another way, language, which pre-exists the infant, identifies us first as boy/girl, daughter/son. Language orders masculinity and femininity, they are positions which shift between and within discourses. The infant takes up these positions and moves between them as s/he journeys through the oedipal trauma, which marks the entry into human culture for every infant. The infant is compelled to acknowledge the significance of sexual difference through the presence or absence of the phallus – the primary and privileged sign of sexual difference. Neither little boys nor little girls possess the phallus; they are placed in a different relationship to it through the threat of castration and prohibition, which have different implications for femininity (lack) and masculinity (loss). The relationship to the phallus is mediated through fantasy; recognition of loss/lack, absence/presence is prefigured from birth as the infant differentiates itself from others – the absence/presence of the desired object (breast/mother); the look and speech of others. Fantasy fills the void left by the absent object. Castration and prohibition represent human law, within which every infant has to take up a place, initially as masculine or feminine, and never without a struggle. A struggle, because it is around these moments –

absence/loss, pleasure/unpleasure – that the libidinal organization of need, demand and desire is shaped.[14]

Subjectivity, and with it sexual identity, is constructed through a process of differentiation, division and splitting, and best understood as a process which is always in the making, is never finished or complete. In this sense, the unified coherent subject presented in language is always a fiction, and so susceptible to disruption by the unconscious (or in collision with an alternative concept of the self in language). Everyday speech with its discontinuities, hesitations, contradictions, indicates on the one hand the process itself, and on the other, the difficulty the individual subject has in aligning her or himself within the linguistic order, since there are as many different orders as there are discourses to structure them and always the possibility of more. A difficulty which is underlined for the little girl/woman by the impossibility for her of taking up a positive or powerful place in a culture which privileges masculinity and therefore men. Subjectivity and sexual identity are always achieved with difficulty, and the achievement is always precarious. The unpredictable effects of that achievement remain inaccessible to conscious thought in the repressed wishes to be one with the other, to belong to the other sex, as well as envy of and desire for the other sex. Both subjectivity and sexual identity are therefore unstable and involve antagonism and conflict in their very construction. Antagonism and instability are lived out not only within the individual psyche and its history, they mediate all social relations between women and men; they prefigure and cohabit with class antagonisms, and, as the history of feminism demonstrates, may well disrupt class solidarities.

Post-Saussurian linguistics' non-referential theory of language and insistence on the arbitrary nature of the sign, marks these instabilities. Meaning is produced through the chain of signifiers – the way words are strung together and organized into narratives, analysis, systems of thought – and may be gleaned from the study of those, rather than from reference to the objects and phenomena which they only designate, leaving them always open to dispute and redefinition[15] (a salutary, if familiar, reminder to the historian that historical reconstruction of the past is always through interpretation of the sources, which serve like memory traces for the psychoanalyst, as the primary sources from which and over which we impose our own interpretations and causalities). There is no relation of sex, Lacan cautions us (meaning no natural relation: no relation that can be read off from anatomy, biology, or the demands of procreation) except, I would emphasize, as it is articulated in language.

It is partly because feminism enquires into the self in its concern to distinguish woman from man as a social category, and because one of the points of that return has been a dissatisfaction with historical materialism's privileging of class (narrowly defined) as the determining social experience, economic relation and agency of political change, that the limits of Marxist history's notions of social being, consciousness and politics, and the articulations between them are so clearly revealed. Feminist history has to emancipate itself from class as the organizing principle of history, the privileged signifier of social relations and their political representations.

Marxism and other sociological theories of social being are resistant to any psychology which could be read as proposing a universal human nature. If they allow for a human nature at all it is one that is produced by the environment (shadows of the Enlightenment). The subjectivity of psycho-analysis does not either imply a universal human nature, it suggests that some forms of mental functioning – the unconscious, fantasy, memory, etc. – seem to be so. Subjectivity in this account is neither universal nor ahistorical. First structured through relations of absence and loss, pleasure and unpleasure, difference and division, these are simultaneous with the social naming and placing among kin, community, school, class which are always historically specific.

Why open up history to the unconscious? But historians are as familiar as the analyst, poet, philosopher, everyone in their daily lives, with the power of the imaginary: dreams, fantasy, desire, fear, envy, pleasure. Historians of pre-industrial society have fewer inhibitions about speaking of myth, ritual, magic and their significance in human organization. Perhaps the fear that by introducing the unconscious and fantasy into social history is to open a Pandora's box, to deny the rationale of political and social life, is stalled by the distance of pre-industrial societies from our own. Against these reservations, I only suggest that the persistent problem of femininity and the presence of feminism indicate that the box is already wide open.

It is not my intention to reconstruct the individual unconscious, or individual subjectivity (which maybe glimpsed nevertheless by the historian through autobiography, memory or speech). But merely to emphasize that the symbolic sets the terms within which any social group must position itself and conceive of a new social order and that the symbolic has a life of its own. And secondly, that human subjectivity shapes, as it is itself shaped by, political practice and language – it leaves its imprint there.

Histories of all mass movements in the epoch of industrial capitalism, reveal the power of language – oratory, polemic, propaganda – both to capture the allegiance of the constituency addressed, and to formulate social visions, to translate need and desire into demand. In so far as the political vision is in combat with the present rule of law, then the question of strategy, how that law is to be encountered and negotiated, will depend on the relative balance of visionary aspiration and concrete political demand within a political movement. The strength of desire in utopian visions of transcendence means that there is little room for negotiation with government, law, or any of the existing domains of authority. We may glean an insight into the mentality of transcendence from Lacan's exploration of desire, which is predicated on loss/absence, is always in excess of demand, and is produced through language. The desire for harmony, a world free from conflict, is – like the unified subject – a wish whose realization is elusive, though a wish that compels. Since even utopian visions, when translated into living communities, must impose their own moralities and laws, they too become open to challenge from those who wish to disobey, or to imagine another order. What happens when the visionaries become the lawmakers?

Both feminism and psycho-analysis suggest (in different ways), and history appears to confirm their findings, that antagonism between the sexes is an unavoidable aspect of the acquisition of sexual identity, and one that can be explained neither by anatomy nor environment alone. If antagonism is always latent, it is possible that history offers no final resolution, only the constant reshaping, reorganizing of the symbolization of difference, and the sexual division of labour. The questions for the historian of feminism are why at some moments does sexual difference and division take on a political significance – which elements in the organization are politicized, what are the terms of negotiation, and between whom?

ACKNOWLEDGEMENTS

Raphael Samuel's provocative criticism and enthusiasm helped me in the writing of this essay. Gareth Stedman Jones and Barbara Taylor have been both critical and encouraging. Special thanks to Tony Wailey and Kate Shuckburgh.

NOTES

1 The phrases are those of John Knox, John Keats and G. D. H. Cole respectively.
2 Shulamith Firestone, *The Dialectic of Sex* (London, 1971); Kate Millett, *Sexual Politics* (New York, 1970). For a survey of feminist theories of patriarchy, see Veronica Beechey, 'On Patriarchy', *Feminist Review*, 3 (1979), pp. 66–83. For a disagreement among feminist historians, see Sheila Rowbotham, Sally Alexander, Barbara Taylor, 'Debate on Patriarchy', ed. Raphael Samuel, *People's History and Socialist Theory* (London, 1983).
3 For an account of the LNA's campaign, see Judith R. Walkowitz, *Prostitution and Victorian Society, Women, Class and the State* (Cambridge, 1980), Part II. For its effects among women and the Women's Movement, Ray Strachey, *The Cause* (1928; Virago reprint, London, 1978), pp. 196–8.
4 Eleanor Rathbone, *Milestones* (London, 1929), p. 28.
5 Histories of the suffrage movement pursue a fairly straightforward narrative of the achievement of women's suffrage. The more comprehensive histories focus on the intellectual components of feminist thought, and the class composition of the feminists. There is a general consensus: the former derives from Protestant individualism, Enlightenment thought and philanthropy; and the feminists were overwhelmingly middle class (e.g. Richard Evans, *The Feminists*, London 1977; Olive Banks, *Faces of Feminism*, Oxford 1981). Feminism's middle-class character has led to its neglect by socialist historians. A valuable exception is Juliet Mitchell, 'Woman and Equality', in J. Mitchell and A. Oakley (eds), *The Rights and Wrongs of Women* (Pelican, 1976), pp. 379–99. No recent histories of British feminism have surpassed two classic studies: Ray Strachey's *The Cause* (1928) and Sylvia Pankhurst's *The Suffragette Movement* (1931), both reprinted by Virago. Written by protagonists in the Cause, both view the struggle as a study in human progress. Ray Strachey, a liberal socialist, gives a brief, but comprehensive, survey of the Women's Movement from the mid-nineteenth century to the 1920s. Despite Sylvia Pankhurst's tendency to shape her narrative around the achievements of her family (beginning with her father), *The Suffragette Movement* is nevertheless a mine of information on the early radical, socialist and labour movements, is full of fascinating thumb-nail portraits and packed with analysis. The reader is swept along by the messianic vision of the author, the elements of idealism, sacrifice and martyrdom that characterized the 'Cause'.
6 Keith Thomas, 'Women and the Civil War Sects', *Past and Present*, 13 (1958), pp. 42–57. Christopher Hill, *The World Turned Upside Down* (London, 1972), ch. 15.
7 For a feminist reading of the GNCTU, Barbara Taylor, *Eve and the New Jerusalem* (London, 1983), ch. 4.

8 For a recent example of that 'stretching', Ellen Ross, 'Survival Networks: Women's Neighbourhood Sharing in London before World War One', *HWJ*, 15 (Spring 1983), pp. 4–28.

9 Karl Marx, 'Preface to a Contribution to the Critique of Political Economy', Marx and Engels, *Selected Works* (London, 1970), pp. 180–5, is the most succinct statement.

10 V. I. Lenin, *What is to be Done* (Moscow, 1969).

11 E. P. Thompson, *The Making of the English Working Class* (Pelican, 1968), Preface.

12 Juliet Mitchell, *Psychoanalysis and Feminism* (London, 1974), Introduction p. XV.

13 Juliet Mitchell's Introduction in J. Mitchell and J. Rose (eds), *Feminine Sexuality, Jacques Lacan and the École Freudienne* (London, 1983), p. 5.

14 Juliet Mitchell's and Jacqueline Rose's introductions to *Feminine Sexuality* are lucid accounts of Lacan's project. J. Mitchell's *Psychoanalysis and Feminism*, parts 1 and 2, give a careful reading of Freud's account of the acquisition of femininity. The most useful essay on fantasy is Jean Laplanche and J.-B. Pontalis, 'Fantasy and the Origins of Sexuality', *International Journal of Psychoanalysis*, 49 (1968), Part 1, pp. 1–17. Sigmund Freud, *Femininity* (1933), Standard Edition, XXII. 112–35, though controversial among feminists, is still – for me – both riveting and convincing. For aspects of that controversy, Elizabeth Wilson, 'Psychoanalysis: Psychic Law and Order', *Feminist Review*, 8 (Summer 1981), pp. 63–78, and J. Rose, Femininity and Its Discontents', *Feminist Review*, 14 (Summer 1983), pp. 5–21.

15 The use I make of Lacan's Freud, and the significance of language in the production of meaning and the construction of the subject are my own responsibility. Useful essays are Jacques Lacan, 'The Function and Field of Speech and Language in Psychoanalysis', and 'The Agency of the Letter in the Unconscious or Reason Since Freud', *Écrits* (London, 1980), pp. 30–113, 146–78. E. Benveniste, *Problems in General Linguistics* (Miami), chs. 19, 20 and 22. Ferdinand de Saussure, *Course on General Linguistics* (London, 1981).

9

'The Serious Burdens of Love?' Some Questions on Child-care, Feminism and Socialism

DENISE RILEY

I

Sometimes it seems absurdly daring to go on speaking out, in all this bleakness and poverty, for choice, flexibility, humanity in the having of and the care of children. Campaigns for more and better state child-care continue in the face of cuts by central government on capital expenditure for nursery building, and by local authorities on upkeep. Is this persistence in campaigning a quixotic refusal to face economic realities? These feminist and socialist virtues cost money, whatever else. Where there is no money, or where the distribution of funds is controlled by a different ethic, a different understanding of needs, then child-care sinks to the bottom of the list. There is not even the embittered grim consolation of ascribing this neglect to the hardness of a calculating capitalism, which we shall see pass away into a more generous socialist dawn. It is not merely a problem of Thatcherism coating a false image of the family with marshmallow tones, while at the same time it acts mean-spiritedly. That is there. But there is no automatic opposite – a socialism of abundance which would pay full and imaginative attention to the needs of women with children; plenty does not spontaneously flow from a new socialist order, any more than refusing public welfare provision is a timeless characteristic of capitalism. Political conservatism, in the narrowest sense of 'political', and conservatism of the spirit may frequently run together, but they need not absolutely do so.

Reprinted, with permission, from *What Is To Be Done About The Family? Crisis in the Eighties*, edited by Lynne Segal (Penguin Books in association with the Socialist Society), pp. 129–56, copyright © Lynne Segal, 1983. It is reproduced by permission of Penguin Books Ltd.

A few years ago, it seems many years ago, British feminists used to puzzle aloud over the 'contradictions' of welfare capitalism, and look to Sweden where some of our aspirations appeared to be met; but then distance, we reflected, must be deceiving us, for we knew that the heart of capitalism was set against the interests of women with children. Now to write that is to caricature, to reduce those reflections of the mid-1970s. We never held, as socialist feminists or as feminist socialists, such unshaken beliefs in the smooth matching of economies – capitalist or communist – and public virtues and vices. And as for this 'we', this writing about 'our' history, and suggesting that 'we' might turn our minds to, there are drawbacks to this device. It can have an irritatingly parochial ring. Who is being addressed by that 'we', except for 'others of us'? And why should anyone not feeling herself implicated in the pronoun put up with it? It also imposes an unconvincing unity of socialist feminism, as if this were a single and programmatic doctrine; whereas, used so generally, it only really acts as a gesture of distancing from radical feminism, again undefined. Nevertheless, I am going to go on making use, with apologies, of this risky 'we'. It is very hard to circumvent, since these remarks are made out of and back to a specific set of concerns about child-care, voiced by British socialist feminists over the last ten years and more. They are intended to suggest ways of contemplating these concerns – although contemplation must be urgent when both feminism and socialism are so hard pressed.

But now, as British conservatism behaves like some cartoon rendering of itself, it is all the more necessary to hold on to the liveliness of our scepticism about the wills or abilities of any governments untouched by any feminism to deliver the social goods. Not that the writing in of feminist language to social programmes guarantees everything. To take the obvious example of Russia in 1917; Alexandra Kollontai, as a leading Bolshevik, effectively amended that fine Leninist slogan, 'Revolution, Electrification, Peace', to include demands for crèches, communal kitchens, divorce, abortion – demands temporarily realized, despite or more accurately including their sturdily conservative vision of The Mother. Looking back after the Stalinist enthronement of the ideal family as 'the sacred nucleus of triumphant socialism', Trotsky wrote in his *The Revolution Betrayed* that: 'You cannot "abolish" the family; you have to replace it. The actual liberation of women is unrealizable on the basis of generalized want. Experience soon proved this austere truth which Marx had formulated eighty years ago.'

Yet it is evident from Trotsky's own account (even if that were all we had to go on) that the reversing of the earlier social aims of the Communist Party cannot be put down to a lack of means, to national devastation through war and 'backwardness' alone. Imaginative poverty cannot, of course, be held to be utterly independent of brutal shortage; the free spirit needs to eat, too. But one strength of feminism is its potential for keeping alive a voice which speaks over and beyond the recognition of practical necessities and austere truths, and which goes on arguing for the reordering of what is to count as need, what social priorities could be – even, if it has to be, in the teeth of what would seem a sensible cutting of coats according to cloth. Especially where much to do with gender is concerned, we suffer from far too much received 'common sense' already, and would suffocate from generating more of it.

But couldn't it be retorted that now is no time for wayward assertiveness about the imagination; that this line betrays only a disguised and silly nostalgia for a decade ago, of charm only to its faithful survivors? I don't myself believe that this retort would be to the point. I want to plead the need, instead, for feminism and socialism to respond to the 'current crisis' by being both far more impassioned and more analytical about questions of child-care particularly; to throw them more widely open, and to flee from solidifying into new orthodoxies. For everything tempts us into retreating now, and sometimes it looks as if withdrawing from possibly shaky ideological terrain might be better than an undignified scramble, or at best a scorched-earth policy, in the face of rapid conservative advance. And there is no doubt that the ground held by feminism 'as a whole', so far as there has ever been such a creature, has been terribly uncertain. I am going to say that this, though, does not *very much matter*; but only to the extent that we are fully aware of it, and not caught out by surprise and despair. That awareness would mean that we would not be so up against our own uncertainty, and be so liable to hang on doggedly to familiar inadequate repetitions of the current claimants to the feminist socialist 'line'; we would be in the far more gratifying and flattering position of developing or revivifying so many lines that we could run them round whatever unsupple opponents we found. This may sound as if all that is needed to solve problems of the state and child-care, feminism, conservatism and socialism is some self-delighted mental quickness, and, of course, it is not a contest of ideas only which is being fought. None the less, child-care is peculiarly susceptible, as a question, to the opposite risk: the risk of being relegated as an already completely understood set of wants to the practicalities of campaigns; as if theorists chased around in a fine thin air, while dogged workers pushed on in earlier agreed directions.

At the same time, though, as the questions seem hedged in by the dictates of good sense, the possibilities for a feminist understanding of them can look increasingly vulnerable – or, less generously, implausible. There has always been, since the beginnings of the women's liberation movement in Britain, a strong anxiety at work concerning child-care. The desire not to run any risk of confirming the identification of feminism with anti-child, let alone anti-mother, sentiment, has uneasily accompanied the refusal of belief in maternal destiny, in the naturalness and inevitability of who does what in the kitchen. We have always been told that feminism is indifferent to the problems of mothers and children; and that charge has not ever been true. We go on saying what we have repeated for years: no, feminists aren't against mothers; we include mothers; we want 'the right to choose' to have as well as not to have children. Engineering for 'choice' does not mean forgetting that the fundamental choices are founded on having money, a room, a job, some help, and also on the liberty to reflect, to analyse. Even though considering the emotion which pulls many towards child-bearing may do little to clarify the nature of its tug, that time to think, to read, to discuss was in itself an important element in all those conditions for 'choice' which lay, massive and monstrous in their intractability, behind the sparse legal options we necessarily had to focus our attentions on. There was the stubborn hanging-on to whatever accidents of 'choice' our lives had thrown in our way; the recognition that defending the 1967 Abortion Act was an inescapable but partial task.

Why, then, has it been such an enduring charge, that feminism has nothing to say to or about women with children? An impression of child-dumping was conveyed, for some, by one of the original four demands of the women's liberation movement: that for 'twenty-four-hour nurseries'. This was, I think, conceived in the wish for some unchallengeable flexibility for mothers, as well as on the principle of going for the maximum possible; but its phrasing has caused some embarrassment. Against that, though, can be set the far greater evidence of extensive feminist work, not only against the myth of 'maternal deprivation' and the rosiness of domestic life, but, for instance, for child benefit to go on being paid to mothers, for better conditions for unsupported mothers, and, critically, for the legal and financial independence of women. Standards of training and pay for nursery workers have not escaped feminists' attention, either; nor have the chances for improvements in what goes on in local authority nurseries. Despite such work, there has not been a single and resonant feminist 'answer' to problems of child-care; there are very good reasons for this silence on something which can't take one 'answer'; but in a period of gross cutbacks in social provision, it can seem as if we had in the past indulged in empty ideological or utopian thinking ourselves. The wish to dissociate ourselves from being considered toughened abandoners of children returns in force. All the apparent weaknesses of the old debates flood back now. Were we perhaps wrong not to have championed childminders more; and was it after all sometimes truly desolate in the local authority nursery? Bedevilled with vacillating between blaming the recession, or a retrograde national consciousness, or the shortcomings of our own earlier analyses, and unsure – not surprisingly – of how to imagine all of these operating together, a 'feminist mother' may well wonder if she can truly exist as that being. In addition to the suspicion that socialist feminism might be mistaken in its aspirations to produce an all-embracing story of the problems of motherhood, that perhaps there will always be something 'in excess' which can't be fully named by the political descriptions available, there is also the vehement appeal of realism.

For, as women's jobs disappear, the chances of combining work and child-care look increasingly slim. Nursery places wither away unless you can plead exceptional circumstances, 'social deprivation', and then you have nothing guaranteed but a waiting list – unless, indeed, you live in one of the counties which has cut away its facilities altogether. So it may seem almost wilful for feminism to go on concentrating on state provision; should not the tactics change with the hardness of the times? It is not just the faltering of earlier hopes about the liberating crannies to be gouged out of the accidents of the Welfare State. Along with the new wry realism is a new emotional tone. There is more weight, hard to describe except impressionistically, on the elements of pleasure, of love in having and caring for children; an insistence that it's not merely a mournful laborious duty. The 'creative' aspects of motherhood are celebrated again, as they often have been, but without incurring the confident feminist derision of recent years. And, in a way, that is quite right; but it is not an interesting or encouraging kind of rightness. It tells us what we already know: that there are passions and surprises bound up with child-care as well as the exhaustion and isolation dwelt on by women's liberation. But it tells us in a debased language which produces a flat sociology of the emotions, and does so at the expense of thought about practical needs. Meanwhile, throughout the drifts of theories, individual solutions are hit upon, or accidents intervene, and children grow. The tiredness of being on your own with young children can mean that you no longer have the stamina or the heart to go to political meetings. But campaigns, fortunately, go on; the National Childcare Campaign is the current central organization.

One sideways comment: the very term 'child-care' has a dispiriting and dutiful heaviness hanging over it which resists attempts to give it glamour or militance alike. It is as short on colour and incisiveness as the business of negotiating the wet kerb with the pushchair; and it has some of the awful blandness of the 'caring' voiced in the language of psychologized social work, and, increasingly, by anyone else wanting to lay claim to possessing a professional humanity. 'Child-care' has the ring of something closed off, finished, which some people — mostly mothers — know all too much about, and from which other people shy prudently away. Like recommendations for anti-sexist behaviour, it makes the private heart sink a bit, while public socialist heads nod a half-automatic assent, as if recognizing, these days, its inevitability. Can we really offer anything more lively and engaging than the good sense and hot dinners advocated by pre-war Fabians? It is uphill work; but beneath the dull surface of child-care there are profound analytical difficulties and interests; and excitement can be got out of it. What I want to indicate is the range and the volatility and the peculiar attractiveness of the questions which child-care can put to a feminist socialism. And, to repeat, there will not be an exhaustive canon of answers — but this does not so much matter.

II

One way of considering these questions and these answers is to look at their life and their transformations in feminist and socialist work and thought. The effect, though, of looking at history may be the production of a gloomy sense of there being little new under the sun, ideologically speaking. To glance back and discover that many of the anxieties and debates of the contemporary women's movement have occurred spasmodically over the last sixty years may give an impression of intimacy with past politics, but it is one stripped of consolations. Or where the arguments from the side of feminism or from women's labour organizations have visibly

altered, the final effects of the actions of central government or
local authorities over child-care provision may well have been the
same over a long span of years; as with the withdrawals, after both
world wars, of nurseries for the children of women war workers.
One outcome of investigating these movements and backtrackings
is the savage evidence of difficulties obstinately recurring, depri-
vations persisting, official refusals ossifying.

The speed, too, with which enthusiasms among socialists and
feminists themselves can flicker in and out of being may bring about
cynicism, or mournfulness. Dreams of Soviet Russia as the ideal
of benign communism which would liberate women through
enlightened public child-care repeated themselves for feminists in
the 1920s, the 1930s, and to some extent in the 1940s; although
hopes of sexual liberation and of collectivism did indeed take on
different forms over those decades. The general dream of Russia
was superseded in the 1970s by a brief dream of China. The
women's liberation movement looked to the nurseries of the
Cultural Revolution; that generation of feminists did not need to
have Maoist convictions to be touched by those rows of shining
children, any more than their predecessors had needed Stalinism to
support their visions. Common to both enthusiasms was a search
for the truth of politics lived in another country, and an indifference
to the general question of the nature of the state as well as a
straightforward lack of information about the nature of those
particular states. How to think about child-care – let alone about
contraception, abortion, population control – in relation to both
central and local governments is a perennial difficulty. For who are
nurseries for? If allotted for the good of 'social hygiene', for the
children of 'deviant mothers', for the easier flow of a temporarily
needed female labour force, for permitting the employment of
women who would not be able to survive without, say, monotonous
and badly paid work on top of their domestic work – how are these
possible conditions of state bestowal of child-care to be understood
and, where need be, contested by feminist campaigns? What were –
and are – the engagements and interests of various forms of the
state in the sexual, maternal, parental actions of its citizens; and
should feminism, less systematically committed to analysing states
than various socialisms, always take up an oppositional stance?

It has been the question of the education rather than of the care
of children which has brought about the adoption of a clearer if
simpler 'line' on the state. The women's liberation movement, at its
start closer as a whole to libertarian socialism, was sympathetic to
the ideals of non-authoritarian, community-controlled education

advanced by free schools and children's rights groupings. To these aims, the particular feminist theory of anti-sexist learning was added (and whatever the uncertainties of that as a theory, the spreading outside the formal confines of feminism of the idea that boys need not be boys must have been one of the most thoroughly beneficial bits of popularization that feminism has ever managed). This early broadly libertarian leaning of women's liberation was overtaken as campaigns spread, diversified, linked up with other work. Both political and organizational changes of emphases saw a concentration on labour organization; the feminist infiltration of union policies occupied the prominence formerly given to 'community politics'. In the name, often, of the rights of women workers, demands for free access to abortion and the defence of existing if inadequate laws, as well as demands for child-care, were voiced at Trades Union Congress level – and at earlier stages by the Working Women's Charter. The *TUC Charter on Facilities for the Under-Fives*, produced in 1978, embodied many feminist aspirations in its call for 'a comprehensive, mandatory service', to include free nursery centres which local authories would be statutorily bound to provide, and a reform of child-minding and of nursery-staff training schemes. In its guarded attitude to workplace nurseries – 'transferring such responsibilities to the employer would be a reversal of the policies of the whole labour movement for a century or more' – the *TUC Charter*, although too sweeping about the coherence of past policies, had drawn the lessons of the post-war period. Between 1945 and 1948, union politics as well as governmental politics drifted well away from commitments to local-authority nurseries for all, leaving it instead up to individual employers; one outcome was that the reputation of child-care outside the home fell, along with ambitions to meet social needs. The vagueness and ambiguity, too, of the 1944 Education Act's wording on whether or not local authorities were obliged to provide nurseries according to local wants was also tacitly referred to in the TUC's General Council's wish to see a clear statutory duty enforced. It is horribly striking that this document, only four years old, should now sound like an impossibly dated utopianism. It recommends the consideration of the pay and conditions of part-time work in order to allow 'flexibility' to parents, instead of being forced into formulating a strategy on part-time and unemployment. It could still debate social need, and make claims for the introduction of 'services which enable parents, especially mothers, to make a free choice – whether to work or to stay at home to look after children'.

What are the needs, and what are the choices now? Over three million officially unemployed, and unnumbered thousands of women, unregistered unemployed, do not make the contemplation of these questions a redundant philosophical luxury. They have a persistent life which is especially vexing for a feminism torn into ideological tatters. To assert flatly the needs of women, children and men is of no help here: such claims only serve to increase the vulnerability of a harried feminism to self-doubting revisions, and drive it back on to the conservatism of common sense, the only familiar ground. Instead of asking, in the name of the latter, whether we had not been wrong in our criticisms of the family, we can ask what needs are; where they come from; and who is attributing what to whom. The clash, for example, between the 'needs' of women for (hypothetically or polemically) sexual expression; or to move in search of work; and the needs of children for (in the same vein) 'security' – is that a real clash? It is a feminist commonplace to mention a conflict of 'interests' between men and women – a commonplace open to well-enough founded attack – and yet it is hard to reconcile this with the supposition that children's and women's needs are, on the contrary, in some automatic harmony.

These difficulties do have resonances for feminist political understanding, and can not be dodged as being trivially philosophical. To do so is to lay open a regressive anarchy of competing political rights and needs – of children, of fathers – all set clamouring for attention against those of mothers. I can only mention this problem here and not pursue it; generalizations will not work. Adults' needs and children's needs are neither necessarily consonant *nor* necessarily incompatible; not everything can be accurately read off from the categories of men, women and children. It is likely to be an increasingly sharp question, though, for feminism, since more 'rights' may be increasingly named and laid claim to by more contestants. Who and what is a 'parent', for instance; is there a genuine democracy of parents, inclined harmoniously over the child? Or instead are there only 'mothers' and 'fathers' who are, because of their different powers, capacities and histories, always irreconcilable? Neither alternative, I think, is right. Meanwhile lives get lived out in some admixture of making do and fortune over the matter of whose interests and wants are pursued – and with prayerful wishes that our children won't grow up to turn round and reproach us with sacrificing their well-being to our ideological convictions. The feminist mother, that uncertain person, may well tremble at *The Woman Who Did*, Grant Allen's novel of 1895. This is the tale of dashed hopes: a terrible daughter who so burned with frustrated social hopes when she realized her own principled illegitimacy that her high-souled mother had only one means of freeing her for respectable marriage. The mother, the woman who did pursue the logic of her own objections to marriage, cleared the path for the conventional child's ambitions by committing suicide.

III

One of the agonies of Grant Allen's heroine, as she arranged herself for the death which, the novel suggests, lies in wait for those who follow through their moral convictions, might have been self-doubt. Composing the lilies across her breast, she could have pondered the question of fashion. Had her life been lived according to principles merely given to her by the transient accidents of styles, fashions of belief? Refusing marriage as a legal shackling of hearts whose only obligation must be spiritual – was that a passing piece of nineteenth-century feminist moralism which, when lived, had only succeeded in disturbing the child of free love? Within a year of its first publication in Britain and America, the novel had reached its twenty-fourth impression. If we translate the anxiety it embodies into contemporary terms, it emerges as the question of how we manage to bear the vicissitudes of socialist and feminist ideologies. For it is not just a task of opposing a capitalist ideology always 'out there', but also of deciphering our own changing manners and articles of faith.

This is the difficulty entailed by wondering if there are general and distinct socialist and feminist objectives in the care of children, or a quintessentially feminist set of demands to be made. Perhaps nothing can be said which is not traceable to somewhere else; to humanist or liberal beliefs, or even to some spreading of lay psychoanalysis. What about, say, hopes for community control of child-care – who is the community? Or for the 'socialization' of child-care – what are the connections there with conception? What about contemporary China, which is trying to reduce its birth-rate, attempting to make conception itself subject to community planning? Or do we want to say that to conceive a child is private, but to rear it must be the responsibility of the community – doesn't that, though, suppose other conditions? Why should child-care be the province of non-parents too? For the sake of some social generosity? If there are not distinctive and original arguments emanating from a socialist feminism on these speculations which could not be derived from other, occasionally antithetical, political beliefs, we might worry about the consequences for socialist feminism, feeling ourselves at the mercy of fashions in all their volatility. The weight of the passing of time here can seem outrageous. Two years ago, 'we' adhered firmly to such and such a line; and now 'we', probably a compositionally altered 'we', must instead adhere to another. Not only that, but perhaps there are no coherent lines anyway to bear very much examination; perhaps there is only a broken scatter of items from here, colourings from there.

It does seem to me that this despair is misplaced – or rather, that its expression need not run to a devastating outcome. There *will* be a kind of eclecticism about formulations on child-care. Political thought always, in a way, comes from somewhere else; there's a necessary stitched-togetherness at work, even though the dream of a pure and unique place of ideals is not to be forgotten in the name of a modest practicable daylight. For, however much history can demonstrate our lack of originality, the recognition of that need not entail a resentful surrender to 'common sense'. Nor need it render pointlessly 'theoretical' any attempts to take up eclecticism into some clearly delineated feminist ideal, even if all the accidents which have coincided to generate the latter are fully admitted.

So, on the question of what is the socialist feminist understanding of child-care now, the inescapable glances back at the determinations of present assumptions do not have to induce pessimism. They can be cheerfully ironic, perhaps, or puzzled; or sobered by the complexities of things, which is not the same as pessimism. There is entertainment to be had, too. Even the impression that there is nothing new under the sun (and so the sharpness of the question of how to produce a socialist and feminist programme which does not merely react to Thatcherism, but possesses some independent dash of originality) – even that impression can result in relief as well as gloom. You can derive consolation, for instance, from the free-floating nature of the attachments of socialisms and feminisms to psycho-analysis and psychology. The consolations lie in the release from having to suppose that there is something necessarily congruent between them which has at all costs to be 'worked out'; and also in taking this very supposition of congruence to have a considerable history and political interest in its own right.

The drifts of both feminist and socialist harnessing or rejection of psycho-analytic theories of child-rearing, in particular, can be scanned to this end. Various feminist persuasions have fought since the 1960s against Freud; or have, through Lacan, espoused Freud; or have been repelled by some facets of Reich and charmed by others; and all this is heavily documented. But studious fascinations with psycho-analysis and its uses for a socialist or a feminist pedagogy well predate contemporary involvements. Indeed, terrible solemnities have long been written and spoken in the name of such a pedagogy, and the old 'philistine' gibes at ideals of self-expression which produce monstrous children – and indeed adults – have their place. More seriously, the history of liberal, socialist, communitarian adoptions of psycho-analysis is illuminating in its very fitfulness, as well as in its intensity. Vera Schmidt, from 1921 on, ran a psycho-analytic nursery in Moscow which became a point for political agitation and defence. Both Sigmund Bernfeld and Wilhelm Reich attempted psycho-analytic education in Vienna in the late 1920s – a city which had seen psycho-analysis on the rates from 1918 onwards, when its council had supported the home for juvenile delinquents directed by August Aichhorn, the author of *Wayward Youth* (1925), to which Freud added a preface. These moments of meetings in capital cities between municipal socialism, or at least liberalism, and educational theories touched by psychoanalysis were not enduring.

But free-thinking pockets of Europe became beacons for British socialism between the wars, although most British experiments in education were privately financed: a psycho-analytic socialism on the rates here was hardly plausible. British feminism of certain persuasions was also close to liberal schooling. Dora Russell ran a school from 1927 onwards, initially with her husband, which followed some of these principles. And the degree of at least intellectual interest among British socialists and educationalists can be gauged – unless their publishers had badly misjudged the market – by the huge numbers of European works which Eden and Cedar Paul translated between 1912 and 1927. These books of Freudian-influenced pedagogy included *The Elements of Child Protection*, *A New School in Belgium*, *Love in Children and Its Aberrations* and *Set the Children Free!* In England, the popular novelist Ethel Mannin produced a 'plea for freedom' in 1931 entitled *Common-Sense and the Child*, a rather honeyed socialistic work. A. S. Neill, as a private progressive, well expresses that blend of simplified psycho-analytic thinking and environmentalism in his introduction to this book: 'When I have a thief to deal with I know at once that he is symbolically stealing love . . . Isn't it a terrible thought that Dartmoor is full, not of natural devils, but of the victims of a wrong education?'

IV

To save the victims, not only of a 'wrong education' and of emotional lack, but of more visibly punishing attacks like rickets and hunger, was the aim of a broad and powerful current of British socialism well before the First World War. To cure through intervening in child-rearing and teaching *now*, rather than wait in the hope of revolution later (however revolution was construed), was the ambition of many shades of socialists, Christian socialists, feminists, Fabians, liberals, eugenicists, educationalists; in and outside of labour organizations, political parties, and religious or ethical groupings. All of these ambitions and campaigns cannot be lumped together as 'philanthropy' in a dismissive sense; although the narrowest philanthropy did have its own life. How to heal poverty, what the state might do to cause or ease it, preoccupied the many socialists and feminists who worried over the depressed lot of working women and children in particular.

To take one prominent campaigner: the work of Margaret McMillan offers the most vigorous instance of a Christian socialism concentrated on child-care. A foundation member of the Independent Labour Party in 1893, she worked for the Bradford School Board, campaigning for open-air schools, voice production, school meals. Her publications include a pamphlet on 'correct breathing' for children and several books, among which are *Education Through the Imagination* (1904), *The Child and the State* (1905) and *Labour and Childhood* (1907). After leaving Bradford, she settled in London, agitating successfully for compulsory medical inspection in schools, and becoming LCC member for Deptford. Best known, though, was her nursery work; her Deptford nursery was formally opened in 1921, and the Rachel McMillan Training College, named after her sister, in 1930. What form did her theories of practical socialism in the care of children take? One of her reasons for resigning her presidency of the Nursery Schools Association in 1929 is revealing here – that it did not emphasize what she took to be the necessity of a nine-hour day in nursery schools serving 'slum areas'. The nursery school should, she believed, be an unassailably large and curative institution, to dispense three meals a day, paid for by parents; it would act, too, as a mothers' social centre. Here is her passion for fresh air, health and school size, exemplified in a broadcast she made in 1927 about 'The Nursery School': 'At 12.30 three hundred little children are fast asleep in little cots where the sun, the blessed doctor in the sky, who cures rickets, can rest on the sleepers. In winter, of course, they are wrapped warmly in red blankets.'

Margaret McMillan's conviction that the best way of altering the damaged lives of 'slum children' was early nursery care sprang from her evolutionary socialism; one also opposed to 'doles' as only sapping the latent enthusiasm of the poor for 'self-development'. Infant schools themselves would, she wrote confidently in her 1926 paper, 'Poverty in the Modern State', make 'class-consciousness' a redundant rhetoric: 'The classes will meet there simply because the upper class girl will train and serve there under the teacher.' Nurseries allowed for social mixing; and observation of the life of infant schools could clarify the vexing question of what ills could be put down to 'wrong nurture' as distinct from heredity, and so be in reach of being cured. Margaret McMillan's lyrical descriptions of the improvements wrought in her nursery children afford extra-ordinary glimpses of a working socialist eugenics in a benign form; this is also from 'Poverty in the Modern State':

> In any other area children who have the same chance would look as they look, and be what they are in a year! They would show the real fibre and pattern of the race, like new-cleaned carpets. A crowd of them in St Paul's, or elsewhere, would give pause to the blackest pessimism. It is not possible to believe today that we fairly *see* each other. For nothing hides so well as poverty, and many are poor.

This diction of 'the race', quite congruent with many socialist and feminist persuasions until as recently as the end of the last war, has been heavily played upon – either instrumentally or with true conviction – in reform work for the care of children. Nurseries have been fought for in what 'we' would take to be deeply conservative or reactionary language. What 'we' would understand to be evidently anti-socialist, anti-feminist sentiments about child-rearing, maternity and the state have been wrapped around results which fit with 'our own' aims; what is to be made of this?

Look, for another quick example of a contrasting approach, at Anna Martin, writing *The Married Working Woman* in 1911 as a piece of polemic for the National Union of Women's Suffrage Societies. She is concerned to defend the native good sense of working-class mothers, their capacity to 'manage' under the most disheartening circumstances. That free school-meals system which has so exercised the imaginations of many socialists, she wrote, 'excites neither enthusiasm nor gratitude'; for working women were 'sincerely apprehensive of the demoralization of the men';

indeed, they might get given less housekeeping money as an outcome of such public funding. Medical inspections, for which Margaret McMillan had done battle, only served, Anna Martin claimed, to lay extra burdens on the mother, who must cut her already tight spending on food to buy medicines, with doubtful gain. But give working women the vote, she argued, and their influence would not be bent to what others short-sightedly held to be self-evident socialist ameliorations in their and their children's lives. With things as they actually were, to raise the school-leaving age would only cause dismay in the home at the loss of an income. Keeping children out of pubs by law, another well-meant intervention, would do away with the moderating influence of the presence of mothers on drinking men. And, she wrote firmly in *The Mother and Social Reform* in 1913, those women who themselves drank might at least square up to their husbands' violence, and be more vivid than 'colourless submissive drudges'. Her point was that the working wife and mother suffered from more profound grievances than her middle-class critics had supposed or understood. As a result:

> . . . 'mothering' the children of the poor became almost a fashionable sport . . . Grave legislators debate the material of which the baby's nightwear should be composed, and endeavour to lay down the principles which should regulate its sleeping arrangements. Local authorities decide the hours at which Annie may earn two pence by cleaning steps or Johnnie add to the family income by lathering chins.

These benign interferences, said Anna Martin, were, like the machinery of school meals and medical inspections, effective diversions from the political powerlessness of the unenfranchised working-class women. What was really wanted was legal redress instead of pieties when husbands wilfully failed to support the family: 'Let her nominal right of maintenance for herself and her children be transformed into a real one, and it will be found that her supposed passion for working ten hours a day in a jam factory for a mere pittance is a figment of men's imagination.' The Labour Party, whose 'leaders wax eloquent over the grievances of the sweated industrial female workers', was notably silent on the question of the wife and mother in the home. For unlike the woman waged worker, she lacked any guaranteed recompense, however inadequate, for her labour; and she had no means of protection against the violence of her husband-employer.

So there is Anna Martin, critical, under the banner of the

National Union of Women's Suffrage Societies, of attempts made in the name of socialism and women's rights to better the lives of working-class mothers and their children; at the same time, among others, Margaret McMillan with the Independent Labour Party agitated successfully for such reforms – school meals, clinics and above all nurseries – as the means of raising those same lives out of hopelessness. Two differently committed campaigners among many. A myriad examples might be traced of other understandings of what constituted the best approach to the question of the lot of the working woman and her children: an urgent and far-reaching question.

How were, and how are, the needs of mothers to be raised without making a fetish out of 'motherhood', all too capable of conservative capture? This was a difficulty for women's labour organizations, suffrage groups, the Women's Co-Operative Guild, women in the Labour Party and other political parties, Fabians, feminists – a difficulty which some of them sometimes registered or more often were not aware of. The 'sexual division of labour' was not enunciated as a problem; improving mothers' working lives was, especially given high rates of maternal morbidity, an obvious first task. Campaigns before and between the wars agitated for the 'endowment of motherhood' or family allowances, for access to contraception and health care, for the better state of kitchens; all these made claims to speak for the most pressing needs of women and children.

For some, it was freedom from repeated unwanted child-bearing which must be won first. Dora Russell, in her *Hypatia* of 1925, held that the question of 'feminist mothers' demanded one clear response: access for all classes of women to contraception, and sexual enlightenment: 'with birth control, in two years a determined mother can completely restore her nerve, her joy in life, and her full muscular powers.' Without it, how should the working woman, badly fed and ill housed, be expected to tolerate going on bearing children? In *Hypatia* she wrote: 'The working mother today looks straight from her kitchen, if she is lucky enough to have one, on to one of the most complex situations in history.'

Dora Russell's understanding of women's and children's needs at that point of historical complexity led her, with others, to a vision of an emancipated motherhood which combined sexual freedom with liberal child-rearing. A practical socialism, she believed, might be brought about by means of the sympathetic influence of the educated mother. She was among those whose aim, in the Worker's Birth Control Group formed in 1924, was for contraceptive information and supplies to be universally available through clinics. And Naomi Mitchison's pamphlet of 1930, *Comments on Birth Control*, also proposes the radical powers of democratic access to birth control to undercut class injustices. It, too, expresses a conviction integral to its feminism – a conviction no longer heard – that a happy heterosexuality, child-rearing, and, later on, paid work, must and could combine. In this spirit, Dora Russell, in her *Defence of Children* of 1932, again inquired, 'What is a civilized mother in the modern sense?' and provided her own answer: '. . . mothers are seeking the liberty to do work of their own and wider choice in loving'.

Who would take care, though, of the children did not pose such a problem. The shadows of the housemaid and the cook flit unmentioned behind that ordered creativity of the emancipated socialist mother, so vigorously drawn in *Hypatia* and in *Defence of Children*. Look also at the awkward knots of opinion in this paragraph from the latter with its stress on maternal maturity and its serious pleasures:

> . . . female non-acceptance of maternal responsibility is deep and wide, whether it take the form of the painted adolescence that continues to the age of fifty years, or the grim feminist savagery that may be seen in a body of European working-class women revolting against the home, and demanding scientific advice that will set them free of the burden of the hated baby. Career women, seeking not to be women at all; alimony women, using female charm and prestige to keep afloat in a sea of liberty and pleasure – all are in flight from the patriarchal female pattern of dutiful daughter and self-sacrificing mother, all are in flight from the withering and dying that inevitably follow on from giving the body to the serious burdens of love. All, in fact, like many men today, do not want to face the burden of growing up.

A savagery, one might think, to be espoused, and a growing up to be fled from. The 'responsible mother' had her contradictions, which inter-war feminism was not fully able to confront.

v

Here again is Dora Russell in 1932: 'There are times in history when we can no longer "broaden down from precedent to precedent" like the English law, and I fear that this is one of them.

Everyone feels bewildered and insecure, whether as wage-earner or employer, wife or husband, mother or father.' Fifty years later, what can be said in the name of socialism and feminism to problems which continue to hang in another aura of 'insecurity'?

There is at the outset the question of whether a socialist feminism need object to the implied democracy of the spread of 'everyone's' insecurity. However indifferent to gender unease about the times may be, it is the case that the strain of day-to-day responsibility for the care of children does rest, on the whole, with women. Anna Martin in 1913 was decisive here: 'It would be a great gain if the word 'parental' could be banished from the language for a few years. The term may refer to the father, the mother, or to both, and this ambiguity of meaning has afforded much welcome cover for obscure and confused thinking.' This is from *The Mother and Social Reform*; she had in mind the speculations of blinkered philanthropy which blamed the defects of one parent on to the other, not noticing those sharp differences in the conditions of living which were bestowed according to the sex of the parent. Her object was to pull into the light the specific position and hardships of working women as mothers; and their abilities, too. This is still an object of feminism, and it is also at odds with other objects of feminism. Child-care draws together these contesting strands – but not so as to knit them comfortably into a smooth fabric. In brief, it is the tension between refusing to elevate maternity into some engulfing feminine principle, and demanding that the needs of mothers be met. Put so schematically, that is hardly a tension; but practically and in full detail, it is.

One solution, it has seemed to the present generation of feminists, is to argue that children are not the sole responsibility of their mothers, that their upbringing should be shared. There are many possible kinds of sharers: the state in the form of nurseries, for example, the community, friends, non-parents, fathers. I want to comment only on one of these – on 'shared parenting', since it is frequently voiced as an ideal, while its worrying properties are little mentioned. Striking among these is that it rests on the accidents of individual solutions, on individual goodwill: to make of child-care such a hostage to fortune is to depart a long way from socialist aspirations to democratically accessible community services.

The slogan of 'shared parenting' – the assertion that fathers should take equal care of their children – is a curious claimant to being a radical demand, one proper to a socialist feminism. Certainly it would entail great changes in patterns of work; it supposes some even distribution of part-time work between the sexes, and this in all kinds of employment; unless the 'sharing' were to be restricted to those who had the freedom to determine their own hours of work – or who were jobless. Here it would fit well enough, ironically, with a state of high unemployment; the Thatcher government itself has argued the virtues of work-sharing. But the arguments advanced for 'shared parenting' do not rest on its profound implications for the organization of paid work; rather that it embodies the feminist ideal that women should not be solely responsible for the care of those children which they did not, after all, produce by parthenogenesis. What a socialist feminism could have to say to the problems of child-care is hardly exhausted by the reorganization of domestic life envisaged by this particular form of care-sharing.

The redistributive justice of 'shared parenting' does not do away with the stifling couple, the dead hand of the parent: instead, all stays firmly within the family, in a way severely at odds with women's liberation aspirations about 'going outside the couple'. There is the whole question, too, of what may roughly be called power; not the 'power' of motherhood, a doubtful claim indeed, but the results of the unevenness which develops when women and men have, as is generally true, unequal access to money and work. 'Shared parenting' cannot rely on that egalitarianism which its formulation presupposes. The odds are that the sharers will start off their existence as parents on a disparate material footing; an imbalance readily exploitable in any later collapse of the goodwill which sustained the original sharing. 'Joint parenting' is also the triumph of the family-planning clinic: the rational harmonious couple, a pair of ideal social democrats who conceive their children with a truly mutual deliberation. This may be admirable, but it can – if it obscures other concerns – run too close to being a socialist social hygiene.

For where does it leave the single parent; the unhusbanded woman who prefers that state; and all those whose lives do not happen to encompass potential sharers in the upbringing of their children? How will their needs be met? Certainly there is nothing in 'shared parenting' which stands in opposition to the battles for local authority nurseries, say; the more attentions which can be alerted to the shortage of state facilities, the better. But there is the risk that concentration on the parental pair may distract from questions about what is to be done where no pair exists.

And should the sharing couple come to grief, the history of where financial power lies is likely to undermine the democracy of sharing. Once a surface of private domestic harmony is disturbed, the structures of public inegalitarianism emerge harshly. For women do not have equal chances of finding work if they have been at home with children; or of finding well-paid part-time employment. And, in the courts, a double standard of sexual morality asserts itself with a severity which mocks years of feminism; it is still, in general, true that women undergo a trial of their sexual being in a way which is not replicated for men as fathers. The sexual – at least the heterosexual – actions of a man do not throw a whole interpretative aura over his standing as a father in the eye of the law, and paternity is not thereby 'sexualized'. But maternity, though officially remote from the taint of other passions, is, with the custody of children at stake, vulnerable to judgement through the real or imputed sexual life of the mother; whether this is heterosexual, or, more dangerously, homosexual.

These lacks of symmetry between women as parents and men as parents are neither timeless, universally true nor incapable of being eroded. But while they exist they make it forcefully clear that 'parenting' cannot be confined to the private domains of the sharers, their 'personal politics' and the exercise of their wills. What can be done about the care of children is heavily invaded by the state of the labour market for both sexes, by child benefits and taxation and welfare suppositions, by the assumptions of the law courts, social workers, of all the agencies outside the home which keep a foot in the door. This is why 'shared parenting' cannot take over a great deal of rhetorical space in feminist-socialist ambitions for the future of the family. As a slogan it has its uses; but they are circumscribed, and, I think, can be included with attempts at some systematic generosity, like those socialist 'good manners' which indicate that meetings ought not to be monopolized by the most obsessive speaker, that women should be equally heard, and so on. All these are excellent developments. Without them, some of us would still be stuck fast in the nervous silence in which we grew up. I, for one, am too familiar with that condition to be dismissive of any inroads on it.

These observations are *not* attacks on the principle that the existing sexual division of labour in the home and out of it should be undermined. They are cautionary remarks about letting it be implied that 'shared child-care' as a goal is capable of covering those principles adequately; that it can substitute for campaigns for nurseries, play centres, school meals, a better level of child benefit. In theory, certainly, there is no reason why these 'social' or 'community' campaigns should not exist alongside attempts to redistribute the care of children between women and men, to the greater glory of each. But what tends to happen in practice, given the utterly miserable outlook for social provisions for child-care to be extended or maintained under present conservative policy, is a loss of heart for reform in the public domain.

Instead, a fresh and anxious stress on socialist and feminist manners and conduct at home develops. This is fine; but if its limits *are* the walls of the home, then that is a constriction of feminism, which has always to look outside as well. 'Shared child-care' rests on private goodwill; but private goodwill cannot be relied on to sustain a whole politics.

The continuing battle for more, better and more flexible provision for the care of children is not, clearly, a battle to be joined only by women, by mothers. Reaffirming the old 'separate spheres' philosophy, whereby each has her or his place in the social and political order of things, will not help. Even if it is strategically necessary to agitate for child-care in terms of women's rights, to lay claim to new powers for motherhood even, what is at stake will go, in the end, beyond the sectional.

Yet it is true that feminism *is* a sectional movement; in its nature and in the point of its existence, it is 'for women'. And it is those women who are mothers who are, because of their histories, best placed now to articulate their needs; to which the needs of children can neither be simply fused, nor simply opposed. Meanwhile, the formation of a new (or the resurrection of an old) ideal of the 'socialist family' is a development we can do better without. It is *social* provision that is needed. The cry of 1940s' feminism, for paid work *and* having children, is still unanswered. For unless women chance to be protected by the fortunes of an atypically good wage, by privately afforded child-care, by a securely employed and reasonably paid husband, the truth still is that to both work and have children is, as well as a pleasure, a bitterly exhausting fight.

ACKNOWLEDGEMENTS

I am especially grateful to Deborah Thom for her comments, and for pointing me towards some of the books I have used here; to Ian Patterson for his help with references, and his comments and secretarial work; to Jonathan Rée and to Nigel Wheale for invaluable last-minute help with typing, and for suggestions. I also want to thank Carol Kendrick and Jonathan Rée for taking care of my children at times while I was writing, and Lynne Segal and Elizabeth Wilson for their editorial work.

SOURCES

Aichhorn, August, *Wayward Youth*, Putnam, London, 1935.

Allen, Grant, *The Woman Who Did*, John Lane, London and Robert Bros, Boston, 1895.

Mannin, Ethel, *Commen-Sense and the Child*, Harrolds, London, 1931.

McMillan, Margaret, *Education Through the Imagination*, Swan Sonnenschein, London, 1904.

—— *The Child and the State*, ILP, London, 1905.

—— *Labour and Childhood*, Swan Sonnenschein, London, 1907.

—— 'Poverty and the Modern State' in *Present-Day Papers*, No. 3, London, 1926.

Martin, Anna, *The Married Working Woman; a Study*, NUWSS, London, 1911.

—— *The Mother and Social Reform*, NUWSS, London, 1913.

Mitchison, Naomi, *Comments on Birth Control*, Faber and Faber, London, 1930.

Russell, Dora, *Hypatia*, Kegan Paul, Trench, Trubner & Co. Ltd, London, 1925.

—— *In Defence of Children*, Hamish Hamilton, London, 1932.

Schmidt, Vera, and Reich, Annie, *Pulsions sexuelles et éducation du corps*, Union Générale d'Editions, Paris, 1979.

Trades Union Congress General Council, *Trades Union Charter on Facilities for the Under-Fives*, TUC, London, 1978.

Trotsky, Leon, *The Revolution Betrayed*, Faber and Faber, London, 1937.

Index

Index by Keith Seddon